TOWARD THE UNKNOWN REGION

AN APPRECIATION OF THE WORK

OF

RUSSELL SHEPPARD

AND

YOUTH MUSIC IN GLAMORGANSHIRE

BY

JOHN JENKINS

WITH ARTICLES

BY

DAVID EMANUEL, NEIL KINNOCK, TONY LEWIS, ROGER LEWIS
HELENA BRAITHWAITE AND JEFFREY FRANCIS

Published by

John Jenkins

Printed and bound by

Fretwells Limited
Olso Road, Kingston Upon Hull HU7 0YN

ISBN 1-902709-04-7

Dedication

This book is dedicated to the grandchildren of Russell and Karen Sheppard - Karin, Mark, Ceri, Siân, Gareth, Owen and great-grand daughter, Chloe. It also records the memory of those grandchildren who performed so beautifully and with such courage at the funeral services of both their grandparents who died within three months of each other in the Spring of 1999.

May Russell and Karen's love of music continue throughout each of their lives.

Preface

The book is written as an appreciation of the outstanding contribution made by Russell John Sheppard to music and education in Wales.

Affectionately known as *Shep*, Russell Sheppard took up the post of Inspector of Schools to the Glamorgan County Council in 1949. The volume marks the fiftieth anniversary of the formation of the Glamorgan Youth Orchestra and the singular achievements of the County Youth Orchestra, Choir and Brass Band - *the Glam.*

Although the official titles of the Glamorgan Orchestra, Choir and Band were lost after the local authority reorganisations of 1974 and 1996, the author has respected Russell Sheppard's wish that the volume should reflect the continuing growth and development of music in the former Glamorganshire to the present day.

To the end of his life Russell Sheppard remained proud of the momentous achievements of many thousands of players, singers and staff. We, in our turn, were privileged to have been members of

........*the Glam.*

Russell Sheppard ~ Founder of the Glam

CONTENTS

Acknowledgements

I would firstly like to thank the family of the late Russell Sheppard for all their help and support in the preparation of the book. In particular, the financial commitment of Wendy, Pat and Peter has enabled the book to be published and for the Russell Sheppard Trust Fund to be established which we all hope will be of assistance to future generations of young musicians. I am also obliged to Janie Sheppard, Albert, Cynthia and John Gilbert; Joan and Richard Sheppard for providing so much background information and many family photographs. Robert Mitchell has been a tower of strength, particularly in liaising with the publishers in proof- reading and, with Gordon Peterson, in the printing of some of Russell Sheppard's manuscripts.

I am especially indebted to Helena Braithwaite and Jeffrey Francis formerly Music Advisers to the South and Mid Glamorgan Local Education Authorities and to Phillip Emanuel, Head of the West Glamorgan Music Service for completing the history of music in West Glamorgan since my retirement in 1992. Valuable assistance was also provided in compiling material on *"The New Glams"* by Dr. Kevin Adams, Mostyn Davies, Phillip Emanuel, David Hughes and Dewi Jones.

I received a great deal of background information from Mrs. Dorcas Way and Mrs. Nora Huxley both of whom knew the Sheppard family in Mountain Ash during the childhood and studentship of Russell Sheppard. Moreover, the information from historian Bernard Balwin and the invaluable advice of Aberdare and Mountain Ash Public Libraries during the period of research was much appreciated. Former pupils of Holyhead County School, Douglas Williams and Glyn Roberts who both sang with the school choir have provided a number of interesting stories, photographs and other memorabilia. I also received valuable assistance from the *"Cynon Valley Leader"* and the *"Holyhead and Anglesey Mail"* and from Dean Powell and Susanne Smith.

Many colleagues have provided marvellous personal reflections on Russell Sheppard's work and achievement and I am particularly appreciative of the contributions of Maxwell Evans, Godfrey Evans, Dr. Raymond Grant, Stanley Jones, Ieuan Morgan, Alan and Ann James, and Tony Small.

I would wish to complement and applaud Tony Lewis, Neil Kinnock, David Emanuel and Roger Lewis for taking the time, in their hectic schedules, to write such individualistic and evocative introductions. I feel that the book would not have come to life without the reflections of former Glam and New Glam members like Raymond Bowden, Hywel Benjamin, Dr. Ian and Adrian Evett, Diana Griffiths, Gruffydd Harries, Cecily Holliday, Heather James, Angela Mills, Michael Nelmes, Mark and Nicholas Ormrod, and Wayne Warlow.

It was delightful to hear of the interest of composers Karl Jenkins and Mark Thomas whose CDs inspired me in the writing of the book. I am hugely grateful to all the singers and instrumentalists who sent articles and photographs. These include singers Beverley Humphreys, Della Jones, Rebecca Evans, Stuart Kale, Dennis O' Neill, Gail Pearson who have starred in opera houses all over the world. In the same way, contributions were received from leading orchestral and recital players like John Anderson, Gordon Back, Gareth Small and Rhys Owens for their tributes. I would also wish to thank Dr. Peter James, Douglas Bowen,

Ann and Alan James and Katherine Phipps for offering their time and expertise, and Diane Onions of the West Glamorgan Music Office for her support to youth music over many years.

The help, encouragement, abundant knowledge of my contemporary in the Glam, Jeffrey Lloyd was formative in my thinking. The regular meetings with Jeff were immensely stimulating. We were delighted to be joined by Brian Clarke, Phillip Emanuel and Gruffydd Harries in planning concert tributes to Russell Sheppard.

Finally, I owe an enormous debt of gratitude to my wife Wendy for her help, support and forbearance during the writing of the book.

Acknowledgements to publishers

The usage of extracts from Welsh poems is a focal point of the book. In this respect the generous co-operation of the following publishers is gratefully acknowledged:

University of Wales Press

Edward Thomas	Words	

Seren Books

John Ormond	In September from Selected Poems : Seren 1987	
R.S.Thomas	Welsh History from Collected Poems : Dent 1993	

Gomer Press, Llandysul

The Collected Poems of Idris Davies

Free Discipline	Gwalia Deserted	The Angry Summer
Gold	The Retired Actor	

Harri Webb : Collected Poems

Mountain Ash	Hall of Song	

Introduction

Recollections of distinguished former members :

Tony Lewis : The '50s

Tony Lewis

Fiddling with the Glamorgan Youth Orchestra in the 1950s was an adventure, a romance, and a musical education which wove the rich strand of playing and listening for the rest of my life.

Adventure? Ogmore School Camp. I remember waking up one freezing December morning in the old hut we called a dormitory, looking at the long line of beds and seeing hoary heads and every blanket white with frost. Snow had drifted up to the eaves; naked bulbs swung slowly on single flexes. It was forlorn. Zhivago-like. Was this Russell Sheppard preparing us for Tchaikovsky's Fourth? He was nothing if not meticulous. The concert required courage : the acoustics of the Porthcawl Pavilion were such that no one could hear anyone else play a note. We all performed the symphony as if our parts were a solo before the steady baton and fixed stare of Shep. Our parents clapped.

The first concert I ever played in was in the Gwyn Hall, Neath and I was asked, along with other diminutive juniors, to play standing up so that I could see over the top of my music stand .... "Peer Gynt", Beethoven's Fourth Piano Concerto, Brahms First Symphony. The humiliation. How can you be a proper fiddler standing up?

Romance? We were make-believe professional players. Violinists longed to develop hard skin under the chin, the badge of a person who lived life in the wonderful world of resin, re-tuning and wide vibrato. Horn players greased their lips, woodwind players bound reeds and timpanists joined the big-time when they counted a hundred bars rest for the first time in their lives without tapping a shoe or counting out loud. We listened and learned a lot about orchestral playing - one of the great team games in the world. And when we were older we would find time for chamber music too. We had aspirations. Often I would go to bed believing I was a Heifitz or Menuhin, miming the soaring octave of the Beethoven concerto. It was a helluva disappointment to wake up as Tony Lewis, but a boy could dream in the Glamorgan Youth Orchestra. I still do.

My slowish vibrato got faster, however, and I arrived for Ogmore courses with the well-muscled left hand of a cricketer. As my cricket got stronger so did my left hand, and so my violin teacher insisted I did finger-flopping exercises wherever I went. I would stand in my aunt's kitchen, or in the cafe, or in the school library with my finger-tip balanced on a high flat surface, such as a mantelpiece, then suddenly flop them off to prove a complete relaxation or otherwise - a dangerously foppish practice in Neath for a nineteen year old.

Musical education? All over the world I have been the cricket writer-broadcaster who hurtles at close of play to the concert hall. The youth orchestra taught us to listen and ask questions. In the days when I was presenting arts programmes for HTV my producer suggested that I gave Kyung-Wha-Chung dinner in order to find out more about her. Her message was tough - that a performer can never reach playing perfection if distracted by a husband. She promised herself to the single life. I nodded. We recorded a suitably testing programme. She played the Bach Partita No.1 in G Minor as we all tried to do in Ogmore Days. She did not like the first four bars; listened to the recording and did the whole lot again. Better, she thought. It was wonderful to be near to such music and such a musician, especially with the understanding of a violinist.

By the time the programme went out on air, she was married and, it was reported, playing better than ever.

Many Glamorgan Youth Orchestra players became performers or teachers of the highest calibre, but it does not matter how exalted they became. The mention of Ogmore School Camp will still bring a smile of affection to their lips; it is a glowing memory of the music-making which shaped us, tuned our ears and left us forever thankful for the diligence and devotion of Russell Sheppard.

Friends for a lifetime, music forever - a precious experience.

Educated at Neath Grammar School and Christ's College, Cambridge, the well known cricketer, broadcaster and writer A.R. (Tony) Lewis was a member of the violin section of the Glam for several years in the 1950s. Tony, a former Glamorgan cricket captain, who led his side to the County Championship in 1969, also became captain of England. He is a former Chairman and present President of the Glamorgan club. Until 1998 he was presenter and cricket commentator for BBC TV and writes on cricket for "The Sunday Telegraph". Tony holds cricket's highest position, that of President of the MCC. A rugby as well as cricket Blue at Cambridge University he is the author of five books including the MCC's official bi-centenary history - "Double Century". He is in his eighth year as Chairman of the Wales Tourist Board and has also been Deputy Lieutenant and High Sheriff of Mid Glamorgan.

Neil Kinnock : The 60's

Neil Kinnock

Gentle, serious, passionate for what he called real music, contemptuous of anything else, Russell Sheppard was unforgettable.

I was an eager teenage Glam chorister when I first encountered him. He seemed didactic, even prissy, in his approach to the legion that sang their hearts out. That adolescent prejudice quickly melted as I realised that, within a few days, Shep and his marvellous deputies were moulding a real choir out of the bits of musical clay brought together from the huge and disparate County of Glamorgan - Swansea Valley to Gwent Borders, Brecon Beacons to Bristol Channel. Even I, with my inveterate dislike of teachers in general, could recognise a great teacher when I had one (fortunately, I had more than one), and Russell Sheppard really had the gift.

He managed to employ it without seeking popularity or showing wrath. An irritated tap of the baton, or a paint-stripping stare, or slumping shoulders accompanied by a soft "No, no, no - you know how to do better than that," was the nearest he got to fury. But no-one wanted to be responsible for earning that mild admonition. Everyone tried their damnedest. The result was sweet and powerful. It was a delight and a privilege to be part of what Russell Sheppard created.

Praise from him was as scarce as sunstroke in Porthcawl. Even when it came it was a mimed "Good" at the end of a difficult passage or, at the end of a tumultuous concert, a barely audible "You behaved well" - uttered in a slightly tinny voice. The words excellent, brilliant, marvellous were probably in his vocabulary - but they would have been reserved for Ogdon or Oistrakh or the Berlin Philharmonic or the Heavenly Chorale of Angels and Archangels (He's probably got them in rehearsal at this moment). Such acclaim was certainly not for the likes of us young ladies and gentlemen, even in sparkling white shirts and blouses, trousers and pleated skirts with knife-edge creases, brushed blazers and cherubic faces.

Perhaps Shep wasn't fooled. Maybe he knew that music is the food of love (or at least cardiac fever) among post-pubescents. It is possible that he was aware that the desire of both sexes to impress each other guaranteed maximum effort and reasonable discipline. Come to think of it, he must have known as much about biology and chemistry as he did about music. He was abundantly pleasant without being "nice", friendly without being familiar, informal without being relaxed. It was a knack. It worked.

All the kids knew that. And they were an easy crowd to be with. Smoothy Periera, Hawkins the Barry Beatnik, Noddy the Glamorgan County Youth Cricketer, Jeff Young the Hooker, Kenny Green comic volcano, Terry "Dracula" Johns, superb horn player and born comic, Tony Davey, basso profundo at seventeen, Ginger

Davies who was taller than Wenvoe TV mast. And the girls. What girls. Lynwen and Jean, Lorna and Maggie, Ceinwen and Chris, Wendy and Annie and forty more. Cool, crisp in school uniform or late '50s starched petticoats. Exotic creatures who were a four hours each way bus journey from my home town of Tredegar. Out of reach for fifty weeks of the year, and, in the other two weeks, hard to catch.

The choir and orchestra were a handful - several armfuls, indeed. Not that it ever seemed to disturb Russell Sheppard. Calm prevailed in the most blasting chorus or soaring crescendo. Benign he was and always keeping time. "For those who think that syncopation was invented recently by jazz people" (he meant rock and roll bands, but who cared) he declared during a rehearsal of Copland or Sibelius or someone, "this is how it is supposed to sound".

Russell Sheppard even managed to keep his self-control in times of greatest provocation. On a beautiful summer evening at the end of a thunderous concert a certain Chairman of the Education Authority (a position which, in that age, was only slightly inferior to the President of the USSR, but with more power over life and death) moved a vote of thanks. Even music was democratic in those days.This speech by the most avid supporter of music in the County reached its immortal climax as he thanked "Mr. Russell" (ripples of "who?" from the choristers) "is Party" and "is Band." The audience clapped loud and long, this time without prompting from me, and the Glamorgan Youth Choir and Orchestra regarded as about the best of its kind in Great Britain hooted with merriment.

'Is band indeed! We knew that all the hard work that flowed from hours of formal rehearsals into the showers, onto the beach, around the teacups and the (illicit) beer had made an art to be proud of. And the committee is going to hear of it. What next? The Nobel Prize, Royal Academy Scholarships, Welsh Caps would have been mere baubles by comparison.

Shep was glacial. As we went to the buses to sing our way back to Ogmore, he seemed to me to be exuding sub-zero rage. I felt like saying to him "We understand". I didn't. It would have been creeping wouldn't it. But I wish I had. Sometimes everyone needs to hear "Good. You behaved well".

A graduate of University College Cardiff, Neil Kinnock joined the Labour Party at the age of fifteen. Following a four year period as a tutor and organiser for the Workers Education Association, he entered parliament in 1970. His distinguished career led to his appointment as Labour's Chief Opposition Spokesman on Education in 1979. He became Chairman of the party and Leader of the Opposition in 1988 and 1983 respectively. Appointed Member of the Privy Council by Her Majesty the Queen in 1983, he became a member of the European Commission in 1995. He has written various pamphlets, two books and a TV Series for BBC - "The Future of Socialism". Married to MEP Glenys Kinnock, Neil holds honorary doctorates and fellowships of Welsh Universities and is Honorary Professor of Politics of Thames Valley University. He became Chancellor of UC, Cardiff in 1988. He lists music, male choral work, theatre and rugby football amongst his many interests.

David Emanuel : The 70's

I clearly remember being taken by my mother, at a young age, to a concert performed by the Glam and, at the time thinking and saying "I want to be in that!"- Easier said than done!

David Emanuel

For a start, I was only introduced to the violin at my senior school, having mostly studied singing and piano until then. After being presented with a shiny new instrument, I could not have been in better hands. My violin teacher was to be Mrs. Sheppard. She adored music with a passion and her infectious enthusiasm certainly inspired me.

Initially, every Friday evening I rehearsed with the Mid - Glamorgan Orchestra. These practices were socially and musically great fun. But I always frustratedly felt we were in the shadow of the BIG one - the Glamorgan Youth Orchestra. That was the ONE I wanted to be in.

As for senior school, a new, young and energetic music teacher arrived named John Jenkins. He quickly whipped up interest in anything musical as well as organising the school orchestra. He invited me to be the orchestra's leader - I was on my way! At the same time Mrs Sheppard finally gave me her approval to audition for the BIG one.

On the day of the audition, I could not wait to get school work out of the way but when the moment came I was nervous but excited. On entering the audition room I was met by a very tall and distinguished gentleman who introduced himself as Mr. Sheppard. He told me to relax and enjoy the music and after I had completed my pieces he enquired as to who taught me the violin. "Mrs. Sheppard" I answered - to which he simply gave a knowing smile. It seemed an age waiting for the results to be pinned on the school notice board but I and Dawn Jenkins got in that year. Our headmaster even announced it at prayers - I was definitely on my way.

The procedure with auditions for the Glamorgan Youth Choir was similar except that, with nerves, anything can happen to the voice. Eisteddfods and Church choir had not prepared me for this. I performed scales and my rehearsal piece but could tell that Mr. Sheppard was not incredibly happy. He kindly suggested that I sang something I really liked. I sang a traditional Welsh folk song and he simply said the magic words "You're in!!".

Once you won a place in either the Orchestra or Choir the music course consisted of a week's rehearsal in preparation for public performances. Ogmore can only be described as an experience! In my day it was a cross between an army camp and a boarding school! Rows of beds, running outside to the showers and midnight feasts, et al. Added to all this a singing-playing regime meant rehearsing from nine in the morning until well after supper. You were in an environment of excellence with several hundred people working toward a truly wonderful and unique performance. Ogmore also taught you to get on with all types of people and to strike up friendships with people, some of whom, I have still kept in contact with to this day!

My musical highlight was undoubtedly the concert given by an enormous Glam orchestra and choir at the Royal Festival Hall.

Russell Sheppard was an elegant man not unlike Sir Malcolm Sargent. Over the years, I for one never saw him shout or lose his temper. Added to this he was soft spoken with a dry sense of humour. He was the first man I saw who, simply by standing on his conductor's rostrum, could silence and take full control of a full orchestra and choir without saying a word.

It was not until a press reporter had rung my office for a quote on his death that I learnt of Mrs Sheppard's demise just a few months earlier - a double blow !! At his funeral, I learned that it was he who had had the foresight and the drive to introduce his concepts into schools. His models were copied by other authorities. It was he who was the driving force behind the Glam.

For the last twenty years, since graduating from the Royal College of Art, David Emanuel has established himself as a Couturier of International repute - designing clothes for members of the British and European Royal Families and for some of the world's most beautiful women including HRH The Duchess of Kent, Joan Collins, and Elizabeth Taylor. In 1981 he co - designed the wedding gown for Diana, The Princess of Wales. The ceremony was watched by an estimated 700 million people worldwide. David established the label "David Emanuel Couture" in 1990 and has also developed a flourishing career in photography, television, the theatre and as a writer. He has supported many charitable events including Fashion Aide with Sir Bob Geldorf and has been a most supportive figure in the appeal to maintain Ogmore Camp as a residential centre of excellence.

Roger Lewis : The final years

I close my eyes and the memories come flooding back. The music, the people, the concerts are indelibly etched on my soul. The emotional and intellectual impact of those times - although not appreciated at the time - are very meaningful to me today.

Roger Lewis

I can see us standing in the car park at Ogmore, outside Mr. Davies the Headmaster's office excitedly catching-up with friends not seen for months who came from all over Glamorgan.

I can still picture the bright red siren in the office and the Nissen-hut accommodation. Friendships built then still last today and will forever continue.

When we meet we still recount the stories of the Glam to each other - bitter and sweet, funny and wicked. The story telling lasts long, continuing well into the night as it did all those years ago.

And the concerts. Ah! the concerts. "Rhapsody in Blue" at the Parc and Dare Hall in Treorchy, Bruckner 4 in the Pavilion, Porthcawl. Verdi "Requiem" in Tabernacle Chapel, Morriston and Tchaikovsky 4 everywhere!

Mr. Sheppard for the most part appeared gentle and unassuming but at times he could be hard and uncompromising. You crossed him at your peril. Undoubtedly, he reigned supreme and unchallenged on the podium - not an easy achievement when one thinks of the many outstanding future professional players who chose to rehearse and perform under his baton throughout their student days at the major conservatories. His iron resolve was unshakable. Even when challenged on one occasion by one student who caustically inquired as to whether Mr. Sheppard would like the wind to play the dotted rhythms of the Rex Tremendae from the Verdi Requiem as written or as the choir were singing it. You could have cut the atmosphere in the hall with a knife. It took Mr. Sheppard just one word, which he frequently used to put over-assertive college students in their place, to win this particular skirmish.... "fathead!" Game, set and match to Shep.

It is amazing to think that the immense achievements of music in Glamorgan were all due to the vision, dedication and commitment of one man, Mr. Russell Sheppard; and we all took it for granted. The music structures and systems built up throughout Glamorgan by Mr.Sheppard and his team seemed to us as solid as Tusker Rock and as consistent as the ebb and flow of the tide over it. Only now we realise, and, hopefully not too late, what an extraordinary achievement was accomplished then in Glamorgan and over such long and economically challenging times.

Look around the orchestras of the UK and you will see faces from the Glam. From my generation alone a significant number, including Huw Jenkins (Horn), Albert Dennis (Bass), Hywel Davies (Violin), Gareth Wood (Bass and Composer of note), Griff Harries (Flute and fixer), Phillip Thomas (Accompanist), Martin Bowen (Bassoon) and Dai Miller (a very fine Lutenist) etc, etc, etc. have reached the top of the tree. John Evans heads Radio 3, Peter Sheppard is a well-known teacher and sports' broadcaster, Gareth Jones is a distinguished lawyer and both Phillip Emanuel and John Esaias are Heads of instrumental Services.

But look further to the countless thousands in all manner of walks of life who experienced those times and still treasure those moments today.

His legacy really does live on. Our respect and admiration for him is immeasurable.

Roger Lewis, who played the French Horn in the Glamorgan Youth Orchesta and sang in the Glamorgan Youth Choir over a period of six years from 1969 to 1975 is now Managing Director and Programme Controller of Classic FM. He is also an executive director of Classic FM's parent company GWR Group plc. Immediately prior to this he spent eight years in the record industry as Managing Director for EMI and President of the Decca Record Company. During the 1980s, he worked in radio, firstly at Radio Tees and then in Capital Radio before joining the BBC where he became Head of the Radio 1 Music Department. Roger read music at Nottingham University, went to Cynffig Comprehensive School and also played in the National Youth Orchestra of Wales. He is Chairman of the Trustees of Ogmore Centre which is dedicated to maintaining residential courses for young people.

1.

Overture and Beginners

§

1. Overture

The lady of the valley, soon to know fame
Among an age of iron, coal and flame.

Mountain Ash : Harry Webb

Like Dylan Thomas, Russell Sheppard was born in 1914. However, the "reminiscences" of the the latter's childhood would recall the "ugly, lovely town" not of Thomas' Swansea but of the mining town of Mountain Ash, in the Cynon Valley, South Wales. The third Sheppard baby, Russell John, was born on the 30th September to Mark Edward and Isabella Maud Amelia Sheppard at 38 Upper Forest Level, Newton, Mountain Ash.

Russell Sheppard's father hailed from Somerset and found work in the valleys as a miner, principally in the Deep Dyffryn colliery. Mark Edward met Isabella Maud Amelia Fry - whose family was related to the Fry's of chocolate fame - at a Dance in Bristol. Her parents, Jonathan and Sarah Ann Fry moved to Mountain Ash where Isabella Maud was christened at St. Margaret's in 1909.

1914 was in many ways an apocryphal year, which heralded not only the outbreak of the Great War but also the birth of actor Alec Guiness and the boxer Joe Louis. In the world of the arts, Shaw's "Pygmalion" had its London premiere and Diaghilev's Ballet Company danced Fokin's choreography of Rimsky Korsakov's "Le Coq d'Or". In the same year, James Joyce's "The Dubliners" was published.

It would be difficult to find a more cultured and musical society and environment into which a musical child might be born than that provided in the Cynon valley in the early years of the twentieth century. Gareth Williams describes the valley as "confident, enterprising and radical" and recounts that "It was in Aberdare - only a few miles from Mountain Ash - that, by common consent the first cymanfa ganu (singing festival) had been held in 1859". He also points to the fact that :-

"Other towns boast memorials to military heroes and political tribunes, but for the cultured residents of Aberdare it is a choral captain who is commemorated by the statue paid for by public prescription".

There is evidence that Russell Sheppard's musical mother worshipped with his grandmother at St. Margaret's Church in Mountain Ash. Of her four children, Beatrice and Austen were more than competent string players and Russell was to excel as a pianist and organist. The youngest child, Douglas, displayed little enthusiasm for music. It is likely that the children, when visiting Aberdare, would have gazed at and admired the statue of Griffith Rhys Jones, "Caradog", under whose baton the South Wales Choral Union carried all before them at the Crystal Palace in both 1872 and 1873. These events were celebrated tumultuously when the choir returned to Mountain Ash and Aberdare railway stations.

Everyone in the locality with a love of music would have been aware of the winning of the first prize in the 1906 National Eisteddfod by the Cynon United Male Voice Choir. In 1908, a singular honour was bestowed on the Mountain Ash Male Voice Choir. On their tour of America, the choir, under the conductorship of T. Glyndwr Richards, sang "Martyrs of the Arena", "Nidaros" and Parry's "Pilgrims" in a special concert presented to President Roosevelt at the White House.

A study of the pages of the "Aberdare Leader" of January 1914 reveals a vast panoply of cultural activity with a vibrant network of choral, orchestral, brass band and eisteddfodic endeavour of very high quality.

Competitive events were held even on Christmas Day and Boxing day in such venues as the Cwmbach Public Hall and Bethania, Zoar and Bryn Seion chapels. At the chief choral competition held at the Pavilion, Mountain Ash later in April, choirs competed for the princely sum of £100. The eminent adjudicators included the celebrated composers Granville Bantock and Morfydd Owen. The arts in the area were in no way parochial. An international flavour also prevailing with appearances by the famous Covent Garden Tenor, Joseph O'Mara, The Royal Italian Circus, and the celebrated Italian violinist Clary di Rubadi with her accompanist Vera Olganov.

Throughout 1914, the pages of the "Leader" were filled with advertisements for piano tuition in Aberdare, with schools of music at Monk Street - Mr. T. Jones and Mr. Haydn Jones - and Stuart Street - Professor Tom Davies. Freed's Musical Warehouse in Mountain Ash offered six months of lessons, a piano stool, a five shilling tutor and 12 months tuning free of charge for every piano purchased. Similar advertisements were regularly placed for pianos and the "Marathon Gramophone" by S.J Parr and Harmston and Company of 7 Cardiff Street. There was keen competition from Bevan and Company of Cardiff, Pontypridd and Swansea who offered pianos from 15 to 40 guineas.

The first reference to the outbreak of "Britain at War with Germany" appeared in the "Leader" on the 30th August. There followed an outburst of artistic activity in the form of patriotic productions at the Moss Empires - "Chained to the Enemy, A True Story of Anglo German Marriage and War" - and at the Colosseum, Aberdare - "England Expects, Sons of the Sea" - a bugle call to patriotic citizens.

This zealous fervour found an outlet in the weekly publication of martial poems, the banning of the playing of German music by local bands and frantic activity in the arts events organised for the Prince of Wales War Fund. Nowhere was the prevailing antagonism against the enemy more clearly exemplified than in an advertisement placed in the "Leader" by the Gadlys Piano Stores:

The Aberdare Leader

THE WAR AND THE PIANO TRADE

"Business as usual" is our motto, and we strongly advise all intending purchasers to have nothing whatever to do with German Pianos.

For more than 12 months we have stocked nothing but the **Best British Pianos—The Best in the World** to-day.

Our stock includes instruments by **Chappell, Cramer, Collard, Allison, Russell,** and **Justin Browne,** whose factories in London are working full time, and who were among the first to subscribe thousands of pounds to the Prince of Wales' Fund.

As a contrast to this, the leading German piano firm in London—Bechsteins—on the 11th of this month barricaded their windows, and their manager is to-day back in Germany fighting against us as an officer in the German Army, as reported in "The Piano-maker."

Beware of German pianos likely to be foisted on the public under assumed or altered names. In such cases buyer and seller are liable to prosecution.

Don't be nervous about the result of the war. In more ways than one we are going to come out on top.

Don't be nervous about ordering your new piano. You are quite secure in dealing with us. Our terms protect you in all times of stress and we are waiting to supply you with really genuine bargains, whether for cash or easy payments.

If you already have a piano, may we tune it? Our charge is 3s. 6d. To Reservists or Territorials serving with the Colours we make no charge.

Catalogues of all instruments and music free.

S. J. PARR, GADLYS PIANO STORES, ABERDARE.

2.
Beginners

§

For freedom is a noble thing, beloved from day to day,
When boys are free to pick and choose of either work or play.

Free Discipline : Idris Davies

It was into these turbulent times that Russell Sheppard was born. His parents provided a supportive, encouraging environment, deeply rooted in the principles of the church and a strong work ethic. All the children were encouraged to take up musical instruments. Beatrice became an accomplished violinist who graduated in music at University College, Cardiff. Similarly, Austen developed into a no mean viola player. After graduating in Latin, Austen held teaching positions, finally settling in Bedfordshire with his wife Joan. Austen eventually became Deputy Headmaster at Redbourne School in Ampthill where he regularly organised and conducted school concerts and plays. An early accident with a firework cut short Douglas's musical aspirations and he was destined for a career in environmental health in London, Shropshire and Hampshire.

The polarities of life in the valley at the time of Russell Sheppard's birth are vividly illustrated in two articles from the "Aberdare Leader" of the time. At the one extreme, it was reported that Mrs. Louise Hutcheson of South Kensington and wife of Dr. John Hutcheson of Aberdare left £20,399 in her will. In dramatic contrast, in the Mountain Ash court, William Cole applied for administration of his debts of £30.34. Cole was engaged at Cwmpennar Colliery and earned 30s.10d a week, the cost of a holiday suit advertised by Stewart's of Cannon Street, Aberdare. The average wage agreed by the council Surveyors Department was 28/- per week. Mrs. Dorcas Way who is now ninety, and who still lives in Mary Street, Mountain Ash has spoken with admiration for the absolute dedication and sacrifice of Russell's parents. She clearly recalls that the children were rarely seen at play. Whether or not they chose to devote their time to their studies is open to conjecture. Beatrice, Austen and Russell performed regularly as a trio. Russell and his sister were also engaged for a summer season by a hotel in St.Austel. (Plate 1.)

As a collier, Mark Edward Sheppard would have experienced great difficulty in supporting a family of four children. Nevertheless, he was still able to provide his children with opportunities to take music lessons and to encourage them toward a university education. In a year when the Ynysybwl District Council was criticised for poor conditions and attendance figures, Councillors citing excessive sickness due to scarlet fever, and regular reports of deprivation as the cause, the singular dedication of both parents to providing their offspring with an extended education is remarkable.

The financial uncertainties of the epoch were regularly to impinge on the Sheppard household whose delight at the birth of a third child would have been tempered by the news of the strike of four hundred workers at the Abercwmboi Colliery. Even with butter reduced to 1/- a pound, bacon priced six pence halfpenny at Pegler's Stores and Illtyd Williams Ladies Millinery offering smart hats at sensible prices, weekly budgeting would have been a nightmare.The family would certainly have been in no position to respond to the Sheen's Garage offer of a two seater Ford car priced £125 (the three seater version retailing at £133).

Having moved to 33 Mary Street, Russell attended the elementary school on the opposite side of the road. When he was seven his mother arranged his first piano lessons with Cissie Collier, a cinema pianist who was related to Joseph Collier the lecturer at Cardiff University, with whom Russell was later to study. Despite his innate musicianship, this studentship was not a success and was discontinued when Isabella Maud discovered that her son was, in his own words, "getting by" playing by ear rather than learning music notation. Fortunately, Russell established a strong and lasting musical relationship with his main piano teacher Mrs. Sarah Richardson, passing his early examinations with distinction after only a few months tuition.

Family life centred around St. Margaret's Church, where Russell Sheppard recalled accompanying a singer called "Flossie" Fluke, who, as it turns out was the cousin of the author's mother. Remarkably, it was Miss Fluke's brother, Ron, who in later years once preached at St. Margaret's and who officiated at the Wedding of Russell and Karen Sheppard's son, Peter to Janie in 1979.

An earnest, studious pupil, Russell gained a scholarship to the Mountain Ash County Secondary School which, following its opening in 1907, had removed to Dyffryn House, the erstwhile home of Lord and Lady Aberdare. He must have impressed W.W. Willams M.A., headmaster of the school for 22 years, with his application to his studies. Although there was no opportunity to study music on the curriculum, Russell was greatly encouraged in his academic music endeavours by Mr. Harries Jones. A Latin teacher, Mr. Jones was himself a talented practical musician who recognised Russell's abundant musical talents tutoring him for the Central Welsh Board Certificate in music which he passed with distinction in 1930.

One of his contemporaries at the school was one, Raymond Grant, who went on to gain a history degree at Aberystwyth University. Later, as Dr. Raymond Grant, they would become collegues as Glamorgan Education Authority Inspectors. He also shared with Russell the distinction of achieving the presidency of the National Association of Inspectors and Educational Advisers. In 1932, Russell gained the Higher Certificate in English and Latin with distinction in History. On June 24th and November 2nd, of the same year the Sheppards would have been delighted to receive letters from T.A.Evans, F.T.A. (Chartered Accountant) who was at the time Clerk to the Governors of Mountain Ash County School. These letters brought the welcome news that Russell had distinguished himself by winning the Sir Alfred Thomas, the Morfydd Owen and The Glamorgan Mus. Bac. Scholarships.

Although there is evidence of his having first played at the age of seven, for his first organ lessons Russell travelled by bus to St. Elvan's Church, Aberdare to which he was to return on several occasions in later years with his excellent Glamorgan Youth Choir. In Herbert Trevor he was fortunate to have an excellent mentor whose encouraging tutorship produced an outstanding executant. The church supported a lively programme of arts events and it was there and in his own church of St. Margaret's that Russell developed a love of organ and English liturgical choral repertoire. At the age of sixteen he was appointed Organist and Choir Master at the Church of St. Illtyd's, Cefnpennar to which he regularly cycled for five years. At this small, though picturesque church, he revelled in the responsibility of organising, accompanying and conducting at the weekly services. He performed an exacting repertoire on the small organ, which at the time was manually pumped. During his fulfilling sojourn at this hill top church he gained a high reputation for his musicianship and was well respected by church members. Plate 2.

His first insights into the wonders of orchestral music were gained when he attended concerts by the Mountain Ash Orchestra and the Juvenile Orchestra. The Conductor, Bob Benton who later became an assistant to Sir Walford Davies, the Master of the King's Musik was to play such an important role in the formation of the Three Valleys Festival at Mountain Ash. A contemporary, Mrs. Nora Huxley (Nee Gibson), who also played in the Juvenile Orchestra and was a particular friend of Beatrice Sheppard speaks of the "wonderful times" in the orchestra. Mrs. Huxley also vividly recalls the Juvenile Orchestra winning the Miners' Eisteddfod at Porthcawl, and the second prize won by that ensemble at the Llanelli National Eisteddfod. Pupils travelled from Abercynon, Hirwaun and Aberdare to Mountain Ash and contributed a shilling per week. Bunford Griffiths visited from time to time and players were in awe of his musicianship. Mrs. Huxley remembers the leader of the orchestra, Betty Styling and includes Trevor Lineham and Norman Griffiths - later to become Rector of Penarth - as particular friends of Russell Sheppard at this juncture. There was also a strong representation from a certain Jones family - Stanley played the clarinet, Glyn the violin and Gethin (violin) who became organist of Bethania Chapel. Plate 3.

Russell might also have heard of the exploits of the Aberpennar Orchestra and the Aberdare Philharmonic who gained first and fourth prizes respectively out of of thirteen competing ensembles in the 1922 "National".

Like Idris Davies' "dreamer in a mining town", Russell's early musical ambitions were nurtured and inspired by the exuberant musical climate of his own locale. Bernard Baldwin provides in his book "Mountain Ash Remembered" an informative account of the extraordinary breadth and scope of music making which was to be the seed corn which would stimulate Russell's future achievements. In 1923 there were no fewer than eight music societies in the town. At St. Margaret's Church, the annual meeting was always held in the presence of a celebrated speaker. On one such occasion, under the baton of

Ben Howells, conductor of the massive Mountain Ash Choir, Sir Stafford Cripps requested a performance of "Myfanwy". He recalled a message from the previous speaker George Lansbury, "ask them to sing this - it will make your day", and by all accounts it did.

Led by Mr. W. Badham - the grandfather of Andrew Badham, the present conductor of the Treorchy Male Choir and former member of the Glamorgan Youth Choir - the sixty voices of the Mountain Ash Girls' Choir were the only choir of the twenty eight competing in the National Eisteddfod to be "staged" three times in a single day at the 1926 National Eisteddfod. At least two local collieries supported their own male choirs. Dr. Malcolm Sargent who directed the Three Valleys Festival held regularly at the 15,000 seater Pavilion described Mabel Linwood-Christopher, the accompanist of the Male Choir and of the festival as the greatest accompanist he had ever met. Indeed, Miss Linwood-Christopher was privately taught in Mountain Ash by no less a celebrity than Sir Henry Wood. She subsequently became a sub - Professor of Music at the Royal Academy of Music and Professor of Music at Cardiff College of Music respectively.

At the turn of the century the Welsh Bard Daniel James (Gwyrosydd) worked at the same colliery that later employed Mark Edward Sheppard and his hymn "Calon Lân" - music by John Hughes - is reputed to have been written in Mountain Ash :

Nid wy'n gofyn bywyd moethus
Aur y byd na'i berlau mân,
Gofyn wyf am galon hapus,
Calon honest, calon lân.

Whether or not the hymn was first sung in Mountain Ash, Russell Sheppard later acknowledged that he gained what the hymn depicts as a musically pure heart (calon lân) as a direct result of the stimulating musical environment in which he was reared. His parents certainly strove to inculcate in their children an aspiration to develop the "honest" and "pure" hearts referred to in the hymn.

Through his parents he would have learnt of the high standards of musical achievement of local singers like Edwin Evans. Following the Baritone's memorable performance in America, the composer of "The Apostles" wrote :

Dear Mr. Evans,

Thank you for your most artistic singing of my work in the Carnegie Hall. Your really reverent and complete understanding joined with your exceptional gifts as a vocalist gave me the greatest satisfaction - Believe me.

Sincerely yours,

Edward Elgar

Russell Sheppard recalled an experience of being taken to the Three Valleys Festival in his teens. This special treat left an indelible impression on the mind of the aspiring young musician. He was unable to remember the programme, but recounted the pleasure of going to the Pavilion with a party organised by a Mr. Dowling. Most of all he enjoyed the many free cakes and sandwiches freely provided - tea was a penny a cup and a jam sandwich three halfpence.

In the quest to ascertain why Russell Sheppard later featured Vaughan Williams's choral masterpiece "Toward The Unknown Region" in so many Glamorgan Youth Choir concerts including those at St. Margaret's and St.Elvan's churches, a remarkable piece of information was unearthed in Aberdare library. In D.L.Davies's "History of the Cwmaman Institute" 1868 - 1993, there appears the programme for the thirty third Annual Performance given by the Cwmaman Choral Society on Boxing Day 1932. It is remarkable enough that a choir from a small, end of the valley village, near Aberdare, could produce a choir numbering 130 voices and capable of performing the Brahms' "German Requiem" and the "Sanctus" from Bach's "Mass in B Minor" supported by the Western Studio Orchestra of the BBC and conducted by Edward Lewis. It is doubly incredible that the society was able to programme the "Four Hymns" and "Songs of Travel" by Dr. Ralph Vaughan Williams and to attract to the concert the same distinguished composer who stated that the choir was wonderful and exceeded his expectations. The composer himself conducted "Toward the Unknown Region" for a delighted audience, in whose ranks, was none other than the seventeen year old Russell Sheppard who was, in the final weeks of his life, to acknowledge the experience as a seminal influence on his future musical tastes and achievement.

2.

Exposition

§

1. First Subject : The student 1932 - 1936

The Gods of great disasters
May crack the hills tonight,
But one man's dream is greater
To build the world aright.

Collected Poems : Idris Davies

It was fortuitous for the Sheppard family that Russell's latent musical talents had resulted in his winning the three meritorious prizes to which reference was made in the previous chapter. It is certain that without such financial support a university career would have been out of the question for all four children. Mark Edward and Isabella Maud were already making sacrifices to support Russell's elder brother and sister in their university studentship - Beatrice was also a contemporary of her brother in the music department at University College Cardiff which Russell entered in 1932.

Both parents were dedicated to the advancement of their children's futures via higher education and determined to prevent the boys from the arduous toil and health - sapping drudgery of work in the pits, vividly described by F. Hodges as an abysmal deep blackness. These were times of strife and tribulation in the mining industry. Families had suffered great hardships particularly during the General Strike and Miners' Lock-Out of 1926, and there is no doubt that the Sheppard family had themselves been personally scarred by the low wages, strikes and harsh conditions of life underground which Idris Davies described in the poem "The Angry Summer" as an era of strikes and soup kitchens.

In the 1870's Lord Aberdare's antipathy to unionism was revealed in a letter :

"It is with this section (unionists) that the masters have most difficulty in dealing. It is composed of the noisiest and laziest of them all. They are the more rampant of the members of the union - leading a life of idleness".

Even though the owners themselves had their own organisation which united them, their detestation - and fear! - of the unions is indicated in the lengths to which they would go to protect their own self interests. Lord Aberdare wrote in 1902:

"We have had a lovely time since you left. Forty soldiers quartered at Mountain Ash, forty at Aberdare, besides some twenty of the 14th Hussars. Their presence had a very quieting effect. The strike would not have lasted half the time, had not the weather been so fine".

There is no direct evidence to link Mark Sheppard with industrial action and, indeed, he was to become a district manager for a time. Neither is the cause of the accident which cut short the career of the bread winner of the Sheppard household clear. What is certain is that the family suffered what Russell Sheppard described as periods of "abject poverty". His proud father, a leading figure in the St. John's and Church Benefit movements, was driven on by the determined "mam" of the household who ensured that all of the children were able to better themselves and develop more secure careers. The parents must have considered that:

We are a people wasting ourselves
In fruitless battles for our masters.

Welsh History : R.S.Thomas

None the less, the uplifting musical life of the village continued to be a source of inspiration for the intending student. Bernard Baldwin states that it was a stroke of genius on the part of Sir Walford Davies (who inaugurated the Three Valleys Festival) to recognise that there was no finer singing anywhere on earth than that found in the Welsh valleys. It should be noted that the Festival which ran from 1930 to 1947, and which brought together choirs from the three valleys of Rhondda, Cynon and Merthyr was, in its heyday, arguably the finest festival of its genre in Great Britain.

Where else in the country could an eighteen year old hear a concert presented by an Oratorio Choir of 1,600 singers from eighteen choral societies, accompanied by the National Orchestra of Wales, with a further 1,000 voices in the Massed Male Choir?

On the streets of what other Welsh town could an impressionable youth rub shoulders during the Festival period with artists of the calibre of Elsie Suddaby and Isobel Baille, and bump into conductors of the ilk of Sir Henry Wood, Warwick Braithwaite, Sir Walford Davies and, of course the resident maestro Dr. (later Sir) Malcom Sargent or have the opportunity, at other times, to see Gracie Fields and Paul Robeson at first hand?

Regularly travelling by train from home to lectures, rehearsals, organ and piano lessons, would have afforded him opportunities for studying scores, and for contemplating the sentiments of Sir Walford Davies's prophetic statement. "Musical vision" he wrote "like every vision, only comes to those who climb". This was to be Russell Sheppard's first rung on the ladder of achievement.

At university, he was to be greatly influenced by two outstanding organ teachers for whom he retained such great respect and admiration. He first studied with George Beale Mus. Bac., F.R.C.O. This resulted in the young man's winning the prestigious Sawyer Prize when he passed his Associate of the Royal College of Organists examinations at the age of twenty one. It is likely that he spent the prize money of £1.15s.8d - "to be spent on books to assist further studies in music" - on the voluminous collection of organ music later found in his music library. If George Beale's reference is anything to go by, student and mentor appear to have formed an ideal musical relationship :-

"He has acquired considerable powers as an organist, both in clever technique and judgment in expression. I believe that he has a distinct promise of a successful career in front of him.

Mr. Sheppard is a man of delightful, quiet and courteous bearing, and is bound to make friends both in music and manners wherever he goes".

Dr. (later Professor) Joseph Morgan also penned a short, but telling testimonial of his organ pupil :

"Mr. Russell Sheppard has studied the organ under my direction for the past twelve months. He has worked consistently and well and has made excellent progress. His organ playing is marked by a sense of musicianship far above the ordinary - a quality which has been gained by careful study of all branches of music in his work at the College.

His College examinations have been taken easily and with distinction.

There can be no doubt that he would make an excellent church organist giving every satisfaction, and he has the qualities which should make him popular as a choirmaster and able to carry out his duties with authority and conviction".

Joseph Morgan D.Mus., F.R.C.O.

In order to improve that "clever technique" about which his tutor had commented, and in order to gain a small additional income with which to support his family, he became organist and choirmaster of the church of St. Donat's Abercynon. He was later to speak in glowing terms of the quality of the seven year old Hope-Jones organ at his new church and of the more extended repertoire which it facilitated. The vicar's wife was very enamoured by a popular song of the time and Russell later recounted with a smile the fact that he was required to play "Smoke Gets in Your Eyes" in several church services. He certainly caused an upset in the Sheppard household when, one year, he took a certain Christmas lunch with the vicar, his wife and pretty daughter rather than returning home.

The responsibilities of the post, a determination to succeed and the vagaries of week-day travel, meant that Russell had little time for the student high life. Such application, as the reference Professor David Morgan, Mus.Doc. points out, did not prevent his becoming a well liked and respected student :

"Mr.Russell J. Sheppard entered this College as a Glamorgan County Council Music Scholar in October 1932 and took a very good degree in June 1935.

His collegiate career was particularly brilliant.

The work he produced was of first rate order. An exceptionally able and a splendid worker, he promises to develop into a first rate musician.

A young man of strong reliable character, popular with staff and students alike, he is certain to do well in any post to which he is appointed".

That Russell Sheppard was the outstanding student of the year was confirmed by Douglas Bowen, a contemporary who later became a lecturer at Hull Training College. It was Douglas Bowen who would later invite Russell Sheppard to become a visiting examiner to the College.

David Egan's illuminating commentary "Coal Society" affirms that "for those who decided to stay in South Wales in the 1920s and 30s, the priority was survival". The 1930s was the period of the demeaning means test, and an era when an unemployed man, his wife and three children were expected to get by on a meagre 20 shillings a week. Even toward the end of a decade of depression and despair, when no less a personage than the Prince of Wales commented about Merthyr that "something must be done", a table issued by the Co-operative Wholesale Society in Cardiff highlights the dilemma of a typical unemployed miner, wife and four children scraping by on 39/- per week. And this at a time when rent would have cost 10s.4p leaving precious little for food with prices at :

Butter	*1s.4d. lb*	*Lard*	*7d.lb*	*Cheese*	*9d. lb*
Bacon	*1s.4d. lb*	*Eggs*	*1s. 4d. Dozen*	*Margarine*	*6d. lb*
Tea	*6d. lb*	*Tea*	*2s. 2d. lb*	*etc.*	

These factors would certainly have suppressed the spirit of a lesser nation and would have weighed heavily on the mind of Russell Sheppard for whom the long- term prospect of the teaching profession was an undeniable attraction. As for Idris Davies in the poem "Tonypandy", the people spawned a determination and iron resolve which :

> *Remind us of the toil of blistered hands, And courage and comradeship of man.*

In order to extend the gamut of his formal qualifications he also took university seminars in classics. In 1936, Mr. Richardson his Latin Lecturer wrote of the care and taste of his Latin Prose Compositions. Also taking finals in History and subsidiary English, Professor of Education, Dr. Olive Wheele, recorded his excellent progress in school practice. Complimenting his effective teaching approaches the Professor and A.Donald Amos, M.A.,B.Sc., confidently recommend him for a post in any type of elementary, central or secondary school:

"He has a quietly charming presence and a businesslike way of handling the class, which ensure perfect discipline. During the course of his lessons, he never wastes a moment, yet there is never any sense of urgency.

He contrives to impart his quiet enthusiasm to his classes, and his lessons are a delight to watch".

The family would have been as proud of this reference as they were of the acknowledgement of three of their progenies excellent academic records which appeared in the Parish of Mountain Ash : Parish Magazine (Volume 356), published on August 1934.

"We heartily congratulate the following upon their examination successes :-

Mr. Austen Sheppard who has added a 1st class Teaching Diploma to his B.A., Mr Frank Rees and Miss Beatrice Sheppard upon passing the subsidiary examinations to the B.A.and Mus. Bac, degrees respectively. Mr.Russell Sheppard upon completing his B.A. course and subsidiary".

In the same magazine there appeared illuminating articles on "Training for Ordination", "Trollope and The Victorian Novel", the third in the series on "The Four Cardinal Virtues : Justice", "In a Japanese City", advice on mothercraft and "Household Tips" in the Section : "The Woman At Home". As she neatly signed her copy of the magazine, Mrs. Sheppard may well have recalled, reading with satisfaction within its pages, Plato's dictum that:

"According to the proverb, the beginning is half of the whole; and we all praise a good beginning".

Might she also have shared in a quiet moment with her husband a sense of a family job well done? Despite all the hardships, they had succeeded on behalf of their children in fulfilling the maxim, also described in the Parish Magazine :

"The great purpose of every Christian home is to raise up labourers for God's vineyard".

2. Second Subject : The Teacher 1936 - 1949

§

Sow an activity and you reap a habit,
Sow a habit and you reap a character,
Sow a character and you reap a destiny.

The Teacher : Charles Reed

Although a signed postcard of the period indicates an interest in at least one other teaching post near Leeds, Russell Sheppard gained his one, and only full time teaching post under unusual circumstances. Finally leaving Aberdare, depicted by Alun Lewis as "our stubborn, bankrupt village", his journey north took him not to the Headmaster's study in Holyhead County School, nor to the hallowed environs of the local council offices, but to the mediaeval town of Chester.

As Russell Sheppard later recalled, in order to minimise costs the venue for the interview with Mr. J.M.Hughes B.Sc. was arranged not at the school in Holyhead, but in the Waiting Room of Chester Station. His successful application was for the post of Assistant Master in charge of Music. 431 other applications for the were received. On appointment, his salary was the princely retainer of £19.14s. 2d per month.

1936 was the year of the inauguration of President R.F.D.Rooseveldt's second term of office and, as in the year of Russell Sheppard's birth, the clouds of impending war were gathering over Europe. This was the year in which Germany abrogated the Versailles and Locarno Treaties and occupied the Rhineland - a milestone on the perilous road to the second World War. Early corroboration of Hilter's inhumane philosophy relating to Aryan supremacy, which later manifested itself in the holocaust of camps such as Belsen and Auschwitz was witnessed in the 1936 Berlin Olympic Games. Hitler left the Olympic stadium rather than present the four gold medals to Jessie Owens, the winner of the 100m, 200m, sprint relay and long jump.

In the arts Russell Sheppard would have read - probably in his beloved "Telegraph" - of the premiere of Chaplin's "Modern Times" and may have marvelled at the voice of Paul Robeson singing "Old Man River" in the film "Show Boat". The year marked the birth of Glenda Jackson and the death of Rudyard Kipling. T.S. Eliot's "Four Quartets" were published and Prokofiev's "Peter and the Wolf" was first performed.

Having, in the final months of his life, confessed that he could in no way match the sporting prowess of his wife, who was especially adept at tennis, he would probably have been far less interested in the news that Fred Perry had won his third Wimbledon title. However, the startling revelations that Edward VIII had announced his intention to marry divorcee, Wallis Simpson, and the king's subsequent abdication on December 10th would certainly have been a topic of conversation in the staff room of his new school in Holyhead.

Russell Sheppard, true to his later form, wasted no time in laying down firm foundations for the remarkable growth and blossoming of music at the school. On his arrival, there was very little in the way of instrumental or choral work of high standard and the subject had a very tenuous credibility in curricular terms. His brief was to activate many extra-curricular activities and to develop an interest in and demand for music as an examination subject. In this regard, he was to quickly repay the confidence and trust of the headmaster, who, in 1945, wrote :

"He was appointed to organise the music of the school. Until then one choral lesson was given per week and that only to Lower forms.

He at once commenced to teach Theory of Music as well as singing to the pupils. In the shortest possible time, pupils sat the First School Certificate of the Central Welsh Board in music with very conspicuous success and have continued to do so ever since.

In due course, pupils were prepared for the Higher School Certificate with very marked success, and these successes have been outstanding ever since.

He organised at once a school choir which gained four first prizes at the Anglesey Eisteddfod and has also broadcast on three occasions. Mr. Sheppard also set up a school orchestra and this gained first prize in the Anglesey Eisteddfod. A man of great keenness in matters musical, he is an excellent colleague".

By February 18th, 1938 the commitment and enthusiasm of the young music master was being recognised in the local press. The "Holyhead and Anglesey Mail" records the contribution of the school's music to the success of the prize day presentations when pupil, Master Jack McDougal performed the Bruch Violin Concerto with a depth of feeling and mastery of technique surprising in such a young performer :

"The choir opened the programme with "Huwcyn Cwsg" by Brahms but their chief contribution was Percy Fletcher's setting of "The Blue Danube". This was given by special request, and was further proof, if any were needed, that the choir has improved beyond all recognition".

Success followed success as the reputation of Russell Sheppard's school work spread both locally and nationally. His work was applauded by the Board of Education and the Central Welsh Board Inspectors, and the local newspaper which reported very favourably that newer subjects were already doing well.

"One pupil took music successfully at the first school certificate stage last year. A large number will be doing so this year.

Additional out of school activities very worthy of note are :

1. *Two concerts held by the school choir in the Central Hall of the school.*
2. *The performance last term of the operetta "The Princess Zara" for two nights at the Town Hall, supported by a few outsiders and the school orchestra augmented by members of the Town Orchestra.*
3. *The appearances of the school choir and the school orchestra in competitions at the Anglesey Eisteddfod held at Gaerwen, when both secured first prizes.*
4. *The appearance of the school choir at the National Eisteddfod at Machynleth".*

The same edition of the "Mail" carried the story that "gas masks for every person in Europe will soon be an an accomplished fact. England has 26,000,000 in stock and is still producing 65,000 a week". It also reported "Another Record Year for the Halifax Building Society whose total assets amounted to £122,626,007". Leading advertisements were placed by H.Pari Jones (optician), Braid Brothers; the largest suppliers of automobiles in Wales, and Jay's Furnishing Stores, who offered a splendid variety of pianos at prices from 23 guineas or 3s.6d. weekly.

Russell Sheppard might also have read of the activities described in the article, "Welsh Nationalists" when it was decided by the Denbigh Executive that it would be more profitable from the point of view of propaganda if Mr. Saunders Lewis, the president and nominee for the University seat, were to contest another seat. In his new environment Russell Sheppard, who was brought up in a monoglot family, quickly realised the importance of learning Welsh. His collection of papers of the time show that he gained a good mastery of the written word, preparing as he did scripts in Welsh for various lectures, adjudications and presentations. He worked hard to develop a reasonable oral proficiency and might have enjoyed the humour of an article published earlier in the "Aberdare Leader" which reported the hilarious case of Thomas Lewis of Aberaman who was fined 10/- for swearing. Lewis claimed that he was speaking in Welsh. However, on discovering that the defendant was unable to speak the language, and on reading a script of the expletive used by Lewis, the magistrate decreed that this is Anglo Saxon not Welsh. Russell Sheppard was quick to innovate the practice of mounting school operatic productions. For his first venture in the genre he chose, produced and conducted "Princess Zara" by Arthur Sommervell - a challenging work for any amateur society and a monumental task for school resources. The production was staged at the Town Hall on December 14th and 15th 1937, and among the orchestra was a talented and attractive violinist, Karen Williams - of whom more anon. This tradition of mounting productions was to continue throughout his teaching career with works including his own composition "The Vagabond Student" (1939) and Coleridge Taylor's "Hiawatha's Wedding Feast" in 1946. Plate 4.

Glyn Roberts, a pupil of Russell Sheppard in Holyhead sang in several school concerts at Holyhead County School. He now lives in Tonna, near Neath, and was delighted to be able to visit his former teacher in the final months of Russell Sheppard's life. His former music master was overwhelmed to renew old acquaintances and was greatly moved by the experience. It was Glyn who contacted the "Holyhead and Anglesey Mail" who published the following tribute to teacher Shep, which encapsulates Glyn Roberts' esteem and admiration for the young, inspirational music teacher.

Fond memories of former music teacher Shep

By GETHIN JONES

OLD Holyhead County School pupils would have very fond memories of their former music master.

Originally from Mountain Ash, Russell Sheppard came to the school in 1936, and Glyn Roberts was a pupil there at the time.

Mr Roberts, who now lives in Neath, saw the man everyone knew as 'Shep' in a nursing home in Porthcawl before his death last month, aged 85, and talked at length about the musical life of the school.

A brilliant pianist and organist it was at Holyhead that he really first made a name for himself, as Mr Roberts recalled.

"Shep conducted the school choir and we made two radio broadcasts," he said.

"One of the highlights was the performance of an operetta *Princess Zara* for which he wrote the music.

"He also conducted the Messiah and Accio Galatea with pupils Eurwen Roberts and Douglas Williams singing soprano and tenor," he added. "Shep also composed the school song."

He became a music inspector for Glamorgan Education Authority, starting the Glamorgan Youth Orchestra in 1949.

"To those who loved music Shep was an inspiration," said Mr Roberts. "He was a man of immense integrity and honesty and those of us who knew him will never forget him."

His son-in-law, John Jenkins, who is also a music inspector, is writing a book on Shep's musical influence throughout Wales.

Mr Roberts said he would gladly pass on any memories or photographs of Russell Sheppard that ex-pupils may have of him.

☎ Anyone who can help can contact Glyn Roberts at 18, Pen-y-Bryn, Tonna, Neath, SA11 3JS.

By great good fortune, the article was read by Douglas and Carys Williams of Trearddur Bay, near Holyhead. Douglas immediately contacted both Glyn Roberts and the author. Douglas' scrap book of his performances as a noted treble soloist in Russell Sheppard's school choir is highly illuminating. The young boy soprano sang as soloist in "Messiah", "Christmas Oratorio" and "Acis and Galatea". Also featured in a photograph of the time were school pupil Eirwen Thomas and Blodwen Williams a local teacher whose "sweet voice", the "Holyhead and Anglesey Mail" affirmed, was "capable of producing fine renderings of difficult solos". The town's Electrical Engineer Llewellyn Lewis reached great heights and was greatly appreciated. Douglas Williams' performance of Bach's "Christmas Oratorio" and Mendelssohn's "Hymn of Praise" earned paeans of praise: Plate 5

"Master Douglas Williams charmed the vast audience with the clarity of his singing. He is a young singer with a wonderful voice".

Newspaper articles provided by Douglas Williams confirm that by 1944 the school choir had grown to 143 voices. At a more personal level he recounts :

"Although I have not seen Mr. Sheppard since the late 1940s, when I called on him in Pontypridd whilst on my National Service in Wiltshire, I have often thought of him and enjoyed many nostalgic conversations with other old pupils of Holyhead County School. We recalled him driving a fire engine during the war, which always raised a hearty cheer from any pupils nearby. In one rehearsal one of his famous Shepisms caused hoots of laughter when he told the cast to "make a circle around this square" .

I find it hard even with hindsight to realise that RJS was still in his late twenties when I entered the school. Although I did not study music formally, I was always a chorister and soloist and can say, as many others can, that he was clearly the most influential teacher I had.

At school we felt that RJS went into a form of hibernation between concerts. This was quickly dispelled as, during a packed school assembly, we witnessed the amazing sight of him sprinting from the piano to catch a fainting girl before she hit the floor - in those days we all had to stand because the hall was far too small for the size of the school. Piano students would be amazed to hear calls from a distant Shep, who, with his amazing perfect pitch, would call out corrections like No! its a Bb not a B natural! and other corrections.

RJS was also an excellent private music teacher. One of my friends, Gwenno Puleston-Williams, was very grateful for the extra support he gave her when she first played the organ in Hyfrydle Chapel - and she was by no means the only one to benefit. We owe him a debt of gratitude for the love of music he engendered in us - a love that still endures".

In addition to his school based work, Russell Sheppard was to play a prominent role in the musical life of the area. Appointed conductor of the Holyhead Orchestra in 1936, he gained invaluable experience in learning the orchestral repertoire as he continued this conductorship until 1948. Although members of this orchestra were to occupy a central position in the accompaniment of future school full-scale performances of major oratorios like "Messiah", "Hymn of Praise" and Bach's "Christmas Oratorio" (1937-1943), "Messiah" (1944), "Samson" (1945) and "Judas Maccabeus" (1946), he actively encouraged any talented school instrumentalists to perform in such works.

The large choir's reputation had now been established and the conductor's popularity in the area is evidenced by the fact that the choir's ranks were usually augmented by what the programmes described as friends of the school - talented singers, former pupils and colleagues at the school (mainly Tenors and Basses) who were delighted to appear under his direction. Rehearsals were held on Friday evenings at 6.30 pm at the school. The attention to minute detail and thoroughness of his preparation which was to be a focal dimension of his later work is abundantly evident in the note books he kept at the time. Meticulous registers of attendance at rehearsals, accurate stage seating plans for choir and orchestra, letters to vocal artists and orchestral members and imaginative programme notes are all indicative of the thoroughness and complete dedication of the man. Plate 6.

As previously mentioned, the standard of academic success at Holyhead County School was enormously enhanced by the quality of his mentoring. No doubt inspired by his academic brilliance, several pupils were to gain music scholarships to universities and music colleges. These included many distinctions at both School and Higher Certificate stages, the Lady Verney Music Scholarship to University College, Bangor won by two students, scholarships to the Royal College of Music and numerous LRAM and ARCM Diploma passes by his students. Referring to his Music Syllabus : "A Five year Course" , HMI reported that :

"The music master has real ability as a teacher and is fully alive to the possibilities of his subject as a vital factor in the corporate life of any school there is little doubt that the scheme is clear in its purpose and thorough in its plan".

That the school had become what his second Headmaster, Mr.T.Lovett M.Sc., A.R.I.C described as "undoubtedly the foremost in the Principality in the encouragement of a love of music in its pupils" is reinforced by the educational recognition bestowed on Russell Sheppard at the time. He organised one day Music Schools at Holyhead, presented evening and youth classes in the town and was invited to give evidence to the 1943 McNair Committee for the Training of Teachers concerning the state of Music Teaching in Welsh Schools. On behalf of the BBC he also organised concerts by the BBC Singers directed by Leslie Woodgate. From 1938, he was the Welsh member on the Music Committee of the BBC Central Council for Broadcasting which organised broadcasts to schools.

There is little doubt that the experiences he undoubtedly gained as Secretary of the Anglesey Branch of the Graduate Teachers Association were later to stand him in good stead in his sterling work both as a general inspector and for the National Association of Inspectors and Educational Advisers. The war years were spent as a Leading Fireman in the National Fire Service and despite these, and his school duties, he still managed to spare the time to serve as Vice Chairman of the Anglesey Association of Secondary Teachers.

The author was surprised and delighted, when, a few years ago he visited the Holyhead school to inspect the music department, to be welcomed by the Head of Music who immediately spoke warmly of the affection and regard with which Russell Sheppard was still regarded in the school and the area. Upon being ushered into the school assembly the first notes of music heard were to be those of the former music master's composition "Cân Ysgol" (School Song) written on his arrival at the school and which is still performed to the present day. The story was relayed to Russell Sheppard who was not unexpectedly equally proud of the fact that his music was still being sung by pupils several generations later. He also recalled the contribution of the author of the words, G. Prys Jones, the colleague with whom he was to collaborate over several years during his time at Holyhead.

The reference from Dr. D.E.Parry Williams, Director of Music at University College, Bangor provides a fitting summative eulogy for this fruitful and productive period :

"His success as a teacher of music at Holyhead Secondary School is well known. Some of his pupils have become students in my department and I have reason to think very highly of his teaching. He also takes a wide view of his responsibilities and has gifts of leadership which have become apparent in his many and varied activities. He has been particularly successful in connection with choral and orchestral work in Holyhead and has been able to give concerts which provide a testimony of his musicianship, public spirit and steadfastness".

3.

Codetta : Performer and Composer

§

Make me content
With some sweetness
From Wales
Whose nightingales
Have no wings

Words : Edward Thomas

By 1947, Russell Sheppard's achievements as a teacher at Holyhead County School, had gained him a national reputation in the field of music education. No doubt the additional £75 approved by the Anglesey Education Committee and sanctioned on April 1st by the Ministry of Education would have been welcomed by the then family man. A year earlier his ambition to seek an even more challenging career in which he might be able to harness those "gifts of leadership" acknowledged by Dr. D.E.Parry Williams led to three job applications. At this time, he showed an interest in a Headship at Penarth County School, the post of Superintendent of Music at Stoke on Trent and in the post of HMI for music. Fortunately for the future of music education in Wales, and, particularly for music in the County of Glamorgan, he appears to have been too young to have been considered suitable for appointment to any of these positions.

Throughout the years in Ynys Môn (Anglesey), he continued to perform as an accomplished organist and accompanist. For several years he was organist at Hyfrydle Church in Holyhead. He performed in radio broadcasts as the organist of the Holyhead United Singing Festivals (Cymanfa Ganu Undebol, Caergybi) in February 1944, May and July 1945 and again in June 1946. As an accompanist, he was to impress in recitals with such eminent artists as Elsie Suddaby, Frank Titherington, Edith Coates and Eva Turner and on one occasion he also acted as a consultant to the Halle Orchestra and Choir.

A much sought after adjudicator, he was able to use what Professor J. Morgan Lloyd described as "his diligence, taste and sympathy" in this capacity both locally and nationally. He was adjudicator at the Caernarfonshire Youth Eisteddfod and the Anglesey Youth Eisteddfod for five and three years respectively. Additionally, he officiated at Urdd Eisteddfodau.

In 1943 - the same year that he gave evidence to the McNair Committee - he successfully submitted compositional work for a M.Mus. degree at University College, Bangor and throughout his working life he was to demonstrate an enthusiasm for composition and arranging which, regrettably, did not achieve the plaudits which his abundant talents and the "insight and scholarship" - described by Dr. Parry Williams-richly deserved. Amongst his many compositions (See Appendix 3), he wrote a number of admirable part songs and arrangements for Holyhead County School which were performed and broadcast on numerous occasions. On March 30th, 1939, the "Holyhead and Anglesey Mail" published a two column review of Russell Sheppard's operetta. Under the title of "Mr.Sheppard Composes Operetta : County School Society's Triumph", the reviewer, "SF" eulogised lyrically in praise of the new work "The Vagabond Student" written for the school. He initially revealed that :

"Fine musician though I know Mr. Sheppard to be, I must confess to a feeling that, on this occasion, his ambition had proved greater than his ability. I therefore, was constrained to possess my soul in patience until the appointed date when the whole conspiracy was to be revealed to the world, or at least that part of it which could be crowded into the Town Hall on Wednesday and Thursday evenings.

Let me say here and now that it was a resounding triumph and one that should echo far beyond the borders of Anglesey".

"SF" went on to describe the intricate plot of the work which involved over 150 pupils and friends of the school commenting at length on some delightful lyrics written by Alex Jones, a close friend and colleague of the composer, who also assisted Russell Sheppard on many occasions in mounting school concerts and other events. Mr. Jones also sang the role of "Barba" in the production. With costumes for the pupils made by the parents and those for the principals hired from the Meirion Welsh Ballet Company, the operetta was an outstanding success.

Russell Sheppard's aspirations as a composer were to suffer a major set back, when, in 1946 he submitted a major work for double chorus and large symphony orchestra to the National Eisteddfod. By a strange quirk of fate, it is ironic that the Eisteddfod that particular year was staged in his home town of Mountain Ash. The adjudicators for the prize were D.E.Parry Williams, Haydn Morris and the eminent composer Grace Williams whose works remain in the orchestral repertory. Such was the storm which the panel's decision caused in their adjudication - or lack of it - that the Western Mail carried an article, part of which is cited below :-

A Disagreement : Western Mail August 9th 1946

"No adjudication beyond the announcement of the award was given in the contest for a composition to Welsh words for choir and orchestra. Only half the prize was awarded (£25) to Russell Sheppard, Holyhead, who was formerly associated with Mountain Ash.

It is understood that the three adjudicators, D.E.Parry - Williams, Haydn Morris and Grace Williams were not wholly in agreement, and that Grace Williams felt the full award should be made to Mr. Sheppard".

Russell Sheppard's choice of a pseudonym "Hyder" (confidence) was unfortunate and the actions of the adjudicators might have done much to shatter the confidence of this aspiring composer. That the composition entitled "Cymru Fu, Cymru Fydd", which took as its text the words of Sir John Morris-Jones was worthy of winning the prize was illustrated not only in the verbal support given by Grace Williams at the time but also in the comments she made on the full score manuscript. It remains a tragedy that Welsh audiences have been deprived of the opportunity to hear such a magnificent work to the present day. Even more disconcerting must have been the petty and often unnecessarily destructive comments later written by one leading musician who, despite his undeniable intellectual eminence, is long since forgotten as a major composer. In this regard, I have respected Mr. Sheppard's wish that the musician in question should not be named in this volume.

Not even the successful performance of his Trio for Violin, Cello and Piano written four years later could have compensated for this disappointment. Entitled "Myfyrdod" (Meditation), the Trio was premiered by the London Harpsichord Ensemble at Van Road Congregational Chapel, Caerphilly and displays his imaginative personal style and his ability to explore the lyrical qualities of the instruments for which it is scored.

Amongst his most endearing works may be numbered the undated song cycle - "Daffodil", "Ai Damwain Yw", "Yr Ehedydd" and "Cwn Y Gwynt", several manuscripts of organ compositions, including the "Ceremonial March" written for the bridal procession at the wedding of his eldest child, Wendy in 1965 and the Fanfare on C and D and setting of "God Bless The Prince of Wales" commissioned for the visit of Charles and Diana and the concert given in their honour by the West Glamorgan Youth Choir, Orchestra and Dance Company in 1981.

In 1965 Oxford University Press published "Emynau a Gwasanaethau i Ysgolion Cymru" - "Hymns and Services for Secondary Schools in Wales" - and for this edition, which was to become the standard hymnal for schools in the Principality, Russell Sheppard was the composer - arranger of by far the greatest number of hymns and hymn tune arrangements in the Hymnal. As appendix 3 indicates, the volume contains five of Russell Sheppards original hymns together with fifteen harmonisations, adaptations and arrangements.

In this work he owed a considerable debt to Karen, his wife, whose academic excellence in Welsh he acknowledged. The serene carol "Sanctaidd Faban" (Holy Child) with music and words composed by husband and wife respectively is quoted in tribute over page :

Sanctaidd Faban

Geiriau gan Catherine Sheppard

Russell Sheppard

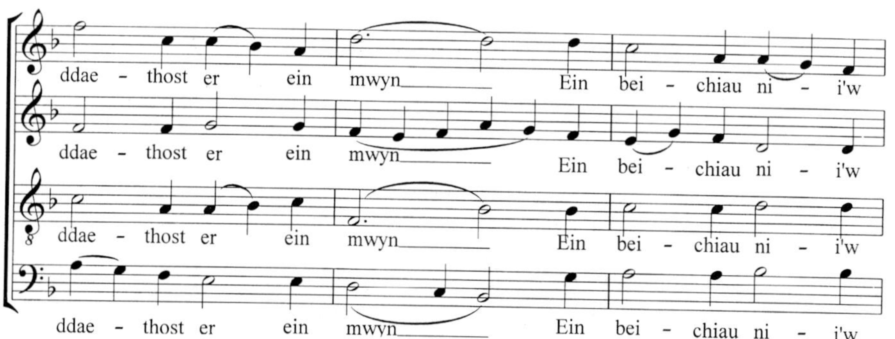

4.

Con Amore

§

Again the golden month, still
Favourite, is renewed;
Once more I'd wind it in a ring
About your finger, pledge myself
Again, my love, my shelter,
My good roof over me,
My strong wall against winter.

In September : John Ormond

For almost fifty nine years Russell Sheppard was fortunate to have found love, support and comradeship through his wife Catherine Ellen. Known as Karen, this endearing lady was the daughter of Thomas Edwal and Jane Williams (Nee Griffith). At the time of their wedding at St. James Church Bangor on June 1st 1940, Karen's father was a mail boat officer at the Port of Holyhead. In earlier times he had travelled the world under sail, becoming a sea captain. Karen's mother was a qualified teacher and as a photograph of the wedding of Karen's sister Betty to Stig Rikof illustrates, the family included the acclaimed actor Huw Griffith in its ranks.

This talent for acting was also to manifest itself in the two Williams girls. Betty was well known for her dramatic talents, and as the photograph shows, Karen was to play the role of Gladys in the Bangor University English Dramatic Society's production of "The Admirable Crichton" by J.M.Barrie at the Prichard Jones Hall in December 1936.

Early programmes of the time include the name Miss Karen Williams in the violin section of the the orchestra which accompanied the Choir of Holyhead School in concerts under Russell Sheppard's baton. Karen also played in the Town Orchestra and it is likely that romance blossomed even further when Mrs. Jane Williams arranged for Russell Sheppard to provide extra coaching in music for her daughter's university course.

Karen Williams - 1st left front row

Karen successfully graduated in French and Russell Sheppard was also proud of her sporting prowess.

She played representative matches in both lacrosse and tennis. However, it appears that she only once competed in the latter sport against her future husband who later confessed to a certain ineptitude - and decided lack of puff - in sporting pursuits. However, without a shadow of doubt, Russell Sheppard was certainly more than competent in accompanying his wife-to-be in her musical endeavours and Karen's musical accomplishments resulted in her passing the ARCM violin diploma in 1938.

After their wedding in 1940, the couple established their home in Orcades Villa in Holyhead and, during the war years, Russell Sheppard's father and mother moved to Anglesey and established their final home near to their son and his family. Karen became a successful peripatetic teacher of children with learning difficulties and also taught the violin.

It was in Holyhead also that Russell and Karen Sheppard's two daughters- Wendy and Patricia, were to be born and to enjoy their early childhood. Under their mother's direction both were to learn the violin. Uniquely, both daughters later became leaders of the National Youth Orchestra of Wales. Although born in South Wales, their younger brother, Peter, who is currently a teacher and broadcaster, would complete a "Nash" family trio as a horn player. Plate 7.

3.

Development 1949 - 1974

§

1. Subject : Inspector of Schools

§

Darest thou now, Oh soul
Walk out with me toward the unknown region.
Where neither ground is for the feet,
Nor any path to follow.

Toward the Unknown region : Walt Whitman

1949 was the year in which the Soviet Union detonated its first atomic bomb and the Council for Europe and NATO were established. In the arts, Arthur Miller's "Death of a Salesman" and Rogers and Hammerstein's "South Pacific" received their premieres and John Wayne starred in "She Wore a Yellow Ribbon". In the same year, the birth of Meryl Streep might have passed by without notice, but Russell Sheppard would certainly have read of the death of composer Richard Strauss. A short article in the "Daily Herald", although hardly front page news, drew to public attention the national reputation which Russell Sheppard had earned for himself.

As the newly appointed Inspector of Schools to the county of Glamorgan, Russell Sheppard's qualities, qualifications, experience and credibility were unquestionable. Not withstanding this, the Director of Education of the time, Emlyn Stephens and the councillors who exhibited trust and confidence in a young man of thirty five could scarcely have anticipated the exceptional and unique distinction and recognition in the field of schools and youth music which the newly appointed Inspector would bring to their South Wales Education Authority.

The County Councillors would have been impressed by the supportive testimonials and references they received from the headmasters of Holyhead County School. The retired Head, Mr. Hughes complimented Russell Sheppard's power of "encouraging the love of his subject in his pupils" and regarded him as "a very willing, conscientious and hard working colleague, who is prepared to state and stand by his definite opinions". Mr. Lovett, the principal of the time wrote in the most glowing terms of the achievement of their outstanding head of music and commented most favourably on the fact that :

"He has a marked organising ability in musical affairs His control of large choirs is excellent".

Leading academics, Dr.Parry Williams of Bangor and Professor David Evans of Cardiff universities also celebrated the meritorious achievements of their former student. Of Russell Sheppard, the former wrote :

"Being a Master of Music of the University, he is fully qualified for the post he seeks, and would, if appointed, discharge his duties with characteristic skill and thoroughness".

A number of key characteristics which were to typify the work of the new Glamorgan Education Authority employee are defined in the statements above. From the start, Russell Sheppard's single mindedness of purpose, determination, outstanding organisational skills and flair, coupled with his enviable energy, drive and amazing work ethic were to set an example which would be impossible for others to match.

The governors of Holyhead County School were naturally reluctant to release such a talented music master a day earlier than necessary. In point of fact, Russell Sheppard's successful interview had taken place in July of the previous year. Matters were finally resolved so that the Inspector with Special Qualifications in Music was able to commence his duties in Glamorgan on January 1st 1949. The letter of appointment, dated 28th July 1948, indicates a salary of £800 rising annually by £25 to £1000 per annum.

It is particularly important to record that, throughout virtually the totality of his tenure of office in Glamorgan, his specific music duties comprised only a part of the requirements of a county-wide brief. Upon his family's moving to their new home at 5 Lanelay Crescent, Pontypridd, Russell Sheppard not only immediately set about establishing a pattern of schools and youth music which would quickly become the model which many authorities would follow, but was also required to fulfil a general educational remit in both the Pontypridd and Neath district offices. With this in mind his musical feats appear to have been even more remarkable.

As mentioned in Chapter 2, the vibrancy and excellence of musical life in the Cynon valley during Russell Sheppard's childhood and youth provided salient stimulation in crystallising the development of music in Glamorgan. Firstly, he was later to acknowledge the influence of the pioneering work of William David Christopher in the field of group violin teaching in the Mountain Ash area in the 1920s and 30s. Secondly, he kept until his death several programmes of the Cardiff Schools' Music Festival in which very large orchestras of school pupils performed under the conductorship of Bunford Griffiths - Russell Sheppard had actually taken a few early piano lessons with Mr. Griffiths. Thirdly, the outstanding choral standards which Russell Sheppard would have experienced in the Cynon Valley and the success of his choral work prior to 1949 stood him in good stead for vocal developments in Glamorgan. Finally, the breadth of his work in both his musical and teacher association activities whilst at Holyhead would provide a pivotal platform for his contributions to music and educational politics post 1949.

2. Counter Subject 1 : The Glamorgan Youth Orchestra

§

O young man, so ardent, rich in your dreams
Make precious each hour, and grasp while you may,
And give ear, O give ear in the cool of the dusk,
To the magnificent orchestras of our history.

The Angry Summer : Idris Davies

Like the mover and shaker of O'Shaughnessey's poem, " The Music Makers ", Russell Sheppard, or Shep as he quickly became familiarly known to all future members of the Glam, wasted no time in establishing a county youth orchestra which over a thirty five year time span would become a focal point in the lives of thousands of instrumentalists. Those who were to perform under his ever vigilant eye, and who would respond enthusiastically to the usually precise movements of his baton were encouraged to realise that :

We are the music makers, And we are the makers of dreams.

The Music Makers : O'Shaughnessey

To assume that Russell Sheppard's orchestra was the first instrumental ensemble made up of young people in Glamorgan would be a misconception. In the programme issued for the twenty-first anniversary of the West Glamorgan Youth Orchestra(GYO) Russell Sheppard, himself, commented :

"It has not always been appreciated that instrumental music has been provided in secondary schools since 1924 when the Glamorgan Authority decided to broaden the music curriculum. It was reported in July 1926 that there were orchestras of varying strengths in the following schools : Aberdare Boys, Barry Boys and Girls, Bridgend, Mountain Ash, Pontypridd Girls and Garw".

In earlier chapters reference has already been made to the orchestras which existed in the Aberdare-Mountain Ash area in his youth. The Mountain Ash Juvenile Orchestra of the 1930s had, according to Mrs. Nora Huxley, been "pipped at the post" on several National Eisteddfodau occasions by the orchestra of Cwm Ebbw Vale and the Cardiff Schools Music Festival of the 1930s could also boast a large string orchestra. Principally, these were orchestras comprised mainly of string players. Young people could also readily find performance outlets in a number of predominantly adult Orchestral Societies including those in the Cynon Valley. A good example of this type of ensemble also existed in the Rhondda Valley, where in 1927, the Porth and District Orchestral Society could boast an almost complete symphony orchestra of about fifty players, although it is strange that the orchestra was unable to find trombonists in an area renowned for the quality of its brass bands.

What is unique is the fact that Shep was able to create and sustain a full symphony orchestra of ever growing size and stature, harnessing and consolidating as he did examples of existing good practice, and developing and extending a county network of instrumental tuition and regional centres which was to become the best of its type, certainly in Wales and, debatably, in the United Kingdom.

Upon his arrival in Glamorgan in 1949, Russell Sheppard quickly became aware of the pockets of orchestral excellence extant in the County. As is shown in Plate 8, in Pontypridd, Mr. Clifford Langham had inaugurated a string orchestra in which Russell Sheppard's first daughter, Wendy, was to enjoy playing the violin. At Neath, music master John Hopkin Jones - firstly with string teacher Valmai Williams and later, in the Boys' Grammar School working in accord with the outstandingly influential string teacher, Freddie Herbert - created a sizable school orchestra. Similarly, in the late 1940s and early 50s, Gowerton Boys' Grammar school orchestra was able to tackle an ambitious repertoire under the direction of Cynnwyd Watkin. This orchestra included in the ranks of the viola section the distinguished composer, Alun Hoddinott, who was subsequently to be appointed Professor of Music at University College, Cardiff. That such a large number of excellent cellists were produced in the same area is a tribute to the eminent player Duval. Consolidation of string teaching at Gowerton was to be undertaken with great success by the talented violinist and teacher Morgan Lloyd.

The development of string teaching in the Maesteg and Bridgend districts in the early years was entrusted into the capable hands of Nesta Garfield who also gave lessons at school to Russell Sheppard's two daughters. Additionally, at the turn of the decade there were examples of instrumental playing of county standard in Mountain Ash, Port Talbot - the base for Aneurin Edwards' future work - and in Barry. In the Barry area, the work of Tom Jones was to be consolidated by Betty Mabbs. In the Garw, Ogmore and Maesteg Secondary Modern schools, Stanley Saunders who eventually became Chairman of the Music Faculty at the University of Ontario was an influential force encouraging players such as Jeffrey Lloyd and William Rogers.

From his first year as an inspector Russell Sheppard had the full support of the County Council in establishing the first Glamorgan Youth Orchestra. He was later to pay warm tributes to the teachers previously mentioned and quickly set about soliciting the support of key headteachers through whom the appointment of string teachers of high calibre would become possible. He also made speeches in several school concerts in the early 1950s and was able to convince influential politicians such as Degwel Thomas in Neath and, even more importantly, Llewellyn (later Lord) Heycock of Port Talbot of the social as well as cultural benefits which the development of music in the county could bring.

Dyffryn House was chosen as the centre for the inaugural course of the Glamorgan Youth Orchestra. It was to this beautiful country estate near Cardiff that the band of thirty nine intrepid orchestral pioneers travelled on the 17th of September, 1949. The founder members of the Glam included :

VIOLIN 1

Maureen Abraham	Mountain Ash	Cecily Holliday	Maesteg
Marjorie Bowen	–	Daphne Jago	Neath
Dorothy Brown	Gowerton	Margaret Protheroe	Ogmore
Brian Campbell	Mountain Ash	Nansi Rees	Caerphilly Girls
Doree Clompus	Neath	Derfel Richards	Gowerton Boys'
Joel Clompus	Neath	Clive Thomas	Gowerton Boys'
Valerie Davies	Mountain Ash	Dilys Thomas	Neath Girls'

VIOLIN 2

Brinley Davies	Student	Donald Kitt	Caerphilly Boys'
William Greenway	Port Talbot Intermediate	Eifion Evans	Ystalyfera
Donald Mogford	Gowerton Boys	William B Evans	Student
Jeffrey Francis	Port Talbot Secondary	Ann Powell	Garw
Roger Galliford	Cowbridge Boys	George Brian Selwyn	Aberdare
Megan Thomas	Neath Girls'		

VIOLA

Peter Evans	Gowerton	Marion Lloyd	Neath
Joan Hugh	Tonypandy	Ronald Parry	Gowerton
John Rees Jones	Mountain Ash	Jean Waygood	Student

CELLO

Valerie Davies	Neath	Geraint John	Gowerton
Hannah Eimsheimer	Student	David Williams	Caerphilly Boys'
Alan Hugh	Tonypandy		

BASS

J.P.Clarke	Caerphilly Boys	Cymfelin Roberts	Maesteg

HARP

Ann Griffiths	Maesteg

The principal tutors on this course were Stanley Popperwell (Violin), Gordon Mutter (Viola) and George Isaac (Cello) of the distinguished Cardiff University String Quartet. Later R. Bossart became a tutor, and in future years, violinist Alfredo Wang coached the first violins on many courses. The quartet were to contribute significantly to the successes of future courses for many years to come. The tutorial staff was completed by Mrs. Nesta Garfield. The Glamorgan Education Committee also granted approval for the secondment of Miss Ivy Morgan of Gadlys Secondary School in order that she might undertake residential duties on the course. Plate 9.

Due to an error in the letter sent to schools the first course attracted only string players. The programme for the first concert, held on Sepember 23rd at Glamorgan Training College, is shown overpage.

GLAMORGAN EDUCATION AUTHORITY.

Programme

of a

CHORAL AND ORCHESTRAL CONCERT

to be held at the

GLAMORGAN TRAINING COLLEGE, BARRY,

on

FRIDAY, 23rd SEPTEMBER, 1949.

CONDUCTOR:
R. J. SHEPPARD.

NOTE

The performance is given by an orchestra consisting of pupils of secondary grammar schools and members of youth centres in Glamorgan who are attending an orchestral music course at Dyffryn Education Centre in co-operation with the Choir of the Barry Intermediate School for Girls.

Part One.

Orchestra:	Eine Kleine Nachtmusik A. ALLEGRO B. ROMANCE C. MENNUET D. RONDO	MOZART
Orchestra:	Andante Cantabile for Quartette (OPUS 11.)	TCHAIKOWSKY
Orchestra:	Serenade from "Hassan"	DELIUS
Orchestra:	The Londonderry Air	ARR HARTY
String Trio:	(a) Allegro Moderato in B flat	SCHUBERT
	(b) Theme and Variations	BEETHOVEN

STANLEY POPPERWELL - VIOLIN; GORDON MUTTER - VIOLA; GEORGE ISAAC - VIOLINCELLO.

Part Two.

Choir:	Y Bore Glas	
Choir and Orchestra:	Gloria in Excelsis Deo	E. THIMAN
Orchestra:	Concerto Grosso in G (OPUS 6 NO. 1.) A. TEMPO GIUSTO B. ALLEGRO C. ADAGIO D. ALLEGRO E. ALLEGRO	HANDEL
Choir and Orchestra:	(a) Sheep may safely graze	BACH
	(b) Sleepers wake	BACH

HEN WLAD FY NHADAU
GOD SAVE THE KING

Following the success of the September course, the minutes of the Glamorgan Education Committee afford ample proof that music was on the move in the county. The committee approved sponsorship of violinists Hilary Squire's fees of £6.6s.6d. and train fare to the National Youth Orchestra of Great Britain Courses held at Leeds and Bath respectively. Leonard James' request for subsistence of £1.18s.7p to travel from London to the National Youth Orchestra of Wales Course held at Caerleon and Wrexham earlier in the year was also approved. Both applicants were leaders of the Glam. In the same minutes there appeared an advertisement for a part-time instrumental teaching post for wind instruments at Gowerton Boys' Grammar School and reference to the reimbursement of £1.10s.0d for seven scholars involved in cello playing instruction.

A second course was held at Dyffryn Residential Centre in January 1950, when a few wind players would facilitate a more ambitious programme which included Bach's Piano Concerto in F Minor, the Minuet from Mozart's "Jupiter" Symphony Orchestra and "Christmas Music" from Handel's "Messiah" performed with the Whitchurch Secondary Modern School Choir.

An interesting account of the early courses is provided by Jeffrey Francis, a second violinist on the first course. Jeffrey was later to lead the Glam and to succeed Shep as the Music Adviser in Glamorgan.

"On the morning of the first day of the first course held for the Glamorgan Youth Orchestra a number of us assembled in the oak-panelled room in Dyffryn House. My parents drove me there. After a short time a car could be seen travelling along the drive. In made an unusual sight as the top of a harp could be seen sticking out through the open sun - roof. The car was driven by Mr. Griffiths a headteacher of a school in Maesteg. He and his wife were conveying their daughter Ann to the course. Years later she became a very well known harpist.

It must be remembered that when the first course was being held, the war had only ended four years previously and that Dyffryn House and gardens were in a very run down state. However, we were given a guided tour of the gardens by one of the gardeners who certainly knew the Latin names of all the trees. On the early courses members of the orchestra were forbidden to walk in the gardens after dark. One disobedient soul broke the rule and promptly fell down an open manhole with rather smelly consequences. This resulted in his parents having to travel to Dyffryn with a change of clothing,

The girls were accommodated on the first floor and the boys on the second. Miss Ivy Morgan looked after the girls and Mr. Sheppard made sure that the boys were all in bed and the lights put out. However, this did not prevent clandestine pranks including a fire extinguisher being knocked off a wall. Fortunately, before too much damage was done its nozzle was stuck down a toilet pan.

The first full rehearsal was held in the a large room the walls of which were lined with green brocade. It also had a beautifully painted ceiling. Impromptu concerts were memorable and I vividly recall a viola player, whose nickname was "Soos", performing on most instruments whilst wearing gloves.

It was in Dyffryn that I first saw a full-sized billiard table and we would be down early to try out our new-found skills.

On returning to school after the first course one of my A' level teachers said to me. "Now then Francis, if you want to do well in your subjects you won't be able to take a week off from school to go on courses". Things haven't changed in fifty years".

The following extract from circular (No.57/50) issued by the Glamorgan County Council on the 30th January 1950 again ensured that wind players would be eligible for the third Glam course.

Dyffryn Residential Centre
Course SP.11 - Orchestral Course

Orchestral course for pupils of secondary schools and members of County Youth Centres:-

Applications are invited for players of stringed and wind instruments. Pupils who have attended the previous course will also be eligible for this course.

Applicants should have reached a standard of proficiency at least equivalent to that of Grade V of the Royal Schools of Music.

A charge of ten shillings will be made for each school pupil attending, but such charge will not be made in respect of pupils being on the scale under which they qualify for free schools meals.

The fee in respect of members of youth centres is £3. The authority make a grant-in-aid of £1.15s.0d, and the balance only (£1..5s.0d) is payable to the County Treasurer.

E.Stephens : Director of Education.

Permission was granted in the Secondary Sub Committee to hold a concert held at Pontypridd Boys' Grammar School on April 6th, 1950 and for a further two concerts to be held - following a course at Dyffryn Residential Centre - at the Coliseum, Aberdare and the Gwyn Hall Neath on September 14th, 1950 and January 4th 1951 respectively.

Jeffrey Francis' narrative continues :

"By the second course the orchestra had grown so much that we used to rehearse in the entrance hall - with its fine fireplace. It was on this course that the BBC arrived to record the orchestra. A temporary "studio" was set up in a small office adjoining the hall, and, in order to deaden the reverberation large blankets were suspended between the ceiling and the handrail on the balcony.

In the early years the outstanding player was Leonard James, a pupil of Max Rostal. On the second course, one of the new-comers was a fellow pupil of mine, the pianist, Geoffrey Arnold. Being excited at being away from home we started practising Haydn's Piano Trio which was performed by us at the

Whitchurch concert. Unfortunately, we rehearsed at about 6am on a Sunday morning. In no time our practice was rudely interrupted by Mr. Phillips, the caretaker whose daughter we saw later and who was to become the famous actress, Sian Phillips.

For the first twelve years or so, the strings were tutored by members of the Cardiff University String Quartet"

Of the many talented performers in the early orchestras, the cellist Geraint John would have a distinguished career with the Aberystwyth ensemble, violinist Clive Thomas and clarinettist, John Hempenstall would both play in professional orchestras and cellist Valerie Heath-Davies would sing professionally. In order to broaden the parameters of the orchestra's role and to establish its educational acceptability the Glam also gave schools' performances.

Until January 1952, orchestral courses continued to be held three times annually at Dyffryn Residential Centre. During this period the orchestra was led by Cecily Holliday and Leonard James. These very talented players were to become orchestral players with leading professional orchestras, the former maintaining a distinguished career firstly with the Halle orchestra and until recently with the BBC Philharmonic Orchestra. Both leaders performed concertos with the Glam, the former playing several Handel Concerti Grossi with other parts performed by Jeffrey Francis, Ioan Davies, Marion Lloyd, Graham Jones and Haydn Davies. Leonard James gave outstanding performances of concertos by Nardini and Mozart. Other soloists were Jeffrey Arnold (Piano), James Hargreaves (Trumpet), John Cynan Jones (Organ) - later the conductor of the Treorchy Male Choir and John Hempenstall (Clarinet). Perhaps the most famous personality to emerge from the Glam of this period was violinist Tony Lewis. Tony, who hailed from Neath, would later captain Glamorgan and England in cricket before becoming the Chairman of the MCC and the Wales Tourist Board, President of the MCC and High Sheriff of Mid Glamorgan. Plate 10.

Programmes centred almost exclusively around works of the Baroque and Classical periods. Choral inputs into these programmes will be appraised in the next section of the book. Similarly, details of the orchestra's important performances during the 1951 Festival of Britain year are given in the following chapter on the development of the youth choir.

Shep, conscious of the burgeoning of instrumental music in schools across the county which emanated from the work of an expanding team of peripatetic teachers, was quick to realise that there was a growing need to establish regional orchestral centres. Working with Clifford Langham, the first centre was established in the east of the county in 1951. The Pontypridd centre was to blossom firstly under the direction of Mr. Langham and, later under the leadership of Roger Jones. Nesta Garfield, and subsequently Aneurin Edwards would ensure the success of the Bridgend Centre which was also inaugurated in 1951. A year later a third centre was opened at Neath administered by John Richards, with Freddie Herbert as the chief instrumental tutor. The three centres were to become an institution for hundreds of aspiring "Glamites" and acted as an excellent nursery where school players could tackle a challenging repertoire. Friday night and Saturday morning rehearsals became sacrosanct and the after-glow of the rehearsal was usually celebrated at the local cafes where many a courtship began.

By the September course 1952, the Glam's home was established at Ogmore School Camp which provided ample, if somewhat primitive dormitory accommodation for 58 strings, a well-balanced woodwind section of 16 players, a brass section comprised of 5 Horns, 4 Trumpets, and 3 Trombonists and a harpist. Ogmore was to become the permanent home for the orchestra until 1974 although occasional courses were held at Bridgend and Barry Training College. Amongst the talented players who took the coaches from Bridgend along the picturesque coastal route to Ogmore by Sea were Cecily Holliday and Hilary Squire. Like Leonard James who was unable to attend this particular course, they were to lead both the Glam and the N.Y.O.W. Second violinist, Alun John was to become a BBC producer and prominent choral conductor. Viola player Susan Salter would later enter the Halle Orchestra. Anthony Randall's career as a leading horn player, conductor and composer was developing in London and the orchestral dreams of Daniel Hannaby (Trombone) and Ann and Mary Griffiths (Harp) were beginning to become a reality.

During this period the programmatic balance shifted in favour of late classical romantic and early twentieth century pieces. The programme performed at the Central Hall Bargoed and the Gwyn Hall, Neath on consecutive nights in September 1952 included works like Beethoven's "Leonora" Overture No.3 with increasing emphasis on romantic symphonies such as Dvorak's "New World". Shep maintained a populist balance of works from different stylistic periods. Included in the same programme were Debussy's "L' Apres Midi D'Un Faune" Mozart's "Marriage of Figaro" Overture and works by Vivaldi and Mendelssohn. Mozart's Horn Concerto in Eb was played by Gowertonian, Haydn Davies who later in his career became firstly a Music Adviser and later an HMI for music. In other programmes Shep's predilection for contemporary English music is revealed in works like Vaughan Williams' " The Lark Ascending", and Delius' "Walk To The Paradise Garden".

By 1953, the orchestra had trebled in size. For the concert held on April 1st of that year, an orchestra comprised of 77 strings, 18 woodwind, 16 Brass, timpani and harp took the stage at the Town Hall, Maesteg. Soloists in Bach's Brandenburg Concerto No 5 in D were Cecily Holliday, Denise Bassett, Graham Jones, Marion Lloyd and Haydn Davies. John Hempenstall performed Mozart's Clarinet Concerto and Cynthia Coombs was the soloist in the first movement of Beethoven's Piano Concerto no. 4 in G.

In April 1954, the Llwchwr Urban District Council Entertainments Committee were given full value for money in an orchestral concert which featured for only the second time a vocal soloist. Shep wisely selected the contralto Maureen Guy whose local connections and growing operatic accomplishments shone in arias from Saint Saens' "Samson and Delilah" and Handel's "Messiah". Miss Guy had first sung with the orchestra in a concert given by Glamorgan Music Scholarship

Soloists at Dyffryn House in July of the previous year which also featured the soprano Eirwen Mathias. In the Llwchwr concert, as in several other performances of the period, Shep was unable to resist the opportunity to perform his beloved " Walk to the Paradise Garden " and music by Coleridge Taylor - this time the work was to be "La Caprice de Nanette".

Returning to the Coliseum, Aberdare on July 14th, the same year must have been a particularly proud moment for Shep, whose programme was as catholic and all-embracing in its construction as ever :

Overture : Semiramide	*Rossini*
Brandenburg Concerto No 6 in Bb	*Bach*
Trumpet Concerto in Eb	*Haydn*
(Soloist Lawrence Evans)	
Divertimento for Wind Quintet	*Haydn*
Symphony No.1 in C Minor(Movement 1)	*Brahms*

Interval

Occasional Overture	*Handel*
Violin Concerto in D Major	*Wieniawsky*
(Soloist Leonard James)	
The Walk to the Paradise Garden	*Delius*
Demande et Reponse de Nanette	*Coleridge Taylor*
Hen Wlad Fy Nhadau God Save the Queen	

The audience certainly had their full money's worth in this as in all subsequent concerts, and the miscellaneous nature of the Glam programmes was replicated throughout Shep's reign as conductor.

Other outstanding concerto soloists of the 1950s were pianists Geoffrey Arnold, Keith Morris, Peter Rees, Carwen Rees, Heather Lewis, Aldon Rees and Arnold Draper who performed between them no fewer than seventeen concertos and other master works. Alan James performed Handel's Organ Concerto in Bb on the Pavilion organ, Porthcawl despite the vagaries of the electricity supply on that occasion. In addition to pieces already cited, Leonard James continued as a prominent soloist performing the Mendelssohn Violin Concerto and Vaughan Williams' "The Lark Ascending", and Cecily Holliday played the violin part with Kenneth George (Flute) and Keith Morris (Keyboard) in Bach's Brandenburg Concerto No.5. Harpist Ann Griffiths (Debussy : "Danse Sacre"), Violinists Denise Bassett (Beethoven : Romance in F), and Victor Chamberlain (Svendsen : Romance in G), Flautist Kenneth George (Mozart : Concerto No.2 in D), Viola soloist Susan Salter (Handel : Concerto in Bb) , Horn player Anthony Randall (Mozart : Concerto No.3 in Eb), David Ayres and Eric James ("Trumpet Voluntary") complete the instrumental soloists hall of fame of the 1950s. Vocal soloists who appeared in Glamorgan Youth Orchestra concerts of the period include Maureen Guy, Marian Davies, Jean Evans, Yvonne Collins - all contraltos - and Gillian Humphreys - soprano.

Concerto soloist, Heather Lewis (now James) writes:

"I have fond memories of playing Mozart's Piano Concerto K488 in the Gwyn Hall and of sharing the concert platform with other soloists from Neath. These were flautist Kenneth George and the marvellous horn player Tony Randall. My orchestral favourites were the Dvorak Symphonies, Rachmaninov's "Paganini" Variations, Franck's Piano Variations and Tchaik 4.

I think that Shep was a marvellous enabler. Without him we would not have had buses, food, accomodation, staff to keep us in order, music, concerts and above all friends. The music he introduced us to was at such an impressionable age. We never doubted that the courses would go on for ever.

In the years leading up to the Glam's tenth anniversary, the orchestra continued to expand and by 1955 it was providing up to forty members of the NYOW. Significantly, no fewer than five Glam leaders, Leonard James, Cecily Holliday, Hilary Squire, Denise Bassett and Victor Chamberlain also led the NYOW during the same period. The other contemporary Glam leaders Jeffrey Francis and Mark Roberts were also "Nash" players in the 1950s. During the era, the repertoire included symphonies by Beethoven, Brahms, Dvorak, Haydn, Mozart, Schubert, and Tchaikovsky together with a myriad of Shep's "lollipops".

The tenth anniversary was celebrated in style with concerts in Penarth, Aberdare, Bargoed and Bridgend. During the decade, a generation of players had gained invaluable repertoire experience which would stand them in such good stead in their future professional careers. Perhaps even more crucially, a substantially larger number of the Glam Club, as it became known, had been indelibly touched and moulded by the social as well as musical benefits derived from their association with Shep. During the period, the well-being of the students at Ogmore was entrusted to the stewardship of Mr. and Mrs Islwyn Williams. They were later to be followed by Mr.Bert Davies and his wife Ceinwen. Plate 11.

The principal pieces in the tenth anniversary concert revolved around Dvorak' s Symphony No.8 in G Major. Shep included Weber's "Oberon Overture", Handel's "Suite from the Water Music" - this was the bicentennial of the death of Handel - and Ravel's "Bolero" in the Tenth Anniversary Concert held at the Central Hall, Bargoed. Soloists in the performance were pianist Arnold Draper who performed Mozart's Concerto in Bb K450, Contralto, Hazel Jenkins who sang the Habanera from Bizet's "Carmen" and David Ayers in the Purcell-Wood arrangement of the "Trumpet Voluntary". The leader was Victor Chamberlain from Barry and it is interesting to note that this was the first Glam course to be attended by a young oboist, Karl Jenkins who, recently, has had such phenomenal success with his three "Adiemus" recordings. The first of this triptych of music by Karl Jenkins has had an unprecedented reign in Classic Top Ten Charts. In particular Disc 1 "Songs of Sanctuary" recorded with Miriam Stockley and the London Philharmonic Orchestra in 1995 has gained international acclaim. Disc 2 "Cantata Mundi" and Disc 3 "Imagined Oceans" quickly followed. Toward the end of his life Russell Sheppard spoke with gratitude and affection of the contribution made by Karl's father who had acted as a member of staff on several music courses.

Many contemporary players would play in top London orchestras, Sylvia Rhys Thomas would later have a lengthy and successful singing career in Italy and at least two players would reach the top of the tree in careers outside music. Viola player, Diana Griffiths, would become a leading author and Dr. Ian Evett, from the same section, would become an eminent forensic scientist writing important books on DNA testing.The programme included a statement written by Shep which concluded by saying :-

"This year the orchestra celebrates ten years of continuous existence. Since 1949, forty-eight orchestral courses have been held in different parts of the county. At the first of these concerts the orchestra consisted of thirty-nine players; one hundred and fifteen players are taking part in tonight's performance. Sixty-six members of the orchestra have been selected to attend the 1959 Course of the National Youth Orchestra of Wales".

The author is grateful to Mrs. Kathy Phipps (nee Evans), a cellist in the Glam and the NYOW and historian of the latter orchestra, for a description of the tenth anniversary course :

"The Tenth Anniversary was celebrated in July 1959. I was fifteen and attending my second course, sitting in the back desk and leaving out as many notes as I could play. I remember a splendid tea in the Dining Hall, a cake cut by Pat Sheppard and Lewis Chamberlain who were the orchestra's youngest members and a speech from Lord Heycock.

At the Anniversary Concert at Sandfields Comprehensive School he produced a programme from his pocket of a concert he had attended in Prague two years earlier, when the Prague Symphony Orchestra had played Dvorak's Seventh Symphony. He told the audience that he enjoyed our performance far more and we believed him - he was always a good friend to the Orchestra". Plate 12

The orchestral personnel during the tenth anniversary year were :

GLAMORGAN YOUTH ORCHESTRA — 25th March—1st April, 1959.

First Violin			
VICTOR CHAMBERLAIN	*Barry*	BARRIE JONES	*Caerphilly*
JEFFREY LLOYD	*Pontycymmer*	GRAHAM ALLPORT	*Barry*
BRYAN THOMAS	*Ystalyfera*	COLIN CLEAK	*Barry*
BRYAN CROWLEY	*Hengoed*	BRIAN EVANS	*Ferndale*
MOSTYN DAVIES	*Pontypridd*	ERIC LEWIS	*Gowerton*
NOEL DAVIES	*Clydach*	WENDY SHEPPARD	*Bridgend*
MAIR FRANCIS	*Neath*	PAMELA CROKER	*Pontycymmer*
SYLVIA GROSKOP	*Neath*	GEOFFREY REES	*Bridgend*
BARBARA PERRY	*Whitchurch*	DAVID BOWN	*Pontypridd*
LESLEY PERRY	*Whitchurch*	JUNE LARGE	*Barry*
GRAHAM WATKINS	*Barry*	ANTONY LEWIS	*Neath*
Second Violin			
HEATHER LEWIS	*Neath*	GWYN LANGHAM	*Pontypridd*
DIANA WARE	*Port Talbot*	EMYR WALTERS	*Neath*
PETER CHISLETT	*Barry*	HANNAH WHITEHOUSE	*Bridgend*
JOAN FRANCIS	*Ogmore*	DIANNE JONES	*Gowerton*
BRIAN HOPKINS	*Gowerton*	OLIVER BOWN	*Pontypridd*
ANN CONSTABLE	*Pencoed*	JEFFREY GEORGE	*Maesteg*
CARL ANDREWS	*Neath*	MARILYN ROGERS	*Penarth*
JENNIFER THOMAS	*Port Talbot*	MERIEL EVANS	*Neath*
ROSALIND MORGAN	*Porth*	MELVILLE JONES	*Ferndale*

ERYL LANCASTLE	*Bargoed*	MICHAEL O'LEARY	*Ferndale*
MARGARET PENRY	*Maesteg*	MEGAN CASE	*Barry*
SUSAN CASE	*Barry*	PHILIP ROBERTS	*Bargoed*
BRIAN JONES	*Port Talbot*		
Viola			
SUSAN SALTER	*Neath*	IAN EVETT	*Neath*
HUGH GRONOW	*Neath*	GARETH LEWIS	*Maesteg*
DIANA GRIFFITHS	*Neath*	BERNARD HUGHES	*Pontypridd*
SYLVIA THOMAS	*Barry*	DAVID HUGHES	*Pontypridd*
SIAN THOMAS	*Cowbridge*	DINAH WILLIAMS	*Gowerton*
WILLIAM REES	*Port Talbot*		
Cello			
HOWARD THOMAS	*Gowerton*	ROBERT THOMAS	*Gowerton*
WAYNE WALROW	*Pontypridd*	JOHN CHAPMAN	*Pontypridd*
MARY GRIFFITHS	*Maesteg*	PETER LOTWICK	*Neath*
JUDITH HOPKINS	*Gowerton*	KATHRYN EVANS	*Bridgend*
MARGARET DAVIES	*Gowerton*	SARAH WHITEHOUSE	*Bridgend*
FRANK JONES	*Bargoed*	ELIZABETH WALTERS	*Caerphilly*
Double Bass			
ERYL DAVID	*Bridgend*	MARILYN EVANS	*Gowerton*
ALAN SHINELL	*Barry*	GARETH COOKE	*Ogmore*
RONALD JAMES	*Ferndale*	DEREK CHIDGEY	*Caerphilly*
Flute			
MICHAEL AXTELL	*Neath*	ROBERT THOMAS	*Pengam*
RAYMOND BOWDEN	*Neath*	JOHN WEEKS	*Gowerton*
JEAN CONSTABLE	*Pencoed*	VERONICA THOMAS	*Bridgend*
ANNE DAVIES	*Neath*		
Oboe			
JEFFREY DAVIES	*Neath*	LEIGH THOMAS	*Neath*
MICHAEL GRIFFITHS	*Barry*		
Clarinet			
CARYS DAVIES	*Pontycymmer*	LYN REES	*Neath*
JOHN JONES	*Ferndale*		
Bassoon			
DAVID REES	*Neath*	ALAN DAVIES	*Bridgend*
DAVID JONES	*Pengam*	JOHN WARD	*Neath*
French Horn			
VIVIAN DAVIES	*Maesteg*	HOWARD NURSE	*Pontypridd*
WALTER MURFIN	*Gowerton*	JOHN V. JONES	*Ystalyfera*
ARNOLD DRAPER	*Penarth*	K. T. JOHNS	*Aberdare*
DEREK COUSINS	*Gowerton*		
Trumpet			
DAVID AYRES	*Pontardawe*	JOHN JENKINS	*Neath*
MICHAEL JOHN	*Pontardawe*		
Trombone			
KEITH WILLIAMS	*Pencoed*	ANTONY MILLER	*Rhoose*
THOMAS HASELL	*Pontypridd*		
Bass Trombone			
NIGEL KIFT	*Pontardawe*		
Tympani			
RUTH THOMAS	*Port Talbot*	KEITH MORRIS	*Port Talbot*

Qualitex Printing Limited, Cardiff. C5634

By the end of the 1950s sixteen County Youth Centres offered instrumental or orchestral classes. During the 1960's the orchestra was again to grow in size as its already formidable reputation was further enhanced. The first leader of the decade was to be Jeffrey Lloyd. For two years, Jeffrey was a distinguished and hugely popular - and not only with the ladies - musician who also led the NYOW. He was followed by Barbara Perry before Wendy Sheppard succeeded splendidly in overcoming the potential handicap of being at one and the same time leader of the the Glam - not to mention the NYOW - and Shep's daughter. After a three year period, she was superseded by Emyr Walters a minister's son from Resolven. It is fitting that the final leader of the orchestra during Shep's reign, Edward Roberts, would later pursue a career as a leading professional player, having been leader of the NYOW. Another professional player, Phillip Morgan led the orchestra until its final concert in 1974.

Soloists of consistently excellent standard continued to be promoted from within the orchestra's ranks. Reluctant horn player - having perfect pitch and hearing a part a fourth or a fifth askew from the printed score - Arnold Draper became, with Gordon Back (Viola) of a later generation, the soloist in most concertos with the Glam. His performances included piano concertos by Mendelssohn, Mozart, Beethoven, Saint-Saëns, Grieg, Liszt, Tchaikovsky, Rachmaninov and Chopin together with Franck's Symphonic Variations and Weber's Konzertstück. Other Glam members who performed piano concertos or concerto movements in 1960s programmes were percussionist, Peter Rees (Beethoven : Piano Concertos No 3 in C Minor and No.4 in G), opera star Della Jones who, as well as playing the clarinet and percussion in the orchestra, showed her amazing musicianship and versatility in a performance of Brahms : Piano Concerto No. 1 in D Minor and violinist, Geoffrey Eales (Gershwin : "Rhapsody in Blue"). Now an internationally respected professional accompanist, Gordon Back completes the honours board of pianists who also played in the orchestra at this juncture. Gordon, who led the viola section gave distinguished interpretations of concertos by Rachmaninov, Grieg, Mozart, Tchaikovsky and Liszt's "Hungarian Fantasia".

Other orchestral soloists include Flautist Michael Axtell (Mozart : Concerto No.2 in G), cellists Helena Davies (Bruch : "Kol Nidrei") and Wayne Warlow (Bach : "Arioso" and Faure: "Berceuse"); violinists Jeffrey Lloyd (Beethoven : Romance in F, and Bach : Concerto in A Minor), Wendy Sheppard (Bach : Concerto in E Major and Brandenburg Concerto No.5 -with John Weeks and Paul Broom and Peter Rees), Emyr Walters (Bach : Concerto in A Minor), Patricia Sheppard (Bach Brandenburg Concerto No.2 in F - with David Richards, Alan Good and Christopher Weeks) and Edward Roberts (Wieniawsky : Concerto in D Minor); trumpeters John Jenkins, and Tony Small (Vivaldi : Concerto for Two Trumpets) and Kenvin Evans (Addison : Concerto - First Movement), harpist Margaret Rees (Mozart : Concerto for Flute and Harp - with flautists Paul Broom and John Weeks), horn player, David Hughes (Strauss : Concerto No. 1 in Eb), and Flautist David Richards (Bach : Suite No 2).

Pianists who performed concertos or concerto movements with the Glam at the time were Michael Beynon (Mozart : Concertos in A K 488 and in D Minor K466), Geoffrey Hopkins (Tchaikovsky : No 1 in Bb Minor), Michael Jenkins (Beethoven: Concerto No. 5 in Eb), Marion Williams (Beethoven : Concerto No.5 in Eb) and Marilyn Phillips (Mozart : Concerto in Eb K499). Wendy Norman, Sylvia Thomas, Ryland Davies, Audrey Griffiths, Thelma Rees, Stuart Kale, Pamela Field, Anthony Davey, Della Jones, Beverley Humphreys and Mary Davies complete the distinguished cast of vocal soloists who appeared in GYO concerts during this epoch.

Cellist, Michael Nelmes writes of his contemporaries in the 1960s :

"Looking back over old concert programmes, it is interesting to note how many fellow members of the Glam have gone on to make a substantial contribution in the world of music internationally.

The tenor Dennis O'Neill not only sang in the choir but also played along side me in the cello section, a photograph of which I still have. The mezzo - soprano Della Jones played clarinet and was a piano concerto soloist. Double Bass player Stuart Kale has since sung leading tenor roles all over the world.

Trombonist Trevor Herbert is often seen fronting music programmes for the Open University and Beverley Humphreys and Pamela Field went on to operatic careers. A fellow member of the Cello section, Hilary Tann is a teacher in the USA. She had a work performed at the Cardiff Festival some years ago and is a well known composer".

In August-September 1966 the orchestra broke down cultural and political barriers on its only foreign tour under Shep's direction - plans for a later tour to Perth, Australia were aborted. During the tour, Shep was delighted to receive the news of the birth of his first grand-daughter, Karin.

Of the tour to Western Slovakia, a student wrote :

"82 members of the large orchestra of 135 players were finally selected for the tour and undertook an intensive period of preparation at the Authority's School Camp, Ogmore by Sea, during the week 24th - 27 August, 1966. It was a good thing that all musical preparations had been completed before the orchestra left on its tour, because the ensuing fortnight was so packed with a succession of concerts, receptions, visits to places of beauty and halls of entertainment that it became quite impossible to squeeze in more than the very minimum of time for necessary day-to-day rehearsal during the tour".

Shep commented :-

" The Glamorgan Youth Orchestra experienced an overwhelming reception from the people of Western Slovakia. The arrangements made had been very carefully thought out and were carried out with meticulous attention to detail; Concerts were held at Bratislava in the hall of the Czechoslovak Broadcast system at the University of Bratislava, at the concert Hall of the Thermia Hotel, Piestany; in the Music School of Nitra; at the Centre of Culture in Trencin; and at the hall of trade unions in Komaro".

Shep paid glowing tributes to the organisation carried out by Mrs. Ada Cervananska, Dr. Novacek - Director of the Bratislava Conservatoire - Professor Pichler, Mrs Vilimova, Mr. Kupkovic, Mrs Hansikova, and Miss Marqaurtova, concluding his report by saying :

"There can be no doubt that the tour was a valuable contribution to the cause of international understanding."

The comprehensive diary kept by students and staff gives a full and often amusing account of experiences during the tour. Soloist, Della Jones seems to have been especially impressed by the gentleman responsible for the transportation of instruments, one Pan Cebo - known as Samson or Daddy Bear - who, "when carrying a double bass, plus its basket, makes it look like a violin". Tenor, Stuart Kale, noted in amazement how easy it is for the important people to get things done here. Concerto soloist, Gordon Back was not overly impressed on his visit to the Bratislava Academy, considering that "although both excellent students, I felt that they were not as good as the Royal College students who had studied for the same length of time". Internationally acknowledged composer Hilary Tann - then a cellist in the orchestra - was very impressed by the heart-warming dedication to true musical standards of a second year cello student. Shep's daughter, Patricia, evidently suffering acute hunger pains after the outward journey wrote of the first meal at the Modra Harmonia :

"By now, our stomachs had made it clear what time it was - salami sausage, tomato and egg and a cup of weak rose hip tea was served. To our utter relief, this was not supper, but merely tea".

Possibly the longest serving member of the Glam, David Hughes, was principal horn player on the tour. The story of his twentieth birthday, celebrated in Bratislava is highly amusing :

"On my birthday we had no concert, so it was decided to celebrate the event by visiting a local hostelry for a few illicit drinks. To cut a long story quite short, I was caught by Mr. Sheppard and confined to the bus instead of being allowed to attend a show at a nearby theatre. I thought that was the end of the incident but I was wrong.

The following day we gave a concert in a beautiful concert hall in Piestany. During the performance of "Capriccio Espagnole", three bats who lived somewhere up in the ceiling woke up and began dive-bombing the orchestra causing one or two notes to be split. I blamed the bats for my mistakes but Mr. Sheppard had other ideas. As soon as the concert was over, I was summoned to his bus and commanded to sit next to him during the hour-long journey back to our base - Modra Harmonica.

Nothing was said by either of us for several minutes. As the journey continued, it was periodically interrupted by expressions of annoyance expressed by Shep. "Urchin.......Ragmuffin........Guttersnipe" - all uttered with vitriolic expression by the conductor. I waited for the reprimand to continue but he lightened the proceedings, as he often did so well, by asking me if I had noticed that although resplendent in his white tie and tails he had completely forgotten to put on his waistcoat for the concert.

We both had a laugh at his expense and the matter was closed".

Staff members Haydn Davies and Glynne Evans complimented the orchestra's commitment, the former recounting a most arduous recording session and the latter describing the concert at Bratislava University as "an unqualified success". Viola tutor F.J.Herbert - a multi-talented linguist as well as an accomplished musician - was delighted to be able to use his expertise in Russian whilst on a boat trip with the director of the Thermia Hotel, Piestany.

As usual, Shep's programming was highly appropriate. Welsh music was reflected in German's "Welsh Rhapsody" and in Della Jones's rendition of

E.T.Davies "Ynys y Plant". A distinctive Czechoslovakian ambience was created in Della Jones' performance of Dvorak's " Rusalka's Song to the Moon " and in orchestral works by Weinberger, and Smetana. The more cosmopolitan flavour of the concerts was represented in a Mozart Piano Concerto - pianist Gordon Back - and in performances of tenor arias by Handel and Verdi and also in the concluding work, Rimsky Korsakov's "Capriccio Espangnol" .

That the orchestra made an enormous impression on audiences and critics alike is evidenced in extracts from three of the reviews of the time :

"The youth orchestra, a body of enthusiastic musicians, surprised us especially in the compositions of Dvorak and Smetana by their performance which was equal to that of a professional orchestra.

One of the pleasant surprises was the Soprano Della Jones and the Tenor Stuart Kale. The audience were very appreciative of the aria "Song to the Moon" which was sung in very good Czech and the quality and purity of her voice.

Stuart Kale excelled in the ballad of the Duke of Mantua from "Rigoletto". With his sound bel canto voice and temperament he seemed to have come from the sunny coast of Italy and not from foggy Wales.

It is necessary to mention that the soprano played the drums in the orchestra and the tenor played the double bass".

Vecernik 5th September 1966

"Our Welsh guests show us how it is possible to reach high standards through the systematic music education provided at the secondary schools as well as the academies of music".

Lud The People 7th September 1966

"In admiring the success of the orchestra we must also admire the musical education in their school system which allows such an orchestra to come into being.

This kind of music education is for the good of Wales. Some of these youngsters play more than one instrument and some both sing and play an instrument.

For many of these players music is a hobby, because many study science and other arts subjects. Possibly because their playing is a hobby, the players have greater enthusiasm".

Pravda : The Truth12th September 1966

It was in this era that a pattern of Junior and Transitional Courses, held at Ogmore School Camp, was established. Two such courses were organised annually, each attended by about 150 orchestral players. Grade requirements for the Junior, Transitional and Senior orchestras were Grade 3, Grade 3-4, and Grade 5-8 respectively. Thus, the continuity of the Glam was assured and the line of progression through to the senior ensemble consolidated. Shep frequently invited Glam students to tutor on these courses and the experience gained usually became a prized addition to students' curriculum vitae. Many students - the author included - gained their first conducting experience in this arena.

The Glam's coming of age is well documented in the programme notes for the twenty-first anniversary concert. The programme was designed not only to reflect back on the orchestra's history but also to look forward with confidence to a healthy and robust future which Russell Sheppard had assured through the firm foundations of an unique system of progressive orchestral growth. The programme itself also celebrated the twenty-first anniversary of state education and the bicentenary of Beethoven's birth. Its forward looking character was mirrored in three new compositions. Shep himself composed a rousing "Celebration Fanfare" and the Glamorgan Education Authority commissioned the Welsh composer David Wynne to write "Cymric Rhapsody No. 2" for the occasion. Students and staff of the time will remember the difficulty of attuning their ears to the modern complexities of Bernard Rands' "Agenda for Young Players" which received its Welsh premiere. True to form, Shep cleverly balanced the more progressive elements of the programme with conventional concert favourites. After the fanfare, the concert opened with Humperdinck's "Hansel and Gretel" Overture, three movements from Brahms' Second Symphony, part one closing with Liszt's "Hungarian Fantasia" played by Gordon Back. In Part Two of the programme Soprano, Susan Dennis sang Beethoven's concert aria "Ah! Perfido" and the orchestra concluded with a rousing rendition of Tchaikovsky's overture "The Year 1812". The concert was broadcast on Radio 3 in the "Youth Orchestras of the World" series. Plate 13.

The programme highlights the dramatic growth of the orchestra which now numbered 100 Strings, 29 Woodwind, 31 Brass, 1 Harp and 4 Percussion and traces the development of orchestral, choral and band courses over the years. Paying due regard to the work of his instrumental teaching team Shep's summation of the ages, standards of proficiency and potential destination of the 21st anniversary orchestra's players is highly illuminating. The Glam had continued to be the principal breeding ground for the NYOW with 45 members of the GYO attending the Nash that year. Research indicates that a staggering 32 Glam members who sat down to the celebratory meal at Ogmore were to play professionally :

Violin	Hywel Davies, John Canter, Clive Dobbins, Phillip Morgan, Timothy Crossland, Adrian Eales, Susan Croot, Mark Thomas, Robert Tonkin
Viola	Gordon Back (Piano), Stephen Broom
Cello	Brian Clarke
Bass	Albert Dennis, Gareth Wood, Alun Williams
Flute	Phillip Emanuel, Griff Harries, Neil Harries
Oboe	John Esaias, Mark Howells, John Anderson
Bassoon	Adrian Evett, Martin Bowen
Horn	Huw Jenkins, Richard Martin, David Hughes
Trombone	John Hendy, Colin Gummer, Phillip Dando Jeffrey Pearce
Percussion	Phillip Thomas (Piano), Sean Hooper

It is even more astonishing to catalogue the career destinations of several players and staff members who were former Glam members :

Strings	Gareth Adams	HMI (Music)
	Gordon Back	Accompanist with world famous performers; professor at the Guildhall School of Music and Drama
	Edwina Thomas	Now Mrs. Edwina Hart : Finance Secretary : Welsh Assembly
	Mark Thomas	Composer of TV and film music for "Twin Town", "The Aristocrats" etc.
Woodwind	John Anderson	Principal of several leading orchestras - currently ECO. His various concerto recordings are heard virtually weekly on Classic FM
	Martin Bowen	A Principal bassoonist with the BBC NOW
	Dr.Hugh Davies	OU and FE lecturer in music
	Phillip Emanuel	Manager : West Glamorgan Music Service
	Griff Harries	Orchestral Manager : National Chamber Orchestra of Wales
	Mark Howells	Long serving principal oboist of the BBC Symphony Orchestra
	Adrian Evett	Orchestral Manager : BBC Concert Orchestra
Brass	Phillip Dando	Professional player; Director : Welsh Brass Trio
	David Hughes	Advisory Music Teacher
	Roger Lewis	Managing Director and Controller : Classic FM; formerly President of Decca
	Peter Sheppard	BBC Sports Commentator, Teacher
Percussion	Dr. John Evans	Director of Radio 3, Music author
	Phillip Thomas	Leading international accompanist; including Cardiff Singer of the World Competition
Staff	Jeffrey Francis	Music Adviser, JP, Choirmaster
	Alan James	Head of Music and Mid Glam Music Centre
	John Jenkins	Music Adviser, University Lecturer, Conductor
	Jeffrey Lloyd	Advisory Music Teacher, Conductor
	Anthony Small	Advisory Teacher, Conductor
	Graham Watkins	Head of Music Department and Music Centre

Also included in the list of distinguished members of the Twenty First Anniversary Orchestra was bass player Gareth Wood. As a young composer Gareth wrote a Suite for Orchestra for the Glam and later was commissioned by the author to write "Margam Stones" for the West Glamorgan Youth Brass Band and also for a Gala Concert for the Prince and Princess of Wales. Gareth has had a long and distinguished career as a bass player with the Royal Philharmonic Orchestra and as a composer of international reputation. Significantly, it was Gareth who composed for and conducted the RPO in Sir Yehudi Menuhin's 80th birthday concert at the Royal Albert Hall.

A report to the Education Committee in 1968, brings into sharp perspective the development of the instrumental music which made possible the achievements indicated in the 21st Anniversary programme. In addition to a permanent member of staff at Neath Boys' Grammar School, 26 full-time and 19 part-time peripatetic staff were employed by the Glamorgan LEA. 675 pupils and 35 staff attended the three regional orchestral centres in East, Mid and West Glamorgan.

A significant feature of the success of the senior orchestra was the phenominal growth of its feeder orchestras. Pupils attending the Junior Orchestral courses increased from 106 in 1963 to 169 a decade later. During the same period, the Transition orchestra numbers grew from 107 to 176. The future of the Glam was thus assured.

A highly complimentary Survey of Instrumental Music in West Glamorgan and Neath Districts, produced on 5th March 1970, is nevertheless, critical of the deplorable accommodation for instrumental teaching in schools. Furthermore, the report goes on to comment on the selection of younger pupils for instrumental tuition:

"Here the experience of the Music Organiser would be invaluable, but as he is concerned to a considerable degree with administrative duties involving general school work in two divisions, he cannot be expected to spare the necessary time to supervise personally the work of all the teachers concerned. With eight divisions and an Accepted District in the county it will be readily seen that, in spite of the excellent organisation provided, there is ample work for at least one more full-time music organiser in the field of instrumental music alone, without taking into account the help and advice needed for young music teachers in their probationary period throughout the county's primary and secondary schools. There is an overwhelmingly strong case here for the appointment of an Assistant Music Organiser".

Within two years of the publication of this report a new era would be heralded in with the appointment of Jeffrey Francis, whom readers may recall attended the first GYO course in 1949. During this interregnum period a signal honour was bestowed on Shep, the GYO and Youth Choir. The combined forces of these two marvellous ensembles were summoned by the Schools' Music Association - Patron Her Majesty The Queen Mother, President Sir Adrian Boult, C.H. - to perform with the Harrow Junior Choirs, the Ley Hill Recorder Group from Warwickshire and the Newham Brampton Infant's School Percussion Ensemble at a concert held at the Royal Festival Hall on March 26th, 1971. In the foreword to the programme for the third annual concert organised by the association, the author writes :

"All that is best in education can be found in music teaching as it makes many demands upon the child - learning, self discipline, team work, and mental alertness of the highest order. It is perhaps one of the few subjects in school which can remain with the child for life".

The memories of this magical experience would certainly remain in the memories of the 320 or so players and singers and would be treasured for a life time. The magic of performing at the hall, the thrill of hearing the rapturous applause from the packed auditorium and the pride at reading the complimentary press reports, will surely, have endured to the present day. A full account of the programme is portrayed in the following section on the West Glamorgan Youth Choir. Plate 14.

During the Glam's history its personnel constantly changed from generation to generation. In the 1960's the average age of the players was 17 years 10 months and it is interesting to note the tangible appeal of the orchestra, not only for school pupils, but also for students in further and higher education which grew from 13% in 1949 to around 30% in the 1960s and 1970s. That such large numbers of players chose to continue in the orchestra's ranks is a tribute not only to the quality of the orchestra itself and to the meaningful appeal of its repertoire, but also to the respect and regard in which Shep himself was held. The figures quoted in the 21st Anniversary programme are typical of the overall scenario regarding take-up of musical instruments. It is to the eternal credit of the authority, its instrumental teaching team and Shep's organisational genius that, of the players on the summer course 1970, no fewer than 85% began lessons at school. Incredibly the Glam grew from 39 in 1949 to 169 by the 1970's.

It is interesting to note the sectional development of the Glam over almost a quarter of a century :

Section	**1949**	**1953**	**1959**	**1965**	**1970**	**1974**
Violin 1	14	21	22	23	24	22
Violin 2	11	27	25	30	36	31
Viola	6	11	11	13	14	14
Cello	5	13	12	15	15	16
Bass	2	4	6	8	8	10
Flute	0	4	7	5	8	10
Oboe	0	4	3	6	7	8
Clarinet	0	7	3	7	11	12
Bassoon	0	3	4	3	3	5
Horn	0	6	7	5	9	10
Trumpet	0	7	3	7	10	8
Trombone	0	3	4	7	11	12
Tuba	0	0	0	1	1	1
Timpani & Percussion	0	1	2	3	4	6
Harp	1	1	0	1	1	3
Totals	**39**	**112**	**109**	**134**	**164**	**168**

The geographical spread of GYO players during the period indicates the exceptionally consistent strength of music making in the western part of the county :

AREA	**1949**	**1953**	**1959**	**1965**	**1970**	**1974**
West Glamorgan	46%	42%	43%	42%	51%	45%
East Glamorgan	36%	34%	34%	34%	30%	29%
Mid Glamorgan	18%	24%	23%	24%	19%	26%

A school-by-school analysis substantiates Russell Sheppard's conviction that the strength of a school's orchestral work is a mirror image of the interest, commitment and enthusiasm of the head of music and the quality of instrumental teaching. This premise is proven in a number of schools which contributed significantly to the consistently high quality of performance produced by the Glam over the years. On the first course, there were significant representations from Gowerton (7), Neath (7), Caerphilly (4), Mountain Ash (4) and Maesteg (3) and Aberdare (3). In the following decade only Gowerton, Neath and, for a shorter period, Maesteg would retain their supremacy. Reference has already been made to the orchestral strongholds at the Gowerton Grammar Schools. The work of Cynnwyd Watkin and his instrumental staff was to be continued in the 1960s and 70s by Huw Jones very ably supported by string teachers, Morgan Lloyd, David Harris and Peter Watts. Derek Fox and D. Anthony Small who provided qualitative and quantitative contributions in the field of woodwind and brass teaching respectively.

Concurrently, Neath Boys' Grammar School became a centre of musical excellence which was highly commended in an HMI report of the period. In this school, under the direction of John Jenkins, orchestras of symphonic proportions won three major prizes at the second Festival of Music for Youth in 1972. Uniquely, the senior orchestra later performed at the Golden Hall of the Musikverien in Vienna. The importance of the work of Freddie Herbert up to the late 1970s cannot be over emphasised. For many years he taught the full range of instruments nurturing and developing many future professional players. Susan Jenkins(Violin), Peter Watts (Cello/Bass), Stephen Benaventi, Edward Howitt and Hugh Phillips (Woodwind) and Idris Rees (Brass) also made a significant contribution to the success of the school's music to 1974. By 1970 Neath Boys' Grammar School pupils made up almost 11% of the GYO, providing, as it did, a mini orchestra of 14 Strings, 8 Woodwind, 5 Brass and 2 Percussion.

The appointment of three other teachers also had a big impact on the composition of the Glam. In Pontypridd Boys' Haydn Davies and his team produced a large number of GYO players. At Sandfields Comprehensive, the show-piece concert hall would be graced by another admirable orchestra. Jeffrey Francis and his instrumental teachers encouraged many fine players, a number of whom became Glam members. The school also became renowned for the many excellent operatic productions in which Jeffrey collaborated with the outstanding dance/ drama teacher Godfrey Evans. Somewhat later, the appointment of Alan James as Head of Music at Kenfig Hill Comprehensive initiated the development of an important nursery of future Glamites. Supported by Deputy Headteacher, John Richards (himself a fine musician) and later by his wife Ann, Alan created a fine orchestra in the school - bassists were never in short supply - and large numbers of his pupils were accepted by the GYO.

In 1974, the last year of the Glam's existence, an unique record was set. In that year, no fewer than 47 players from Neath's Dwr y Felin Comprehensive School (Formerly Neath Grammar) were represented in the orchestra. This represented over 20 % of the orchestra and included 13 Violins, 4 Viola, 5 Cello, 4 Bass, 4 Flutes, 2 Oboes, 2 Clarinets, 2 Bassoons, 3 Horns, 2 Trumpets, 2 Trombones, Tuba and 2 Percussion. The school provided the Glam's Leader, Phillip Morgan, who also led the NYOW in 1973, together with the majority of section principals. Even more remarkably 15 of this band of talented players were accepted by the NYOW. Nine of these would later make careers as professional players. The school also provided a record number of leaders and principal players from a single school. This roll of honour included Timothy Crossland (Leader), Albert Dennis (Leader of the Bass Section), Phillip Emanuel and Griff Harries(Principal Flutes/Piccolo), Mark Howells (a Principal Oboe), Martin Bowen (Principal Bassoon), Huw Jenkins and Alan Lockyer (Principal Horns), Phillip Cowley (a Principal Trombone), David Langford (Tuba). It is possible that this record may never be surpassed.

A principal bassoonist of the period, Adrian Evett has, after a period as a professional performer, been Orchestral Manager of the BBC Concert Orchestra for several years. Adrian comments :

"My best concert memories include hearing John Anderson playing oboe solos and turning around, on a choral course, to see a hundred gorgeous sopranos and altos. I loved the Mozart, Brahms and Verdi Requiems and Vaughan Williams Serenade to Music. I was terrified by Tchaik. 4.

I am sure that we all took Shep for granted, not realising what he was providing by way of experience and inspiration. In more than twenty courses I learnt so much repertoire and was never again frightened by sight reading.

I wish I now had the opportunity to say Thank you, to Mr. Sheppard."

Shep would hand over the reigns of the Glam in 1972, but continued his association with the orchestra and its new conductor, Music Adviser, Jeffrey Francis until the division of the county of Glamorgan into three constituent authorities - South, Mid and West Glamorgan - which occured in 1974. During this period of change Shep regularly appeared as guest conductor with the Mid Glamorgan Youth Orchestra and was commissioned by the author to write a Fanfare on C & D and arrangement of God Bless the Prince of Wales for the visit of Charles and Diana to the Brangwyn Hall in 1981.

His last concert in sole charge of the Glam was given on the 6th of April, 1972 at the Grand Pavilion, Porthcawl. The programme included Weber's "Oberon" Overture, the Allegro Molto Moderato and Finale from Bruckner's Romantic Symphony and Liszt's "Les Preludes". Former Neath Grammar School pupil, Phillip Thomas - who was also an excellent percussionist - and is currently accompanist to Leslie Garret and the Cardiff Singer of the World Competition, performed Shostakovich's Second Piano Concerto. Wayne Griffiths, then a student at the Royal College of Music was the tenor soloist in arias by Handel and Edward German.

During the transition period from July 1972, soloists were Mary Davies, Soprano, John Anderson (Oboe), Phillip Thomas (Piano) and Kenneth Lewis (Baritone).

Shep conducted his final orchestral concerts at the Michael Sobell Sport's Centre, Aberdare on Friday 21st July, and again at the Grand Pavilion Porthcawl on July 22nd,1979. This was also the year in which he retired after thirty years marvellous service to music and education generally. It is fitting that the first of these appearances should have taken place so near to his birthplace, Mountain Ash. The choice of the Symphony in D Minor by Cesar Franck characterised, as it is, by what the programme note describes as its "cyclic genre" of composition brought his fantastic orchestral tour de force full cycle.

Hall of Fame

John Anderson : Oboe

John Anderson

John Anderson took up the oboe while a pupil at Gowerton School. He studied there with Tony Small and subsequently with Derek Wickens and Terence MacDonagh. A career spanning over twenty years with major symphony orchestras has established him as one of the most sought after oboists of his generation.

John Anderson currently combines his work with the English Chamber Orchestra with a professorship at the Royal College of Music.

He is a very busy freelance player both as a solo artist and a studio player recording music for film and television. His many, highly acclaimed recordings, particularly of Baroque Concertos, have made his name a household word, and are regularly featured on radio broadcasts.

"I think I may be speaking for many ex-Glam members when I say that in many ways the achievement of Russell Sheppard and his contribution to all our lives can best be fully appreciated with hindsight. At the time it didn't occur to me that there was anything unusual in having the opportunity to learn an instrument at school and then to have residential Glam courses. We loved the music and the chances to have a fairly riotous time! Many have gone on to pursue careers in music-making or teaching, but I'm certain that everyone who took part in the Glam had their love of music nurtured as well as making enduring friendships.

Shep chose wonderful and always ambitious programmes and was determined to get the very best results. He could be a very demanding taskmaster - "It's too loud ; I'll have to cut you out!" was a frequent cry. We all gained so much from his commitment and his ability to make us play with as much professionalism as possible. Those of us who went on to play professionally were privileged to have such a musical background. I know that I have rarely encountered such a demanding conductor in twenty five years of orchestral playing.

The Glam, with Russell Sheppard at the helm, gave anyone who was prepared to work hard access to an amazing standard of music making. It is the measure of his achievement that he was able to establish and sustain such a structure for so long with such care, commitment and love of music."

Gordon Back : Pianist

Gordon Back

Gordon Back's distinguished career as a pianist has taken him all over the world. He has performed and recorded with artists such as Yehudi Menuhin, Nathan Milstein, Itzac Perlman, Maxim Vengerov, Joseph Suk, Aaron Rosand, Yo Yo Ma, Ko Iwasaki and the Cleveland Quartet. A pupil of Neath Boys' Grammar School, he studied at the Guildhall School of Music and in Italy. He teaches at the Guildhall School of Music and became a Fellow of that School in 1984.

Gordon has participated in many international festivals, and is the Director of the Celebrity Series at the Brangwyn Hall, Swansea. He gives regular master classes in music colleges like the Cleveland Institute of Music, the Curtis Institute and the Royal College of Music.

His recent recordings include the Bach-Schumann Sonatas and Partitas with Jean-Jacques Kantorow (which received a French Grande Prix du Disque), the Schubert "Arpeggione" and Rachmaninov Cello Sonatas with Cellist Daniel Lee (for Decca) and a series of CD's with clarinettist Emma Johnson(for ASV).

"I was privileged to have known and worked with Russell Sheppard. It was he who provided me with the opportunity to perform so many concertos with the Glam. I shall never forget the thrill of my first appearance as soloist in 1967 when I played the first movement of Rachmaninov's Second Concerto. In addition to playing so much music as a member of viola section of the orchestra, Shep gave me many future opportunities to learn the concerto repertoire and for this I remain eternally grateful.

From 1967 until 1970, I experienced the magic of the concert platform in concertos by Grieg, the full Rachmaninov Concerto, the Tchaikovsky, a Mozart Concerto and Liszt's "Hungarian Fantasia". There were so many excellent young players in the orchestra at the time - Mark Thomas, Gareth Wood, Stephen Broom, Albert Dennis, Huw Jenkins, John Anderson, Mark Howells, Roger Lewis, Phillip Thomas, John Evans and many, many more - that the standard of performance was always high. I shall never forget my days in the Glam".

Karl Jenkins : Composer

Karl Jenkins

Karl Jenkins read music at University College, Cardiff which was followed by post graduate studies at the Royal Academy of Music.

Whilst at university he began playing jazz, winning awards in the unusual role of jazz oboist and multi - instrumentalist. He worked with Ronnie Scott and many famous jazz exponents and co - founded "Nucleus" in 1972, which won first prize at the Montreux Jazz Festival. He then joined "Soft Machine".

"Soft Machine" was one of the seminal and progressive bands of the '70's embracing a wide variety of styles from jazz and orchestral rock, including even minimalism before it became widely known as such. Defying categorisation, in various incarnations it played at venues as diverse as The Proms, the Newport Jazz Festival (USA), Carnegie Hall, the Reading Festival and the Montreux Festival.

In recent years, Karl Jenkins has become one of the world's best - selling living composers. His Adiemus series has become the highest ever charting contemporary classical compositions. "Songs of Sanctuary", "Cantata Mundi" and "Imagined Oceans" are a highly original series of compositions each exploring a different aspect of musical styles and genres. He now conducts his music all over the world.

"I have a clear recollection of the first run-through of my first ever rehearsal with the Glam - I think I was about seventh oboe. It was Handel's "Water Music" and the emotionality of the sound, even after playing in a decent orchestra at Gowerton Grammar made a lasting impression.

The power failed during a rehearsal at Ogmore. Wayne Warlow, Principal Cellist lit a match in the packed hall. Shep screamed at him - "Get out you madman! You'll burn us in our beds!!"

My best remembered contemporaries included Terry "Drac" Johns, Tony Small, John Jenkins, John Weeks, Rhian Samuel, Tony Randall and Wendy Sheppard, most, if not all of whom went into music.

I always thought Shep's musicianship to be of the highest quality. He had an excellent ear and showed great musical control, which, in retrospect, would not have been easy with well over a hundred teenagers. His impact and influence on musical life in Glamorgan and Wales was enormous".

Mark Thomas : Composer

Award winning composer Mark Thomas is undoubtedly one of Britain's most diverse and exciting composers with established credits of over 100 scores for film and television. In a successful career as a violinist in the LSO and RPO, he worked on scores with composers such as James Horner, John Barry, and John Williams in the recording studio.

Mark Thomas

Mark is well known and sought after for his ability to score feature films. His credits include "Twin Town" for which he won a Bafta Cymru award for the best original score. He also scored "Up'N Under", "The Sea Change", "Chameleon", "The Big Tease" for Warner Brothers and "Mad Cows" starring Joanna Lumley, Anna Friel and Prunella Scales. Of his compositions, John Williams has written:

"Few composers show the versatility and sheer superb musicianship that Mark Thomas can seem to effortlessly conjure up.He is a composer of proven ability - inventive, stylish - classically trained, yet capable of highly modern sounds that will take us to the next millennium; in fact the perfect film composer".

Mark has scored many popular films, drama series, factual and history programmes and animated films, several of which have won prestigious awards. He scored the commemorative production of Sir Peter Hall's "Man and Superman". In 1996 he was commissioned by The Year of Literature Festival to compose "I've known Him By The Thousands" and, in 1998, he composed the score for the Royal Shakespeare Company production of "Two Gentlemen of Verona" at Stratford.

Mark is proud to have been a player in both the Glamorgan and West Glamorgan Youth Orchestras, where he stated "I was able at an early age to learn orchestration from inside an orchestra". He recalls the 21st Anniversary of the Glam stating that "as the youngest member of the Glam I was asked to cut the anniversary cake at a special birthday party. On my first course I played in what Shep called a sea of violins. I remember the thrill of playing Brahms and the 1812 Overture and although Shep asked the back desks of the Second Violins to omit the triplets in the Prelude to Act 3 of Lohengrin we all respected his friendly, father-like approach. We were often in awe of his disciplined approach but he was a great motivator and commanded our respect".

Those were the days

Cecily Holliday

As the first leader of the Glamorgan Youth Orchestra in 1949, I vividly recall our rehearsals at Dyffryn House. Recollections flood back of Tchaikovsky's "Andante Cantabile" which seemed to be one of Mr. Sheppard's favourite works.

I also clearly remember taking a string rehearsal of Leonora No.3 - rather slowly - and a young lad who stopped the rehearsal to ask me if we were rehearsing at the right tempo. I explained that we were trying to sort out the difficult passages and I also thought to myself, "Cheeky brat!" But afterwards I smiled.

I remember staying at Ogmore and wondering if we were camping in the Arctic. Now Dyffryn House was something else. When we had a fine evening the girls always managed some lively entertainment. We were always reasonably behaved under the guidance of Ivy Morgan, whom we all adored and respected. Naturally, Shep kept a close eye on the boys!

Of my contemporaries I still maintain contact with Denise Bassett and Malcolm Williams who played in the orchestra together and who later married - perhaps the first example of the Glam as a marriage agency! They now live in Kingston Ontario where Malcolm is a Ear, Nose and Throat Surgeon. Both play an active role in the Kingston Symphony Orchestra.

Now, about the man himself - Russell Sheppard. I used to think what a serious person he was, but, on reflection, I know he was a shy man. But this should in no way detract from his dedication and determination to help young people make music. He made the Glam possible through his determination and dedication to help young people to make music. How fortunate and how privileged we were to have the opportunity to have worked with him".

Cecily Holliday lived near Maesteg and initially studied the violin in Cardiff, In 1949 she became the first leader of the Glam. She maintained her connection with the orchestra until 1953 and performed Handel's Concerto Grosso in Bb, the Concerto Grosso in F with Jeffrey Francis, Ioan Davies, Marion Lloyd and Haydn Davies, and Bach's Brandenburg Concerto No.5 with Kenneth George and Keith Morris.

Cecily also led and tutored the National Youth Orchestra of Wales. Following a distinguished career with the Halle Orchestra, she recently retired from her post in the BBC Philarmonic Orchestra

Raymond Bowden

"A flood of memories come back to me about those halcyon days at Ogmore in the fifties. I was never much of a musician, but I can honestly say that some of the greatest feelings of joy I have had in my life came to me when I was sitting at the back of the hall near the stage and the door, surrounded by everyone playing their hearts out. It was thanks to Russell Sheppard that I gained an insight into the pleasures of music.

I remember, too, the excitement - and trepidation that accompanied the opening of those big brown envelopes of music which arrived a week of so before every course. I learned later that Shep used to deal with them all himself.

I can still vividly recall the tension of the full orchestra, the respect commanded by the rostrum, the rare - it has to be said - sign of a sense of humour, all of which provided really valuable experience in later professional life. One course the excellent flautist Ken George did not attend. I had had long experience of sheltering under the umbrella of his confident and extremely talented playing, and had forgotten how exposed one is in the principal's seat. I must have set about it in a second flute mode and not dominated the solo parts as necessary. Result ; a tap of the baton; mini lecture about being timid; about being a small cog in a big machine with a job to do all in the course of duty; no big deal etc. I practised a particularly difficult solo to perfection in the dorm and in sectional rehearsals. Yet every time the full rehearsal came, my pinched lips failed to reproduced the carefully rehearsed piece. Justified exasperation eventually surfaced in Shep who finally suggested that I pass on the solo to another member of the section. This met with my stubbornness to do the job; and he acceded. The tension of the concert; an anxious glare rather than a glance from the rostrum at the appropriate moment; perfect rendering of the solo - or at least it seemed to me! -; palpable relief and an approving nod from Shep ; and relief all round from the orchestra.

Character forming! What a valuable experience that has been. I have remembered it on countless occasions when having to make speeches, do something difficult, or indeed advise others in such circumstances.

Even as I write, I can vividly recall Ogmore rehearsals, the experience and tensions of growing up at the same time, the occasional visits to the beach on summer courses with Viv Davies, Tony Randall, et al and the freezing dashes to the loo and the washroom in mid winter. I often wonder what happened to those seemingly confident people who shared my experiences. However, I reflect more often on how much I owe to that rather remote, conscientious, perfectionist man, Russell Sheppard, who made it all happen. He was one of those few people one is fortunate to encounter in life who make an incredible impression and whose influences changes one.

All these memories are crystal clear now and are destined to remain so, with a tinge of sadness at putting these thoughts on paper when they should have been conveyed verbally in earlier years - even to a person uncomfortable at accepting compliments. I will never forget that face, those days, and the joy of them! "

Dr. Raymond Bowden was a pupil of Neath Boys' Grammar School and a flautist in the Glam and NYOW. He gained his doctorate at Oxford University before becoming a stockbroker in the City of London. Amongst his many achievements, he is Chairman of the International Wine Society.

Ian Evett

"I had played in Neath Grammar School Orchestra and the West Glamorgan Orchestras for a few years before my first Glam course, at the age of fifteen. To say that I wasn't the greatest viola player of my generation would be a wilful understatement. I gained my place through the persistence of my application, rather than any degree of musical ability. Nevertheless, I joined the 100 or so Glam musicians crammed into the rickety main hall at Ogmore. After a prolonged and extremely noisy tuning session - a cacophony of obbligatos from budding virtuosos - Russell Sheppard rapped his stand for silence and, appropriately enough, directed in the "Academic Festival Overture".

As the most junior member of the viola section, I dutifully raised my MKII Outspan to my chin, poised my bow and followed the conductor's downbeat. And I was transfixed. I have never been able to find the words adequate to describe the sensation of being at the heart of the sound that filled every crevice of the hall. Utter enchantment. After a dozen bars or so, I was sufficiently composed to join in myself, and by the time we had reached "Gaudeamus Igitur" I was in a sort of euphoric state that drug takers lust for. How do you describe this experience to someone who has not had the good fortune to play in a good orchestra? I suspect you can't. It is an experience that is still with me, which is just as vivid after more than forty years.

Other memories persist strongly; the rolling beauty of "Vltava"; the ear - splitting dissonance of "Mars"; lush themes of Dvorak; sitting in front of the trombones in "Finlandia". These and many others are treasures to savour. So many pieces evoke memories of those dilapidated shacks perched above the coast at Ogmore. Old friends; good friends; grace sung to the "Old Hundredth"; chocolate (was it?) at 9.00pm; the miserable flatness of the day after the course; Wayne Warlow's grin; Michael Axtell's zany humour; mischief in the dorms; sectionals in the sun lounge; and many others.

I owed so much to the vision and energy of Russell Sheppard. It is my deep regret that I failed adequately to thank him for the effect that the Glam had on my youth, education and life-long memories. I think that at the time we saw Shep as something of a martinet but hindsight shows that he was only as strict as he needed to be - and we could be a pretty unruly bunch. Those who got to know him better saw that behind the stern exterior was a kind man with a keen sense of humour.

Playing in the Glam was always exciting, stimulating and immensely enjoyable. The enthusiasm of youth was tempered and channelled by sensible discipline, astute musical direction and efficient orchestral management. What a magnificent institution. How I miss it".

Dr. Ian Evett spent six years in the viola section of the Glam. He has developed an international reputation as one of the world's most eminent forensic scientists specialising in DNA testing. His brother Adrian was also principal bassoon in the Glam and is currently Orchestra Manager of the BBC Concert Orchestra.

Dr. Evett writes "I would like to pledge my support to a movement to preserve the memory of Russell Sheppard and of the wonderful Glamorgan Youth Orchestra. Just don't ask me to play the viola - the world deserves to be spared that".

Diana Griffiths

When I remember the range of music we played in the Glam - not just the usual Haydn, Mozart and Beethoven, but Tchaikovsky and Dvorak symphonies, "Thomas Tallis", Grace Williams, Vaughan Williams and even a Rachmaninov symphony - I am amazed. Much of that music, now taken for granted, was almost inaccessible to the public at the time - neither available on record, nor in the general concert repertoire.

We were thrown in at the deep end when we went to Ogmore, and it turned out to be no bad thing. From a few hours solitary practice per week, suddenly we were playing and rehearsing together for six hours a day - sight reading, practising, learning to keep up. I remember, at fifteen being bewildered, swamped and lost in the orchestra's first run through of Tchaikovsky's Fourth Symphony ; by the end of the course, at the concert, I could follow all the music and even play some of the notes! That's how quickly we learned.

No matter how old you grew to be, one of the rules at Ogmore was that no-one was allowed out of camp in the evenings after supper. Well, this was a winter course, spanning the New Year and one of the boys (he was 22), who was commuting to the course in his father's car, asked me out for a drink - just to the village. I had never broken the rules before, but I myself was 21 - a true grown-up. So we went out, and there was no problem getting out of the camp because K left at that time every evening. Getting back in at 10.30 pm, however, looked more difficult. " If you cwtch down on the floor of the front seat, K said I'll throw my coat over you and nobody'll see you". And so we got to the gates of the camp - only to be flagged down by Shep, who was there, waiting. He tapped on the passenger window. K leaned over and wound it down. Shep poked his head through the window and said, in his usual gentle way, "Good evening Diana Griffiths - you can come out now". That was all, he never mentioned it again.

Heather and Tony Lewis, Mary Griffiths, Jeff Lloyd, Gareth Jay, Helena Davies, Susan Salter, Keith Morris, Wendy Sheppard, John Jenkins, Maggie Rees and Tony Randall rank highly among the very good friends I made at Ogmore.

For we aspiring young musicians in the 50s, to be chosen to go to Ogmore for a week's playing together in the Glam was our dearest ambition. Just fifteen shillings it cost us for a week's board and tuition by professional musicians, in that idyll of an old army camp on a windy hill overlooking the sea. But, exciting as it was, we didn't really know at the time what treasures we had or how very privileged we were. If we thought about it at all, we would have imagined that something similar happened everywhere. For me, it was only after leaving Wales that I realised that we had been given something very special - unique, in fact.

And it was all made possible by the dedication and enthusiasm of Shep, whom we also took for granted. Because Shep and Ogmore and the Glam were inseparably one and the same. He was always there, up front, quietly in control of the whole thing from beginning to end".

Diana Griffiths did not become a professional musician. She was born in Neath and educated at Neath Girls' Grammar School, the University of Sheffield and University College, Cardiff. She was a member of the NYOW. Diana taught English, and was an examiner for O Level English for eleven years, She is now a freelance radio playwright and adapter. Plays include "The King's Hostage", "Set to Rites", "The Emperors Dream", and "Second Fiddle" (a nostalgic tale of amateur musicians, it includes all the music most people can ever remember). Radio adaptations include "Joby",and "Flambards". Diana is a full member of The Welsh Academy. She has one daughter who also did not become a professional musician.

Wayne Warlow

"Oh Mr. Porter"

"I am sure that all of us who were members would acknowledge the influence of Ogmore on our future in terms of musical and character development. Equally, all will rightly pay tribute to the pivotal role played by Russell Sheppard in creating the orchestra and so ably directing its fortunes over many years. However, none I suspect can have benefited as directly as I once did from the application of his well-disguised expertise as a luggage porter.

At the time I took part in my first Ogmore course in 1955, both the Sheppard family and mine lived in Pontypridd. It was both thoughtful and kind of Shep to offer to drive me down to the camp on the first day. We duly arrived and I trotted off, cello in hand to get my bearings. After a quick circuit of the dining hall, toilet block and main hall, I was comfortably settled in about two-thirds of the way down Dorm C, chatting away ten to the dozen with the then unknown faces who would become best friends over the following years.

I suppose about half an hour must have passed before the dorm went suddenly silent apart from the sound of heavy footsteps - taken at a more leisurely pace than the hundred yard dash technique adopted by the majority of the inhabitants of the dorm.

If the word "gobsmacked" had been invented in those days, it might well have been used to describe the faces of those who stood open-mouthed, brains trying frantically to retain some tenuous grip on reality as their eyes focused on their approaching conductor. Not only was it almost unheard of for Shep to enter the dorms - indeed, I cannot for the life of me remember another occasion when this happened - but he seemed to be carrying somebody's suitcase - Mine!

I don't remember exactly what Shep said to me as he dropped the suitcase on my bed, but I think that memory training, the importance of concentration and the long-term effect of heavy cases on the upholstered rear seats of British saloon cars were all mentioned.

No reference was ever made to this incident by him again. Meanwhile my social standing in the dorm went ballistic as, despite all my denials to the contrary, I became known as the boy who forced Russell Sheppard to carry his suitcase".

Wayne Warlow was a member of the Glam and National Youth Orchestras where, in addition to being leading cellist, he showed his fine musicianship by playing many instruments including the Oboe and Cor Anglais. A student at University College, Cardiff, Wayne has had a busy and successful career as a performer, conductor and very talented composer and arranger. His work has embraced many branches of music and he remains a jazz devotee.

JPR Williams

Music was the one hobby I could not combine as well as I would have liked; although my hands are better known for catching a ball, swinging a racket or even, in later years, wielding a scalpel, at one time, they had tripped along the piano in gay abandon and produced vibrato on my old violin. I had played in the Glamorgan Youth Orchestra as a first violin and had experienced great thrills when we performed well even just when we all finished on the right notes - especially after many hours of rehearsal. It was rather like training hard for an international and running out winners. It's the team spirit and sense of achievement which are common to both.

As is clear from the above extract from JPR : An Anthology, the legendary Welsh full back JPR Williams also had a flirtation with music. It is believed that he was actually taught the violin by Russell Sheppard's wife Karen before entering the Glam. Music's loss was certainly rugby's gain.

Gruffydd Harries

There are so many memories of concerts with the Glam, and they are all good ones. I remember my first with particular fondness. My first concert - the thrill of seeing the bill-board outside the Parc and Dare Hall, Treorchy and thinking how proud I was to be part of it. The journey to the Royal Festival Hall by chartered train and the magic of playing at a venue I had only dreamt about before Shep made it a reality for the choir and orchestra is mingled with the bitter sweet memory of the Glam last concert at the Gwyn Hall in my home town of Neath.

Although most of my recollections carry an x certificate, three are just about printable here. Escaping for one of our illicit visits to the local hostelry (or was it the local curry house) five of us were creeping down the hill back from Ogmore camp when a shadowy figure appeared in the porch of a nearby house. To avoid detection, we laid down on the gravel just as a rather shabby old horse decided to gloriously break wind - loud and long as old nags are prone to do. The sound subsided on the breeze (a force eight gale was considered but a breeze in

Ogmore). It was replaced by a shout of "Oh my God, the horse has f..ted!" and the hysterical laughter of five helpless individuals who, needless to say, progressed no further on their night's quest.

Then there was the traditional dupe for newcomers to the orchestra regarding their concert attire. I can remember many attempts at yellow bow tie making and frantic phone calls home to parents with urgent requests for the same. And then, of course there was the famous occasion, when, in "Rhapsody in Blue" a trombone solo is followed by a silence and then orchestral crash chords. The trombone solo was played beautifully by John Hendy (now a principal with the WNO) who in the aforementioned moment of silence uttered an expletive loud enough to wake up any stone-deaf grandmothers dragged along for the occasion and enjoying forty winks at the back of the hall. Although many incidents have made me laugh at concerts since then, I can never recall being so helpless as, indeed, was everyone around me.

I cannot overstate the sense of gratitude that I feel for Russell Sheppard for giving me the opportunity to join the exclusive club - the Glam - and to enjoy all the benefits that came with membership - the appreciation of music, the performance opportunities, the friends, the social life - the list goes on. The respect that he commanded from me, and from every one of my friends was immense, and that respect grows ever greater with passing years putting in perspective how much he achieved. There was an occasion in 1996 when I met him in a concert, and it must be said that he and Mrs. Sheppard looked old and frail. Seeing him again, even after all the years that had past instantly made me stand upright, check my tie was done up, worry about the length of my hair and make sure that I behaved properly. I made a point of going up to him and introducing myself. To my amazement he remembered me, my instrument, the address of my old family home and the date I first got on the Glam. I like to think that the lessons he taught me, and the opportunities he gave me served me well. He was a remarkable man".

Gruff was a principal flute and piccolo player with the Glamorgan, West Glamorgan and National Youth Orchestras. He has managed several orchestras including the Swansea Sound Sinfonia, the Welsh Philharmonic and the National Chamber Orchestra of Wales and has been responsible for organising the music of many programmes for HTV, SAC and the BBC. In this capacity, he has worked with most of the famous artists of his generation, including Bryn Terfel, Rebecca Evans and Dennis O'Neill. He organises concerts for the City and County of Swansea and the Gower Festival.

Plate 4 : Holyhead County School Choir and Orchestra (Karen Williams - Violin - fifth from the left)

Plate 1 :
The Sheppard Trio
Left to Right -
Austen, Beatrice and
Russell Sheppard

Plate 5 :
Holyhead County School :
"Messiah" 1944
Left to Right -
Russell Sheppard,
Einwen Thomas,
Douglas Williams,
Blodwen Williams,
Llew. Lewis

Plate 3 : The Mountain Ash Juvenile Orchestra : 1930
Mrs. Nora Huxley - Cello - is seated second from the RIght.

Plate 2 : Russell Sheppard - front row, second from the right - is honoured as organist and choirmaster of St. Illtyd's Church, Cefnpennar

Plate 6 : Holyhead County School Choir
Russell Sheppard, centre: Glyn Roberts front row, third from the left

Plate 7 - Karen Williams

Plate 12 : The Glam
Tenth Anniversary Celebrations at Ogmore
Shep responds to speeches of congratulation

Plate 9 - Glamorgan Youth Orchestra -
Inaugural Course 1949

Plate 8 - Mr. Langham's Pontypridd Orchestra
Wendy Sheppard - violin - second row,
second from the left

Plate 10 : The Glam at the Pavilion, Porthcawl
Tony Lewis - violin - second desk of first violins

Plate 11 : Symphonic Proportions
The Glam - Leader : Jeffrey Lloyd - at Sandfields Comprehensive School

Plate 14 : Orchestra and Choir at the Royal Festival Hall, 1971
Roger Lewis and Peter Sheppard are on the extreme left and right of the Horn section respectively

Plate 13 - 21st Anniversary Orchestra and Staff at the new hall, Ogmore

Plate 22 - Bass Section 1961 - Neil Kinnock is standing sixth from the left of the party

Plate 24 - In Concert at the Royal Festival Hall, 1971

Plate 21 - Glamorgan Youth Choir and Orchestra - St. Theodore's Church, Port Talbot, New Year's Eve 1961
Stanley Jones is seated behind and to the right of Shep

Plate 23 - It's all smiles as Glamorgan singers and players board the plane for Bratislava.
Della Jones and Pat Sheppard seem determined to board first whilst staff members
Ann James and Eleri Owen bring up the rear

Plate 30 - Glamorgan Youth Brass Band 1964 - Conductor Aaron Trotman is seated in the centre of the picture.

Plate 19 - Shep conducts the Youth Orchestra and Schools Choir at County Hall, Cardiff in 1958. The Duke of Edinburgh listens with enthusiastic attention.

Plate 29 - *Inaugural Brass Band Course, Dyffryn House, 1952.*

QEP 4020

Choir of
Glamorgan County Grammar Schools

accompanied by a section of the

Glamorgan County Youth Orchestra

CONDUCTOR: RUSSELL J. SHEPPARD, M.Mus.
Inspector of Schools, Glamorgan County Council

VIVAT—a welcome chorus
BUGEILIO'R GWENITH GWYN
NON NOBIS DOMINE
YR UTGORN

QUALITON EXTENDED PLAY RECORD — MADE IN WALES
January, 1959

Plate 20 - *Royal Command Performance - Record cover of the recording requested for Her Majesty, The Queen.*

Counter Subject 2 : The Glamorgan Youth Choir

§

Blessed is a world that sings
Gentle are its songs.

Sir Walford Davies

The history of the Glamorgan Youth Choir (GYC) is inextricably linked with that of the orchestra. From the outset, Shep adopted the policy of including an input from a local school choir in his orchestral programmes. In this way, he was able to assess the vocal talents in the three geographical areas of Glamorgan whilst affording himself the opportunity of working directly with many of the leading singing coaches of the late 1940s and early 1950s. Even more significantly, these ventures provided a platform for Shep to promote and propagate his choral aspirations in the field of school and youth singing which would, eventually, lead to the creation of a first-class county choir and also to improvements in vocal standards in schools throughout Glamorgan.

In 1949, the first invitation to appear with the GYO was accepted by the choir of Barry Intermediate School for Girls who took the stage in the first orchestral concert held at Glamorgan Training College, Barry. Although the names of the school's choral staff are not recorded on the programme, it is evident that the choir was of good standing, singing as it did "Y Bore Glâs" as a solo item and combining with the strings of the orchestra in Thiman's "Gloria in Excelsis", Bach's "Sheep May Safely Graze" and "Sleepers Wake" which concluded the programme.

In January 1950, Shep collaborated, and, no doubt, enthused and inspired, the pupils and staff of Whitchurch Secondary Modern School Choir. The concert was held at Whitchurch school, and because of Shep's confidence in choir trainers Mr. I.Thomas and Miss K.Jones, the choir shared the entire second half of the programme for a performance of the "Christmas Music" from Handel's "Messiah". Regrettably, the vocal soloists in the work were not mentioned. This was to be Shep's first oratorio performance with young performers in Glamorgan and the programme is printed in full over-page :

Pontypridd Boys' Grammar School Hall was chosen as the venue for the third concert on April 15th,1950. The orchestral strains of the "Water Music", Fletcher's "Folk Tune and Fiddle Dance" and Bach's Brandenburg Concerto No.3 in G were juxtaposed cleverly with items by the Girls' Choir who sang "Music When Soft Voices Die", "Suo Gân" , "Sound The Trumpet" and "Geneth Lân Oedd Gweno". Members of the Boys' Grammar School Choir joined forces in "Let us Now Praise Famous Men" and "Praise" and the combined choral and orchestral forces brought the concert to a rousing and patriotic finale with "Britons Sing". The choirs were trained by Mr. H.Meredith and Miss M.Lewis.

GLAMORGAN EDUCATION AUTHORITY.

Programme

of a

CHORAL AND ORCHESTRAL CONCERT

held at the

SECONDARY MODERN SCHOOL, GLANYNANT, WHITCHURCH,

on

FRIDAY, 6th JANUARY, 1950,

by the

Glamorgan Youth Orchestra

and the

Whitchurch Secondary Modern School Choir.

Trained by Mr. I. THOMAS and Miss K. JONES.

Conductor:
RUSSELL SHEPPARD.

NOTE. During the present week members of the Orchestra have attended an Orchestral Music Course at Dyffryn Education Centre, with the Chamber Music Players of University College, Cardiff, as tutors.

Part One.

ORCHESTRA	**CONCERTO GROSSO in G.** Opus 6, No. 1. a. **Tempo giusto.** b. **Allegro.** c. **Adagio.** d. **Allegro.** e. **Allegro.**	HANDEL.
ORCHESTRA	**PIANO CONCERTO in F Minor. No. 14.** a. **Allegro moderato.** b. **Largo.** c. **Presto.**	BACH.
CHOIR:	**CAROLS:** a. **"Beside Thy Cradle here I stand."** b. **"Luther's Cradle Hymn."**	BACH. BACH.
ORCHESTRA	**MINUET from "JUPITER" SYMPHONY.**	MOZART.
ORCHESTRA	**FIDDLE DANCE.**	PERCY FLETCHER.

Part Two.

CHOIR and ORCHESTRA:	**THE CHRISTMAS MUSIC FROM "MESSIAH"**	HANDEL.

1. **Overture.**
2. Recit: **Comfort ye my people.**
3. Chorus: **And the Glory of the Lord.**
4. Recit: **Behold, a Virgin can conceive.**
5. Air & Chorus: **O thou that tellest.**
6. Air: **How beautiful.**
7. **Pastoral Symphony.**
8. Recit: **There were Shepherds.**
9. Recit: **And suddenly there was with the Angel.**
10. Chorus: **Glory to God.**
11. Recit: **Then shall the eyes of the blind be opened.**
12. Air: **He shall feed His flock.**
13. Chorus: **For unto us a Child is born.**

HEN WLAD FY NHADAU.
GOD SAVE THE KING.

GOWERTON CONCERT

Glamorgan Youth Orchestra in West

GLAMORGAN Youth Orchestra had a great music-making at the Gowerton Girls' Grammar School, which the monogram over the stage still calls by the honoured name of Gowerton Intermediate Girls' School. It was a musical marathon done on the relay race principle: when Mr. Russell Sheppard's orchestra had played a couple of concertos Mrs. Bull's choir would take up the running, and a brilliant finish was improvised at the last moment by which they both ended together in "The Heavens are Telling," under Mr. Russell Sheppard.

SOMETIMES SUPERB

Perhaps the greatest compliment paid to the progress of musical education in the schools to-day is that we seriously find fault with these youthful orchestras and their conductors—"He is driving them too hard," "They weren't together" at some point or other. "This soloist has the technique and brain but not the natural gift and lovely singing quality of the other"—an orchestra of teen-agers is accepted as a natural feature of youth work and expected to play like young semi-professionals. And so they do, they play exactly like semi-professionals, sometimes superbly, at others very badly in passages that professionals would have glossed over if they could not properly exploit them.

WEEK AT DYFFRYN

These youngsters aim at the highest, and conductors like Mr. Russell Sheppard pay them the compliment of calling for the full thing and no compromise; hence the brilliant moments, of which there were very many last night, when everything went well; and the critical compliment is that attention has been drawn to scattered patches of unequal performance, which might easily have been ignored with an avuncular blind eye, or should it be deaf ear.

For a week the Glamorgan Youth Orchestra has been coached at Dyffryn by members of the Chamber Music Players of the University College, Cardiff, and paid tribute to Gowerton's contribution to orchestral work by giving their first performance in West Glamorgan in Gowerton. Many members of the orchestra were from the two Gowerton schools.

Presumably one must preserve the anonymity of the programme, but some of the performers were not anonymous when they won at Caerphilly, and these prize winners were among the singers as well as the instrumentalists. There were movements from three concertos, besides the Brandenburk No. 3, and these alone would have been riches enough for one evening. The playing in the Bach violin concerto in A minor was magnificent. They used two very fine soloists, but one had the rhythm and beauty of a true Bach singer. He could not make a discordant sound, and the music rippled from his fingers in an intoxicating stream. He gave a more romantically felt performance in the serenade from the Haydn quartet, with three other Gowerton boys playing the pizzicato accompaniment. To show the quality of the wind section we had an excellent performance in the slow movement of the Mozart clarinet concerto and a delightful Haydn trumpet concerto.

The orchestra's most finished performance of all round excellence, though they played well in the "Water Music" and the Brandenburg No. 3, where they had admirable volume and tone, was the "Carnival of Animals." This was up to many professional standards with glorious playing on the two pianos.

GIRLS' CHOIR

The Gowerton Girls' Choir under Mrs. Bull may have been pace-makers, or front-of-the-curtain turns — they sang from the floor of the hall —but they were by no means secondary to the orchestra. Here was a body of girl singers who produced their voices for beauty of tone. They never let everything go for the fun or excitement of the thing, as the orchestra did in "Handel in the Strand," and in a group of solos and a duet they showed the standard of voices there were among the choristers.

The group who sang the solo and trio passages in "The Heavens are Telling" had a loveliness of tone that will not be easily forgotten. Mr. Russell Sheppard paid this closing chorus the compliment of treating it as an adult performance, and choir and orchestra responded in a great climax to a concert which had covered an immense amount of music from Purcell to Percy Grainger. D.M.I.P.

On 14th of September 1950 the orchestral wagons rolled West for a concert held at Gowerton Girls' Grammar School. Here, the choir coached by Mrs. D.Bull, sang "Siôn a Siân" and, under Shep's baton even more more challenging pieces were performed including his arrangement of "The Heavens Are Telling" and "Achieved is The Glorious Work" from Haydn's "Creation". Before "Handel in The Strand" and the anthems brought the concert to what the "South Wales Evening Post" heralded as a great climax, the choir sang the tranquil setting of "Lully, My Liking". The "Posts" review of the concert provides evidence of the orchestra's speedy development and also of the high standard of singing produced at Gowerton.

During the 1950s, there was a strong tradition for choral singing in Glamorgan Youth Centres. Written at the end of the decade Russell Sheppard's report on "Music Classes Held in County Youth Centres" affirms that the youth of Glamorgan were extremely well catered for in terms of singing.

Division	School	Activity	Evenings per week	Instructor
West Glam	Gorseinon Boys	Choir	1	Mrs.Myra Rees
	Penclawdd Secondary	Choral	2	Mr. E.G.Austin
	Pontarddulais Secondary	Mixed Choral	2	Mr. Noel Davies
	Pontarddulais Junior	Choral	2	Mr. A.Miles
Mid Glam	Aberkenfig(Pandy School)	Choral	1	Mrs. Veronica Rees
		Boys Choir	1	Mrs. Veronica Rees
		Madrigals	1	Mrs. Veronica Rees
	Bridgend(Heol Gam)	Choral (Mixed)	1	Mr. Howell Evans
		Choral (Girls)	1	Mr. Howell Evans
	Caerau Boys' School	Choral(Mixed)	1	Mrs. Veronica Rees
		Choral (Boys)	1	Mrs. Veronica Rees
	Port Talbot Central School	Choral	1	Mr.E.Richards
	Sandfields Junior	Choral Music	1	Mr.G.P.Powell
South East	Cogan Boys' Sec. Modern	Choir	2	Mr.D.W.Jones
	Penarth Victoria Boys' Primary	Choir	1	Mr.T.Thomas
	Whitchurch Secondary	Boys Choir	1	Mr.Wyndham Jones
		Mixed Choir	2	Mr.Wyndham Jones
		Girls' Choir	1	Mr.Wyndham Jones
	Gladstone Road, Barry	Choir	1	Miss Tidball
	Ogmore Vale Infants' (Tynewydd)	Choral Music	1	Mr. V.J.Crocker
	Cynffig Secondary	Choir	1	Mr.B.Jones
Caerphilly	Coedybrain Junior	Choral Singing	1	Mr. A.J.Clarke
	Ffynon Taff Junior	Choral Singing	1	Mr. J.H.L.Mabbit
	Twyn Secondary	Youth Choir	1	Mr. A. Jones
Port Talbot	Baglan Primary	Choral	1	Miss G.Williams
	Llansawel Mixed	Choral Music	1	Mrs. M.R.Davies
	Coedffranc Jnr. Boys, Skewen	Mixed Choir	1	Mrs. A.Davies
	Herbert Road Jnr., Neath	Choral	1	Mr. Snow
	Rhydhir Secondary	Choral	1	Mr. W.Lawrence
Aberdare	Y Gadlys Secondary	Choral	1	Mr.J.Jenkins
Pontypridd	Beddau Sec. Bryncelynog	Choral Mixed	1	Mr. A.Watkins
	Pontyclun Mixed and Infants	Choral	1	Mr. D.T.Evans
	Trefforest Junior	Choral	1	Mr.G.E.Hughes
	Hawthorn Sec.	Choral	1	Mr.T.I.Humphreys

Festival of Britain year, 1951, proved to be an exciting and challenging one in the annuls of the development of a county youth choir. It began with a concert held at the Gwyn Hall Neath on January 4th. James Hargreaves (Trumpet) and local clarinettist John Hempenstall were concerto soloists with the GYO. Winnie Richards-Thomas directed the Choir of Neath Girls' Grammar School in an ambitious programme which centred upon Britten's "Ceremony Of Carols". Her accompanist was Mrs. Edna Morgan and under Shep's baton the choir and orchestra performed excerpts from Bach's "Christmas Oratorio" with Pamela

Oakes, Vera Adams and Marslie Harris as soloists. A repeat orchestral performance, albeit with a much reduced choral content was given the following night by the GYO, and the Choirs of the Boys' and Girls' Grammar Schools at the Coliseum, Aberdare.

Regional concerts of epic proportions were planned and enacted involving the county orchestra and the first embryonic template of the Glam Choir. Shep's organisational flair was put to its ultimate test to date, and, as his letters to "Heads of Certain Schools" proves he was assuredly not found wanting in the task of co-ordinating large scale musical marathons.

The first of these performances attracted a large May audience to the Hall of Heol Gam School, Bridgend. Very much a musical pot-pourri, Shep's programme was to harness the talents of twelve Youth Club Choirs from Glynneath, Penarth, Tondu, Bryntirion, Taibach, Romilly, Senghenydd, Clyne, Pontrydyfen, Skewen, Nelson and Onllwyn together with the choir of Trefforest Girls' Guild and Boys Brigade. County Eisteddfod winners were also given a platform with the GYO. Concert Chairman, Sir Ben Bowen Thomas the Permanent Secretary to the Welsh Department of the Ministry of Education presided and the Festival Choir sang Bach's "Passion Chorale" and music by Elgar and Handel.

In the events centred on the East and West of the county, the unifying ingredient in the programme for both districts was Purcell's "Dido and Aeneas" presented as the concluding half of the mammoth spectacular. Similarly, the GYO performed Walton's "Crown Imperial March" and the first movement of Beethoven's Symphony No.5 in C Minor in all concerts. Instrumentalists from the West and East united in the slow movement from Mozart's Clarinet Quintet.

The Glamorgan Choir performed at the Town Hall, Maesteg on July 9th and gave two repeat performances at the Gwyn Hall. They combined in Beethoven's "Creation Hymn" and Parry's "Jerusalem" and a Mixed Choir - not forgetting the hardworking orchestra - performed Bach's "Sleepers Wake" and Quilter's "Non Nobis Domine". The combined choir of Gowerton Girls', Neath Boys' and Girls Grammar Schools sang the challenging "Folk Songs of the Four Seasons" by Vaughan Williams. Individual school items were presented by ;

Maesteg Grammar	*Flora Gave Me Fairest Flowers*	*Wilbye*
Bridgend Boys' and Girls' Grammar	*When Summer's Merry Days*	*E.T. Davies*
Gowerton Girls' Grammar	*Y Cyntaf Dydd O'r Gwyliau*	*Alawon*
	Fflat Huw Puw	*Gwerin*
Ystalyfera and Pontardawe Grammar	*Sound The Trumpet*	*Purcell*
	Old Mother Hubbard	*Hutchinson*
Neath Girls' Grammar	*Eastern Pictures*	*Holst*
Port Talbot Secondary	*O My Saviour*	*Dvorak*

In his response to the report, "Music in the Schools of Wales" : 1953, Russell Sheppard is critical of the omission of a reference to the importance of mixed choral singing, stating :

"One feature which appears to be omitted in this memo is reference to SATB singing in Grammar Schools. By the age of 16 plus (even 15 plus in many cases) the great majority of boys can be taught to sing Tenor and Bass. Once again, it is important that Grammar Schools should realise that the future bass and tenor singers will have received literally no training unless it is provided at the school. Some interesting SATB singing has taken place in Barry Boys, Aberdare Boys, Pontardawe, Gowerton Boys and Maesteg.

It is, possibly, worthy of mention that a mixed choir of 300 (SATB) sang part songs and chorales including Bach's "Sleepers Wake" at the Festival Concert held at Neath in 1951. This is probably the largest body of mixed voices, pupils of Grammar Schools, which has gathered for such a purpose in Glamorgan and probably in Wales. It proved what can be done in Grammar Schools that have the correct attitude to the subject".

In this respect, Shep later paid tribute to the outstanding choral work of Winnie Richards-Thomas and John Hopkin Jones who achieved amazing standards in Neath Girls' and Boys' Grammar Schools respectively. The Girls' Grammar School Choir also contributed significantly to another Gwyn Hall concert in January, 1955, when they successfully tackled music by Bach, Handel and the Four Choral Hymns from Rig Veda by Holst.

For the Festival Concert held at Alexon House, Hawthorn on July 11th,1951 the GYO accompanied the East Glamorgan Choir in Holst's "I Vow to Thee, My Country", Beethoven's "Creation Hymn", "Codiad Yr Ehedydd", Bach's "Flocks in Pastures Green Abiding", "Non Nobis Domine", "Dwfn yw'r Môr" and "Little Jack Horner." Individual choral items were presented by :

Tonypandy Grammar	Merch Megan	Traditional
Pentre Grammar	The Bells	Roberton
Porth (Dual) Grammar	Nant y Mynydd	Williams
Cowbridge Girls' High School	Y Mae Afon	Protheroe
Barry Boys' Grammar	King of Glory, King of Peace	Bach
	Summer Carol	

The successes of these concerts is indicative of Shep's stamina and administrative acumen. The opportunity to rehearse with staff from most parts of the authority and to rub shoulders with headteachers and political leaders of the time was to prove to be a potent influence in the future inauguration of the Glam Choir. Shep's notes taken from the Glamorgan County Council Festival Brochure indicates the scale of the celebratory events.

Other examples of the GYO collaborating with school and youth choirs continued until 1962. In that year the Glam was joined by Myra Rees' Gorseinon Youth Choir and Ryland Davies. Previously, on July 9th 1958, Shep organised and conducted a County Youth Choir Festival, held at the Gwyn Hall Neath. Choirs representing twelve County Youth Centres joined forces and the programme included music by Dvorak and excerpts form Haydn's "Creation". In January 1952 Bridgend School for Girls performed extracts from Bach's

"Christmas Oratorio" at the Town Hall. Later, in July 1955, the choir of Barry Girls' Grammar, under the direction of Merfina Evans, sang at the Glamorgan Training College. Finally, in March 1956, at the Working Mens' Hall, Nantymoel, the orchestra's guests were the choir of Ogmore Girls' Grammar, trained by Mrs. M.D.Morris.

If these examples represent the choir in its embryonic form, then, metaphorically speaking, Shep's choral egg was - in all but name - well and truly hatched in 1958. Due to the Queen's illness, HRH The Duke of Edinburgh accepted an invitation to visit the Glamorgan County Hall on Tuesday 26th July, 1958, the year in which the Commonwealth Games were held in Cardiff. A performance, to be given in the Council Chamber, was commanded. Shep's response was to instigate county-wide auditions, and organise a residential course at Ogmore in order to prepare for the event. With the help and support of the music teachers of the schools involved, Shep finally gathered together for the occasion 51 Sopranos and Altos and 36 Tenors and Basses whose ages ranged from 16 to 18. Together with the 30 strong GYO, the choir so delighted the Duke, that he requested that a recording be commissioned to be forwarded to the Queen herself. Plates 19 & 20.

Despite the choir's long-winded title - "Choir of the Glamorgan County Grammar Schools" - Shep, in later programmes was to date the creation of the Glamorgan Youth Choir as 1958. A rose by any other name, the Glam choir was to flourish until reorganisation in 1974, and subsequently would develop into the Mid, South and West Glamorgan Youth Choirs. Shep himself, firstly as conductor, and, after 1972, as Guest Conductor would grace many a podium in Glamorgan, London and Czechoslovakia until his retirement in 1979.

Never a person to miss a golden opportunity, Shep organised an immediate sequel to the royal recital. Regular residential courses were henceforth to become as much a way of life for succeeding generations of singers as they were for orchestral and band players. In point of fact, many members of the GYO were to supplement the ranks of the choir when, of necessity, sections of the orchestra were reduced to manageable proportions for accompaniment purposes. Shep was, by all accounts, delighted to include the three items sung for the Duke of Edinburgh in a GYO concert held at the Memorial Hall, Barry and the College of FE, Port Talbot on the 8th and 9th of September 1958.

Under the same name, the choir gathered together in September 1959. Staff and students worked tirelessly in preparation for the first concert of a predominantly choral nature which was held at the County School for the Blind, Bridgend. The first part of the programme included an input by the female section who sang Shep's arrangement of "Bugeilio'r Gwenith Gwyn". Later, the male voices gave a very creditable account of the "Song of the Jolly Roger". Who could ever forget the words of the opening refrain, "Up with the Jolly Roger boys, and fling it to the breeze."? How did we restrain ourselves from singing our own unexpurgated version of a certain unforgettable phrase when we affirmed that we would "chase the <u>beggars</u> across the sea, ha-ha, ha-ha, ha-ha., hee-hee?"

On a more serious note, Shep was to return to an old favourite of his from his days in Holyhead, namely Coleridge Taylor's "Hiawatha's Wedding Feast." Tenor soloist in the lilting aria "On Away Awake, Beloved" was T.Eifion Evans and both Choir and orchestra pulled out all the stops to achieve an undoubted success. The work ends with the evocative lines :

And the wedding guests departed
Leaving Hiawatha happy;
Happy with the night and Minehaha.

Such were the emotions of singers and players - myself included - as they left the concert hall. For we were all "happy with the night" - and Russell Sheppard.

Still without an official county title the ever expanding choir began to scale the heights of ever more ambitious choral masterpieces. At St. Martin's Church, Caerphilly on 12th September 1960, Shep continued the practice of featuring both the female and male sections of the choir, the former singing Schubert's "The Lord is My Shepherd" and the latter Daniel Protheroe's rousing "Laudamus". Those who took part in the concert will never forget the impression made by Holst's Short Festival Te Deum and Mozart's First Mass in C. Soloists in the Mozart Mass, included future professionals Gillian Humphreys and Sylvia Thomas (Sopranos), Jean Lewis (Alto), Stuart Kale (Tenor) and Peter Lodwig (Bass). Other soloists were sopranos Mavis Brown, Wendy Norman, and Carolyn Morgan, altos Wendy Mordicai, and basses Huw Williams, Anthony Davey and Meredith Rees.

At long last, the title Glamorgan Youth Choir was bestowed in December 1960. Possibly remembering the many eisteddfodau which took place during Advent in the Cynon Valley of his childhood, Shep decided, in his wisdom, to schedule this course over the New Year festivities. Most members questioned his choice of Friday 30th December for the first concert at Bethany Chapel, Port Talbot. Everyone doubted his sanity - and most of the brass, at least, the authenticity of his parentage - when it was discovered that the second concert was planned for New Year's Eve. Perhaps it was because most of the music was a repeat of the previous course, or even more probably because Llandaff Cathedral was such an inspiring setting, the concert was an unparalled success. Davy Ayers(Trumpet) and Jeffrey Lloyd (Violin) were the instrumental soloists, and Joan Hockings replaced Wendy Mordicai as one of the Alto soloists. Even after the long journey back from Cardiff there was still time for a short period of official celebration, not to mention a number of clandestine high jinks.

The choir reconvened in July 1961 for two concerts at All Saints Church, Porthcawl and Jerusalem Chapel, Resolven. Unusually, Shep featured three vocal soloists in concert arias - Norma Watkins (Soprano), Joan Hockings (Contralto) and Adrian Perrett (Baritone). The main work was Mendelssohn's "Lauda Sion". Margaret Williams (Alto) made her Glam debut and cellist Wayne Warlow performed Bach's "Arioso". Later that year, the names of choristers were printed in the programme for the first time. Four future professional singers and a leader of the Labour Party appear in this meritorious assembly. They are Della Jones, Sylvia Thomas, Stuart Kale, Peter Lodwick and of course Neil Kinnock.

The maestro persisted with unseasonal scheduling, this time arranging concerts at St. Theodore's Church, Port Talbot, on New Year's Eve and, incredulously, at Windsor Road Congregational Church, Barry on New Year's Day 1962. As if by a miracle, still the audiences came and the performances were both of high calibre. With only very minor modifications to the programme from the summer course, both singers and players virtually knew their music by heart.

May 15th, 1962 was an important milestone in the history of the choir and orchestra, who were both to participate in a royal occasion at Dyffryn Gardens. A thirty minute programme was an appropriate appetiser before the Princess Royal's arrival. Russell Sheppard's "Fanfare for a Royal Occasion" proclaimed the arrival of the royal guest and various dignitaries addressed the Princess Royal, interspersed by short musical items. The programme is shown below ;

SOUTH-EAST WALES Y.M.C.As CAPITAL DEVELOPMENTS

CEREMONY IN THE MARQUEE AT DYFFRYN GARDENS ST. NICHOLAS

TUESDAY, 15th MAY, 1962

Chairman:
County Alderman LLEWELLYN HEYCOCK, C.B.E., J.P.
(Chairman of the Glamorgan County Council)

2.30 p.m. Glamorgan Youth Choir and a section of the Glamorgan Youth Orchestra.
Conductor: RUSSELL J. SHEPPARD, ESQ., M.MUS.

3. 0 p.m. ARRIVAL of Her Royal Highness, The Princess Royal, G.C.V.O., G.B.E.
Orchestra:
"Fanfare for a Royal Occasion" (*Russell Sheppard*)
The National Anthem
ADDRESS OF WELCOME to Her Royal Highness by County Alderman Llewellyn Heycock, C.B.E., J.P.
A bouquet will be presented to Her Royal Highness by Miss Lynda Williams

3.10 p.m. Choir and Orchestra:
" Gloria in Excelsis Deo" (*E. Thiman*)

3.15 p.m. The Chairman will invite Her Royal Highness to receive Token Gifts and will call on D. W. Vaughan, Esq., C.B.E., J.P., Hon. Treasurer of the Royal Appeal, to announce the names of those who are to present tokens.
The Rev. David Williams, B.A., will dedicate the gifts.

3.30 p.m. Orchestra:
First Movement from Occasional Overture (*Handel*)
Choir and Orchestra:
" Non Nobis Domine" (*Roger Quilter*)

3.35 p.m. ADDRESS by W. F. Cartwright, Esq., D.L., J.P., Sponsor of the Royal Appeal

3.45 p.m. EXPRESSION OF THANKS to Her Royal Highness, The Princess Royal, G.C.V.O., G.B.E., by The Hon. J. H. Bruce, C.B.E., K.ST.J., D.L., J.P.

3.50 p.m. Hymn: " Iesu, Iesu rwyt ty'n ddigon"
Benediction
The Welsh National Anthem

4.15 p.m. Tea

The Welsh National Council of Y.M.C.As, take the opportunity of expressing their considerable gratitude to the Glamorgan County Council, through its Education Committee, who generously support Y.M.C.A. Service with Youth and provided the facilities of Dyffryn for today's Ceremony

Photo by Dorothy Wilding

In the early years of the GYC's development, regular members of staff on courses held at Bridgend, Ogmore and Barry included Mrs. M. Morris, Miss M. Morgan, E.Jones, J.Samuel, Alun John, H. Morgan, Mr. P.Rees, M.Burtch and, of courses the ever-present Stanley Jones. Gethin Evans (Aberdare), Huw Jones (Maesteg/Gowerton) and Hilton Richards (Ystalyfera) were to provide many of the Bass and Tenor singers in the choir. Later Alan James, Ann Hughes, Eleri Owen, John Davies, Clive Stubbs, Angela Mills and others would make substantive contributions to the successes of the choir.

Throughout its illustrious history, Stanley Jones served the choir with distinction. A teacher and later a primary school deputy head and headteacher, Stanley will long be remembered for his pioneering work using the recorder as a serious class instrument. He wrote a tutor in Welsh for that instrument which became a standard text in most primary schools and organised many Glamorgan recorder courses, for both pupils and teachers. As Shep's right hand man, his contribution is incalculable. With his infectious good humour he became the perfect foil to Shep on the occasions when the more irascible side of the latter's nature was in evidence. He enacted Shep's course arrangements with aplomb and became an excellent stage manager, interpreting concert arrangements by producing a host of stage plans - all written and sketched with the neatest of pens. Plate 21.

By the start of the 1960s the choir had established itself as a leading British youth choir capable of tackling virtually any work in the choral repertoire with professionalism and achieving standards equal to that of any adult choir. Competition to be accepted for the choir was very keen and once singers were accepted they showed a remarkable disinclination to "retire". That this is the case is demonstrated by the fact that the proportion of students grew from 21% in 1961 to an astonishing 48% in 1967. From that date, the figure settled at a percentage around the mid thirties. From 1961 to 1971 the chief providers of male singers were Gowerton (23), Aberdare (14), Neath Boys' (14), Kenfig Hill (11) Mountain Ash (10) and, especially in the early years, Barry Boys (8).

In terms of the provision of sopranos and altos, the early work of Winnie Richards-Thomas at Neath Girls' Grammar was to continue to be represented thanks to the efforts of Glynne Evans, Noel Davies and others and, in the West, Dyffryn and Glanafan schools were strongly represented. In Mid Glamorgan, Maesteg, Cynffig, and Garw(Ynysawdre) are all well-represented whilst, in the East the principal source was Pontypridd Girls' Grammar School. The impact of Ysgol Rhydfelin from the late 1960s was significant. From its modest beginnings of 90 singers in 1961, the choir numbers steadily increased to average around 130 in the 1960's and 70's.

Schools from East Glamorgan proved to be the most consistent source of singers during the decade although, by 1969, the West was coming strongly into prominence :

AREA	**1960**	**1963**	**1965**	**1967**	**1970**
East Glamorgan	39%	46%	47%	41%	37%
West Glamorgan	27%	32%	27%	33%	39%
Mid Glamorgan	34%	24%	26%	26%	24%

During the 1960s Shep introduced his young singers to a glittering kaleidoscope of works ranging from Handel to Walton and from Bach to Vaughan Williams. The quotation from "Toward the Unknown Region", by Walt Whitman, which is cited at the beginning of this chapter typified the confidence and pride in a sense of achievement experienced by those who were proud to sing in the choir.

Then we burst forth
We float in time and space,
Them to fulfil.... oh soul.

The echoes of this explosion of vocal endeavour were to reverberate throughout the world of professional opera in the most sensational manner. Research based on Richard Fawkes' book "Welsh National Opera" reveals that an amazing number of former Glam singers who sang as soloists with the GYO were to take principal roles with the company. Between 1974 and the writing of the book in 1985, a staggering 75 roles were sung by fifteen former Glamites.

Singer	Number of Roles
Susan Dennis	1
Marion Davies	1
Mary Davies	15
Ryland Davies	2
Meryl Drower	3
Jean Evans	5
Helen Field	19
Maureen Guy	3
Beverley Humphreys	1
Gillian Humphreys	1
Della Jones	1
Stuart Kale	8
Geoffrey Moses	9
Dennis O' Neill	5
Kelvin Thomas	1

Many of these singers have gone on to sing in opera houses and on the concert platforms of the most prestigious concert halls all over the world. Other Glam choir singers of the period who forged successful singing careers were Valerie Heath- Davies, Peter Lodwig, Sylvia Thomas and Lesley Roberts. One wonders if any other county or, in fact, any other region of the world of comparable size and population could match this peerless pinnacle of achievement.

Of the members of the Glam choir of the 1960s who distinguished themselves in the field of singing, records remain of the hopes and aspirations of two young mezzo sopranos both of whom also played in the GYO. Both singers were in their mid teens on the summer course of 1962. The younger hopeful, was Beverley Humphreys, from Maesycoed, Pontypridd who was on her very first course. She was evidently keen at that juncture to follow a career in teaching. However, such were her latent musical and dramatic talents that she was to become equally successful in the world of opera and broadcasting. Della Jones was much more assured of her intentions to follow a musical career.

No application forms were discovered pertaining to other famous opera stars of the future - Helen Field, Stuart Kale etc. By good fortune a photograph of Dennis O'Neill, who is not necessarily remembered in future for his instrumental, prowess as a cellist, was discovered in the process of research. Singer and instrumentalist, Rhian Samuel has, like Hilary Tann, established a fine reputation as a composer. Dr Samuel is currently a leading academic and is Professor at City University and Paul Loveluck was for a long period Chief Executive of the Welsh Tourist Board before taking up a similar post with the Countryside Council for Wales.

Many other choir members proceeded to distinguish themselves in a vast array of future careers. None more so, perhaps than Neil Kinnock, who, as leader of the Labour party opposition, so nearly became Prime Minister. A student at University College Cardiff, Neil from Tredegar, had, by 1962, attended six choral courses and was intent on continuing in the choir. As indicated in a course form, his hopes for a career in industrial relations were modest and he is currently a Member of the European Commission. Plate 22

Later, in July 1966 a young soprano from Pontardawe Grammar appears on the choral register - apparently for only one course. One reason for her brief membership of the choir might have been that, in the same year, she made her first appearance on the television programme "Heddiw" and stardom would soon beckon for Mary Hopkin. Her song "Those Were The Days", released in 1968 would top the pop music charts and she still remains a household name in Wales.

"Lauda Sion", with replacement soloists Peter Carder and Brian Llewellyn (Tenors) and Norman Pereira (Bass) was retained as the principal work for the September course, 1962. Trumpeters John Jenkins and Anthony Small performed Vivadi's Concerto for Two Trumpets at Capel Annibynnol Yr Alltwen, Pontardawe and the choir's new compositional gem, Handel's "Dettingham Te Deum", was introduced. Soloists Lynda Adams, Beverley Humphreys and Alan Badman were added to the traditional line-up of soloists. Shep was enticed back to his mother church, St Margaret's, Mountain Ash the next night and this occasion must have brought back many memories of his childhood. Research shows that the only concert to be postponed - although it was honoured within a few months - was that planned for Tabernacle Chapel, Skewen. The snow could not prevent a memorable April concert at Llandaff Cathedral with Marion Edwards making her debut; the programme replicated that of the previous September course.

Apart from the Verdi Requiem of a later period, if there is a single choral work with which Shep is most closely associated, then that piece must assuredly be "Toward The Unknown Region". Readers may recall, from Chapter 1, that Shep as a youth of seventeen had been inspired when he heard Dr. Vaughan Williams conduct the work at the Cwmaman Institute on Boxing Day 1932.

"Toward The Unknown Region" was a particular favourite of Russell Sheppard and was revisited on many subsequent occasions and it is hugely apt that he chose to perform the piece at St. Elvan's Church in nearby Aberdare on September 3rd, 1963. It was in this church that Shep had received his first organ lesson many years earlier. As the illuminating article from the "Aberdare Leader" recounts, particularly impressive standards were achieved by all the participants, including soloist Della Jones, under Shep's direction :

1,100 CROWDED INTO ST. ELVAN'S FOR THIS EVENT

Memorable musical experience from County singers and players

By E. MORLEY SMITH

ON TUESDAY WEEK, Aberdare was one of the three centres in the county privileged to receive the Glamorgan Youth Choir and Orchestra, and, in the event, to listen to a programme of music that was not only an entertainment but a musical experience of a high order. The venue was St. Elvan's Church, which was filled to its capacity of 1,000, and which accommodated 100 more on improvised seating, a tribute indeed to these talented young musicians.

The choir very quickly established an atmosphere with Mendelssohn's "Hear My Prayer," accompanied by the organ. It was launched rhythmically, in a style that properly reflected the suavity of much of Mendelssohn's writing in this vein and this was maintained by the soloist, Delyth Jones, who sang with verve and an eagerness to shape a vocal line that is not so easy as it might seem. The fall of the final cadence was beautifully poised and indeed was "at rest" in the full sense of the word.

The second item took us back to the sixteenth century to the measured polyphony of Palestrina, one of the great masters of the church music of the period. Here it was the turn of the male voices, who sang a Welsh translation of one of the motets, and sang it very well with a full tone and without loss of intonation. If there could have been more gradations of tone, its development would have been still more effective. But, these very young singers dealt remarkably well with music that would be a test of any mature choir's ability.

MUSICIANSHIP

The girls then sang "Blessed are They that Dwell in Thy House" by Brahms. This also was very effectively done and was a pointer to the quality of the musicianship which was to reach its culmination later in the programme.

Mainly a choral evening, the contrast of an orchestral item gave its quota of enjoyment. This item, best known for the "air" commonly identified as the "Air on the G String," was the Suite No. 3 in D Major by Bach, excellently played. The breadth of the long phrase in the air was well managed by the violins.

Choir and orchestra then joined in one of the main works of the programme, "Toward the Unknown Region," by one of the significant composers of our own century, Vaughan Williams. This work, which has not received the number of performances it merits, was written for the Leeds Festival of 1907 and is a setting of a poem by Walt Whitman. In this work the composer forged for himself a style that links him up with the great tradition of English music, while at the same time reserving for himself a complete freedom of individual expression.

FINE RAPPORT

From the opening chords and the haunting horn call, and the piano entry of the choir, "Darest Thou, O Soul, Walk with Me Toward the Unknown Region," this performance caught the imagination. There was a rapport between the conductor and his forces that led us on through this uncharted land, with a certainty of reaching that bourne where the soul triumphs at last, at a pitch of sustained intensity, through a range of dynamics which built up the tension to the final tremendous chord treble forte, maintained for several bars by the whole weight of the orchestra, finally leaving us seemingly several inches higher in our seats than we had been before. These young singers and players had succeeded in giving us a musical experience rare by any standards, a "piece de resistance" if ever there was one.

Since applause was not to be thought of, the audience was given an opportunity of responding to this inspiration in their own inimitable way. This was their singing of the well-loved hymn of Williams, Pantycelyn, "Iesu, Iesu, 'Rwyt Ti'n Ddigon," to the tune "Llwynbedw" by J. T. Rees. There was a deep sonority about this which was both moving and uplifting, and which testified to the inspirational quality of what had gone before. No greater tribute could have been paid to the high endeavour of these young musicians and their conductor, Mr. Russell Sheppard.

The work to conclude was, in contrast, a "piece d' occasion," the "Dettingen Te Deum," which is by no means Handel at his best but yet represents something that he could do extremely well.

ACCIDENTAL VICTORY!

But for the plans that so often go awry Handel might never have written it. A military gentleman by the improbable name of de Noailles had initiated a pincer movement calculated to destroy the British troops at Dettingen, led by George II, but one of the jaws was stricken with some kind of sclerosis that enabled the King to snatch an unwarranted victory from the jaws of defeat, to give Handel the opportunity of gratifying his royal patron.

Since Handel could not help being himself whatever the occasion, there are glimpses in this work of his quality, in the hints of majestic polyphony in the last choruses, and the occasional sense of power in the climaxes.

Once again the choir and orchestra performed their tasks with certainty and enthusiasm, and the soloists in the trios, quartets, and solos, all gave of their best. They were Marian Edwards, Della Jones, Lynette Howells, Alan Badman, Stuart Kale, David Llewellyn, Adrian Perrett, and Beverley Humphries.

The orchestra, led by Wendy Sheppard, played splendidly and the trumpets rang with an exuberance worthy of the accolytes of Gabriel.

Indeed, at times, the nonchalantly diabolical flourishes of these dedicated cornupcopeans, by name John Jenkins and David Small, might have sent the thoughts of those sitting in the front rows wandering uneasily in the direction of the walls of Jericho! It seems certain that Joshua would have promoted these two trumpeters on the spot. They probably enjoyed themselves as Handel intended they should, and, as he also intended, so did we!

The singing of the "Doxology" brought a really memorable evening to a close and singing of this seemed to have more than its usual significance, such was the atmosphere created on this notable occasion.

EXCELLENT RESULTS

The County Education Authority is to be congratulated on its work in this field, which has borne such excellent results and deserves our gratitude. So, too, do all the tutors in charge of sections, whose enthusiasm for their tasks know no bounds.

Finally, a tribute to the conductor, Mountain Ash-born Mr. Russell Sheppard. Obviously dedicated to his task, he has pursued it with perseverance and has brought a sound musicianship into the integration of his forces all over the county, and forged a musical entity of striking significance.

Unostentatious, his work is done with a calm discipline and a sound perception of the capabilities of the forces under his command.

His achievement here was something in the order of an apotheosis of his work to date, especially in the Vaughan Williams composition. "Toward the Unknown Regions" had had a quality bordering on the apocalyptic in its intensity.

● A COROLLARY to the performance of "The Unknown Region" is the pioneer work and ability of a local musician, the late highly regarded Edward Lewis, Cwmaman. In days when musical education was not what it is today and there was a marked reluctance by choirs to break new ground, Mr. Lewis, who had conducted choral works for 28 years at Cwmaman, conducted two successful performances of this work. The first was in December 1931, and the other in December 1932.

At one of these performances Vaughan Williams himself came down to conduct, and a presentation was duly made to him by the choir. I am indebted to Miss Ivy Morgan for this reminder. Cwmaman readers will no doubt recall the occasion with pride.

The writer had the pleasure and privilege of singing with Mr. Lewis in his Gamut Madrigal Society, and his dedication to music must always be remembered and appreciated here in Aberdare.

At the same period, two other concerts were given at Ebenezer Chapel, Gorseinon and at Hope Baptist Church, Bridgend.

In 1964 the GYC sang excerpts from the "Dettingen Te Deum" and "Toward the Unknown Region" at All Saints', Penarth and Glamorgan Training College, Barry. Delyth Jones sang Mendelssohn's "Hear My Prayer" and Kenneth Green augmented the soloists in choral works. In the autumn of the same year the choir visited that bastion of choral excellence in the Rhondda, Noddfa Chapel, Treorchy which was later tragically, destroyed by fire. At this concert glowing tributes were paid to Shep and his young musicians by two distinguished conductors of the world famous Treorchy Male Voice Choir, John Haydn Davies and John Cynan Jones. John Cynan had performed an organ concerto in the early period of genesis of the GYO and was later a tutor on GYC courses. Susan Dennis, Lesley Roberts and Peter Ballinger were admirable debutantes in Bach's Cantata : "O Praise The Lord For All His Mercies" and the choir revelled in the sumptuous harmonies of Brahms' "Song of Destiny". The "Academic

Festival Overture" by the same composer and Elgar's "Pomp and Circumstance March No. 1" were also programmed together with "Toward the Unknown Region". All agreed with Walt Whitman's sentiments that the choir and orchestra were "equally equipped" for the job in hand - and this in a valley renowned for the brilliance of its male voice singing.

The following January, in concerts at Sandfields School and the Memorial Hall, Barry, the brass section would revel in Mendelssohn's "Festgesang". The young musicians visited St.Elvan's church, Aberdare and the Central Hall, Bargoed. In September, 1965 a certain young tenor, who was soon to become a world - wide operatic star, made his Glam debut in Handel's "Sixth Chandos Anthem". In addition to Dennis O'Neill, this was to be an exalted line-up of soloists all of whom would later sing professionally - Elizabeth Field, Pamela Field, Della Jones and Stuart Kale. Shep's daughter, Wendy, the leader of the accompaniment orchestra performed the first movement of Bach's Violin Concerto in E Major and the programme also included "Y Bumedd Gerdd" by Vincent Thomas.

The conductor rested all but Pamela Field of his vocal soloists for the opening concert of 1966. Instead he arranged a concert platform for the varied talents of Della Jones. This time, instead of the audience thrilling to the dulcet tones of her voice, they were introduced to Della the solo pianist. What an incredible talent Neath had produced! What a challenging choice the first movement of Brahms' Piano Concerto No.1 in D Minor would be for any young pianist. For Della's mother, Eileen Gethin Jones, the eminent teacher who nurtured the talents of so many budding pianists, this must have been a thrilling experience. The performance certainly gave evidence not only of the daughter's all round musicianship, but also of the success of the mother's distinctive teaching technique. The concert at Barry Training College was brought to a triumphant choral climax with Handel's "Zadok The Priest".

As the size and competence of the choir further developed, Shep was able to introduce singers and audience to ever more exacting works. In July, 1966, church concerts at Caerphilly and Resolven saw the arrival of three taxing pieces - Bach's "Magnificat", Arwel Hughes' much neglected work "Gweddi" (Soloist Della Jones) and Parry's eternal "Blest Pair of Sirens". This triptych of pieces was preserved for combined choral and orchestral January concerts held at the Memorial Hall, Barry and the Gwyn Hall, Neath. John Milton's "At a Solemn Music" provides a fitting description of the young musicians as they sang "Blest Pair of Sirens" :

Where the bright Seraphim in burning row,
Their loud, uplifted angel-trumpets blow.
And the cherubic host in thousand quires,
Touch their immortal harps of golden wires.
With those just spirits that wear victorious palms,
Hymns devout and holy psalms,
Singing everlastingly.

At a Solemn Music : John Milton

Shep continued to encourage the audience or congregation to feel a part of these concerts. It had become a tradition to end performances with a joint rendition of the "Doxology" and in many concerts there was communal singing of a popular hymn. This practice of hymnody continued through to Shep's farewell concert in 1979.

Walton's Coronation "Te Deum", and Haydn's Sixteenth Mass were introduced for the summer church concerts at Aberdare and Maesteg with vocal introductions for Howard Handford and John Davies.

Following a visit of friendship by the students' Orchestra of the Bratislava Conservatoire of Music in the August of 1967, the return visit to West Slovakia will long be remembered by the 25 senior members of the Glam choir several of whom were also experienced instrumentalists :

Soprano	Mary Allen, Pamela Field, Della Jones, Ann Morgan, Mary Morgan, Patricia Sheppard(Violin), Angela Williams.
Contralto	Mair Hopkins, Rhian Jones, Lesley Roberts, Avril Thomas Delyth Thomas.
Tenor	Howard Handford, Anthony Hughes, Quentin Jones, Stuart Kale(Double Bass), Graham Marshman.
Bass	Alan Hughes, Dewi Jones(Viola), David Richards(Flute), Alan Thomas(Cello), Richard Vaughan Emyr Walters(Violin), Elwyn Williams(Piano), Paul Williams

Plate 23.

Staff members, Ann Hughes, Eleri Owen and Stanley Jones, the choir and of course Shep himself awoke very early on the morning of September 11th, 1967 for a most successful two week tour of West Slovakia. On arrival at Bratislava the party was warmly welcomed and a highly successful tour ensued. Shep had carefully constructed his programme to reflect a range of Welsh music. As he stated :

"Two short courses were held; sufficient works were rehearsed to provide a number of alternative solo items in the programme. "Canu Penillion" in two, three, and four vocal parts was a feature of the programme. These penillion were specially set for the occasion by our harpist, Eleri Owen. A number of modern Welsh composers were represented by original works or arrangements of works; one such arrangement was the work of a member of the group, Graham Marshman. Concerts were held at the Mirror Hall in the city of Bratislava and at Partizanske,Trenianska, Teplice and Star Tura. Large audiences attended these concerts and gave warm receptions to the singers. After continuous applause at the end of the concerts at Bratislava and Stara Tura, the group sang an arrangement of "Sospan Fach" which was well received. This and other popular Welsh songs were sung on numerous informal occasions and at various receptions, so that Welsh hymns were truly introduced in many parts of West Slovakia during the tour of the music group".

Two short quotations from the daily newspaper Vecernik are worthy of mention:

"The singers displayed their fine voices and were able to give excellent interpretations of the lyrical and ballad songs of their own country. The high quality of their vocal art was also evident in the sacred works".

"The soloists showed us a level of performance which is higher than amateur; we can compare their work with that of a high professional standard".

In the tour diary, one of the party relates what she describes as a Shep "epic" .

"Mr Sheppard was explaining to Mrs Cervenanska about some music which was not of a particularly high standard of composition, viz "Hywel and Blodwen" by Joseph Parry. Mrs. Cernenanska, I might add, could not speak English. Mr. Sheppard's words were - "This music is - dim dobre": ("Dobre" is the Slovak word for "good". "Dim" need not be explained!). As one would imagine, this comment resulted in hoots of laughter from everyone".

Tour Programme

Part 1

Choir	Rhyfelgyrch Gwyr Harlech Nôs Galan Ar Hyd y Nos Hw Mlân
Various Solos	Paul Williams, Stuart Kale David Richards, Howard Hanford
Choir	Dafydd y Garreg Wen Suo Gân Ave Maria (Holst)
Cello	The Swan (Saint Saens) ... Alan Thomas
Various Solos	Ann Hughes, Della Jones.
Piano	Rhapsody No.2 (Brahms) Elwyn Williams
Duet/Solo	Cân yr Utgorn (Purcell) Pamela Field& Lesley Roberts,Rhian Jones
Violin	The Holy Boy (Ireland) Patricia Sheppard/Emyr Walters
Flute	Syrinx (Debussy) David Richards
Choir	Cyfri'r Geifr Un o fy Mrodyr i Hefo Deio i Dywyn

PART 2

Canu Penillion	
Trio	Meditation(Russell Sheppard) Patricia Sheppard(Violin), Alan Thomas(Cello) Elwyn Williams(Piano)
Choir	Deep River Were You There/ Gweddi (Arwel Hughes) Hen Wlad Fy Nhadau

1968, the choir's tenth anniversary year opened with a joint GYO and choir concert at the Gwyn Hall, Neath. The march, "Crown Imperial", a treasured favourite of the conductor proclaimed the passing of a decade in style and the Glam choir reflected back to the GYO's programme of 1949 in singing Thiman's "Gloria in Excelsis". Musical celebrations continued at Eglwys Gynulleidfaol, Panteg appropriately concluding on September 7th 1968 at St. Margaret's Church, Mountain Ash. It may not have occured to many present on this memorable occasion that although Shep chose as the congregational hymn "Blaenwern" by W.P.Rowlands he actually substituted the words of "Calon Lân", because of the connections of the poet Daniel James (Gwyrosydd) with Mountain Ash. As was explained in Chapter 2, James wrote these immortal words whilst living and working a few streets away from Shep's birthplace and Mountain Ash parish church.

Fittingly, the maestro also included another fine work by Vaughan Williams when the "Serenade to Music" was sung by a small choral group. Brahms' "German Requiem" gave an early platform for Mary Davies, who by the present time must be one of the longest serving members of the Welsh National Opera Company, and also to Gaynor Harries, Soprano. The list of players includes Meryl Drower and Margaret Field who would subsequently sing with the WNO. Interestingly, one of the Tenors, Wyn Davies, son of the MP for Gower, who also played the violin in the GYO, was later to conduct WNO productions. As if in a reflection back to the predominance of the Baroque in early Glam programmes, Shep opened the concert with Handel's Overture in D Minor but could not resist the temptation to use a modern arrangement by Elgar. The programme was completed by a performance of the "Romance" from Wieniawsky's Concerto No 2 in D Minor played by leader and future professional player, Edward Roberts.

The "German Requiem" continued as the chief work at the start of 1969 when the choir returned to Neath and, obviously, according to the "Western Mail" article quoted below, both the orchestra, soloists and choir gave a very good account of themselves.

Sopranos score in Requiem

Western Mail Reporter

The richly-voiced young sopranos of Glamorgan made a lasting impression in a centenary performance of Brahms' *German Requiem* at Bridgend Technical College last night.

After only a week's rehearsal at a music course, it was surprising to see that their conductor, Russell Sheppard, had instilled into them such a thorough interpretation of the work.

The *Requiem* is a long and exacting one for such a young group, yet under Mr. Sheppard's direction the 200 members of choir and orchestra made light of the demands upon them.

It was the purity and strength of the soprano voices in particular that gave this concert, one of three given each year, that extra touch of quality.

Baritone John Davies gave a confident display, and his partner, Gaynor Harries, a student, showed considerable potential as a soprano.

Sections of the orchestra again impressed with their concentration and discipline, not least the wind section in *Khachaturian's Lullaby*, and the first violins in some excellent accompaniment of the chorus *How Lovely Are Thy Dwellings* in the *Requiem*.

The choir continued to celebrate the investiture of Charles as Prince of Wales in a September concert held at Sandfields Comprehensive School, Port Talbot. Recapitulating the Choruses from the "German Requiem", with Gaynor Harries, Mary Davies and John Davies as soloists, Shep added a touch of light-hearted spice in three choral items from Gilbert and Sullivan's "HMS Pinafore", "Mikado" and "Gondoliers" . "Toward the Unknown Region" was reintroduced for the grand finale. Shep paid a touching tribute to his former Professor of Music at University College, Cardiff. He set about orchestrating David Evans' "Deffro Mae'n Ddydd " in tribute to the professor. The work was worthy of an occasion which included a fulsome flavour of Welsh music in "A Chain of Welsh Folk Songs" for Female Choir arranged by David de Lloyd and "Two Welsh Nursery Tunes" by the then Professor of Music, Alun Hoddinott.

The distinguished Welsh author, Gwyn Thomas has written of the National Eisteddfod in whimsical fashion :

"It makes its way annually North and South, inflated for the great week and then deflated for its eleven months rest, like a massive lung, which is just what it is"

Shep made several contributions to both the proclamation concerts and to the main Eisteddfod itself organising and conducting massive choirs of school children. There must surely have been years when, with all his other musical and other activities, he must have felt, like Gwyn Thomas, that he had been bombarded by a shell burst of "eisteddfodic activity". This was particularly true of the School Children's' Concert held in Caerphilly in 1950. On the 5th of June Shep sent all schools in the Caephilly and Gelligaer Divisional Executive the most detailed notes on the massed choir rehearsal previously held. He commented that "it is noticeable that a number of units are not yet perfect", stating emphatically that "it is anticipated that words of all items will be known by June 24th". Seeking his usual high standards he goes on to request improvements in diction, particularly the use of the consonant "R" in sections such as "Yr Iôr". "Enunciation has improved considerably", he praised, but continued, "there are, of course, still a number of "foggy patches". The same "Notes" contain detailed instructions as to the train times for schools departing for the second massed rehearsal from Rhymney, Pontlottyn, Tirphil, Brithdir, Bargoed, Pengam, Hengoed, Ystradmynach and Llanbradach. He also planned, with an impeccable eye for detail, the coach arrangements for a further nine schools. Head Teachers of schools in Abertridwr, Cwmaber, Senghenydd and Trethomas were obliged to make their own transport arrangements, whilst the pupils of Caerphilly Boys' and Girls' Grammar, Junior Technical, and Secondary Schools were instructed to walk to the pavilion.

A choir of 1,500 pupils formed the nucleus of the performers at the Barry Eisteddfod of 1968. Of Shep's interpretation of "The Creation" , performed to an audience of over ten thousand people, A.J.Sicluna of the "South Wales Echo " complimented:

"Conducting with the clearest of techniques and a fine sympathetic feeling for the music, Russell Sheppard achieved remarkable results "

Stephen Price of the "Western Mail" was equally enthusiastic in his praise :

Singers thrill by memory

By STEPHEN PRICE

The majority of concerts at the Barry eisteddfod seem to have been built around works with strong biblical connections. Last night proved no exception.

Parts one and two of Haydn's mighty canvas, *The Creation*, formed the first half of the concert given by the Eisteddfod Children's Choir with soloist Marian Evans, Keith Erwen and Raimund Herincx.

The choir was a delight to hear, achieving a feat which experienced choral societies rarely attempt — singing throughout from memory.

Dynamic range was obviously restricted in such young voices; the words, "Let there be light," for example, would have made a greater impact if the opening had been pianissimo.

Apart from this, no criticism is possible.

Inspired soloists

The three soloists were also inspired to great heights and, on the whole, well-supported by the orchestra.

The other work in the programme was *Noah's Flood* by Benjamin Britten.

The libretto is taken from one of the many miracle and mystery plays performed widely throughout Europe during the Middle Ages.

The opera was completed in 1957 and since then has been played many times throughout Europe—one of its salient features being the simple style of presentation similar to the original plays.

Perhaps the most exciting in this performance was the exuberant and professional participation by the children taking the parts of Noah's sons and wives, Mrs. Noah's Gossips and the animals.

There is also a children's orchestra of strings, recorders, bugles, percussion and handbells in the score, again played with aplomb and vigour.

Some most beautiful effects were obtained not only fror the original and bold instru mental textures which we now come to expect of Britten, but also by the action itself aided by expert lighting.

Great ovation

Noteworthy was the representation of the undulating sea and also the dancing of the birds sent out from the ark, to a delicate accompaniment.

Congratulations to all the young people taking part for a stirring and enjoyable evening. The crowded pavilion showed its appreciation with the greatest ovation so far.

Tonight's concert will be given by more young players, the National Youth Orchestra of Wales.

The start of the new decade corresponded with the coming of age of the GYO. It was natural, then, for the orchestra's founder to tilt the balance slightly in favour of the orchestral forces at his disposal. Not withstanding this artistic decision, Shep placed the spotlight on the choir. "Deffro Mae'n Ddydd" together with Gilbert and Sullivan excerpts led to a "Toward the Unknown Region" finale at Bridgend Technical College.

With great confidence in the vocal as well as orchestral forces at his disposal, Shep launched the first of several performances of the monumental "Requiem" by Verdi at an unforgettable Sandfields School concert on July 19th, 1970. Sopranos Ann Hughes(James) and Barbara Clarkson, Mezzo Sopranos Margaret Blacker and Margaret Field, Tenors Stuart Kale and Wayne Griffiths and Bass Kelvin Thomas were the soloists, the concerts concluding with the community singing of the hymn, "Hyfrydol". It is almost incredulous to record that Shep repeated the "Requiem" in Bethany, Treherbert and again in St. Elvan's, Aberdare on consecutive following nights. The work is taxing enough for an adult or semi-professional ensemble, but the young singers, revelling in its mood changes and drama, produced an overwhelmingly moving interpretation. The Glam choir could be said to have established new parameters for the quality of all future youth choir singing and to have set a standard which it would be difficult to match in future years.

In the year following the Investiture a new entrant is recorded as one of the 25 strong tenor section of the GYC. Hailing from Porthcawl school, where in 1963, he had been an excellent boy soprano soloist and leader of the author's school orchestra, David Emanuel was about to launch his highly successful career as one of the world's most famous and respected dress designers. David speaks with fond affection of the courses he attended and of the impact of the music. He also enjoyed his violin lessons with Karen Sheppard and has related the story of how he avoided science lessons by claiming that he was involved in music practices. His love of singing has endured, and, who knows, the public may still hear more of his musical talents. As everyone now knows, David would co-design the highly original dress worn by the future Princess of Wales on her wedding day in 1981.

David's first insight into large-scale mixed choir singing was the Verdi "Requiem", which he would sing again at the Brangwyn Hall, Swansea and in Bridgend in January 1971. As if in recognition of its fine achievement, the choir also travelled to the Royal Festival Hall in March 1971 for the highly acclaimed concert reviewed in the previous section on the GYO. Press cuttings of the period reveal that Glamorgan's youth musicians would make a strong impression on the audience who afforded them the honour of a standing ovation. Plate 24.

"The second part of the programme was presented by the Glamorgan Youth Choir and Orchestra - a wonderfully flourishing group of young musicians who left the audience in no doubt that music is indeed cherished in Wales".

Music Teacher

"The GYO displayed its considerable virtuosity by successfully capturing the magical content of Humperdinck's "Hansel and Gretel" Overture and the exhilarating exuberance of Walton's "Crown Imperial" March, in which nine horns, twelve trumpets, eight trombones and a tuba made an exciting contribution.

Beginning with a suitably restrained performance of "How Lovely Are Thy Dwellings" from Brahms "German Requiem," the choir then gave a performance of the eight-part "Sanctus" from Verdi's "Requiem" which can only be described as superb. For me this was the highlight of a unique and worthwhile concert. Vaughan Williams' "Toward The Unknown Region" concluded the programme",

Welsh Music

"The Glamorgan Youth Choir and Orchestra are well known. Their performances of "How Lovely are Thy Dwellings" from Brahms' "Requiem" and the "Sanctus" from the Verdi "Requiem" would have done credit to any professional choir and orchestra. In particular the clarity of the latter was superb. The orchestra of 160 players showed its paces from the delicate magic of "Hansel and Gretel" to a positively jingoistic account of "Crown Imperial".

Times Educational Supplement

"The orchestra is one of the largest in the country with 165 players which has reached a high standard of performance well shown in works by Humperdinck, David Wynne and Walton and the "Celebration Fanfare" by Russell Sheppard. The Choir sang "How Lovely are thy Dwellings" by Brahms, the "Sanctus" from the Verdi "Requiem" and gave a moving rendering of "Toward The Unknown Region" by Vaughan Williams, the concert ending with "Land of My Fathers". The Welsh have a very high reputation for singing and this choir certainly lived up to and exceeded what might have been expected, being quite the equal of

many of the London Choral Societies. The bringing of such a large numbers of performers to London was quite a feat of most careful and exacting organisation. This is the first concert at which performers have come from Wales, and it was particularly appropriate in that the County of Glamorgan has for many years supported the Association's work.The link with Wales is one which the Association values very much".

Schools' Music Association News Bulletin : Summer 1971

In sharply defined contrast Verdi was replaced by Mozart's "Requiem" for appearances at Pontardawe and St. Margaret's, Mountain Ash with soloists Mary Davies, Margaret Field, Wayne Griffiths and Kelvin Thomas. For this, the September course, Shep also returned to Vincent Thomas' "Y Bumed Gerdd". Both works were retained for concerts at Cymmer Afan and Cynffig Comprehensive Schools in January 1972. As associate conductors, Russell Sheppard and Jeffrey Francis performed Dvorak's "Stabat Mater" in concerts in Ystalyfera,Treherbert, Port Talbot and Aberdare.

Shep's final course as the sole conductor of the Choir occured in September of the same year. In future concerts, until the division of the Glamorgan County Council into three constituent parts he shared the programme with the newly appointed Adviser Jeffrey Francis. Shep became Chief Adviser to the county of Mid Glamorgan.

In January 1973, Bryntirion School and the Town Hall Maesteg were the venues for performances of Dvorak's "Stabat Mater" featuring Mary Davies and Ann James, Soprano, Rhiannon Hopkins and Margaret Field, Alto, Wayne Griffiths and Stuart Kale, Tenor and Kelvin Thomas, Bass.

September concerts were scheduled at churches in Ystalyfera, Treherbert, Port Talbot and very appropriately on September 9th at St. Elvan's Church, Aberdare. It is important to mention that in all previous choral concerts collections had been taken in support of a number of differing charities. In this way the community and fund-raising dimension of the choir should not be under-estimated. Over the years a not inconsiderable amount of money would have been contributed to charities of all types. For the St. Elvan's event, four charities were nominated, these being the British Empire Cancer Campaign for Research, the Children's Society, Christian Aid, and the Malcolm Sargent Cancer Fund for Children. The option of the final charity is even more significant considering Sir Malcolm's long and fruitful association with the Three Valleys Festival at neighbouring Mountain Ash. Returning as soloist by arrangement with the Welsh National Opera Company that stalwart of many courses, Stuart Kale was joined by Ann Hughes, Margaret Field and Kelvin Thomas in an interpretation of Dvorak's "Stabat Mater". This was also a course attended by long-serving singer, Andrew Badham, currently Conductor of the Treorchy Male Choir and by John Evans, author of the definitive book on Benjamin Britten who, at present, heads Radio 3.

Russell Sheppard and Jeffrey Francis shared the podium for the last joint orchestral and choral concert to mark the demise of the Glamorgan Authority. On

Friday 4th January 1974, The Glam performed Berlioz "Marche Troyen", Dvorak's "Slavonic Rhapsody No 3 in Ab" and the "Theme and Variations from the Suite No 3 in G" by Tchaikovsky at the Gwyn Hall, Neath. Ann James, Karen Shelby, Stuart Kale and Kelvin Thomas were the soloists in Verdi's "Requiem". Performing the "Requiem", the choir reached its sixteenth anniversary in the year that the school leaving age was raised to the same age, and as Shep wrote in the programme:

"Established in 1949, the Glamorgan Youth Orchestra attains during 1974 the mature age of twenty-five years. Its flourishing condition has been achieved through the development of instrumental music as part of the curriculum of secondary schools. Several past members have risen to positions of responsibility in a variety of professions. Many have become professional players in the leading orchestras of the country. Five are music advisers.

The enthusiastic choristers take pleasure in studying and performing works which they cannot easily perform elsewhere. Among the highlights in the life of the choir and orchestra were the concert tours of West Slovakia during 1966 and 1967 and their performances at the Royal Festival Hall in 1971. Broadcasts and television performances have also taken place. Courses have always been staffed by teachers of music in Glamorgan Schools.

Orchestra and choir have, throughout their existence been maintained and controlled by Glamorgan Education Committee as an integral part of music education in the county".

Names of students on the final course

GLAMORGAN YOUTH CHOIR

SOPRANO
Karen Badham, Sarah Bassett, Judith Bell, Janet Bowen, Rosemary Berg, Susan Courtney, Joan Davidson, Janet E. Davies, Janet S. Davies, Ceris Deverill, Heulwen Ebsworth, Susan Forrester, Amanda Gill, Jane Grey, Joanne Hanson, Susan Higgins, Bethan Howells, Ann Humphreys, Rhian James, Carolyn Jones, Denise Jones, Pauline Jones, Corinne Kent, Barbara Lane, Marian Lewis, Vicky Lewis, Andrea Little, Gaynor Lloyd, Sian Mathews, Joy Mitchell, Karyl Mumford, Gillian Napper, Marilyn Rees, Sian Stenner, Lorna Stephenson, Elizabeth Stone, Jill Taylor, Catherine Thomas, Ceri Thomas, Lynda Thomas, Elaine Tossell, Alison Waller, Alyson Williams, Caroline Williams, Shelly Thomas.

ALTO
Rhiannon Barrar, Lynda Coles, Maureen Davies, Pamela Davies, Pat Davies, Sally J. Davies, Bernadette Drazek, Sian Dyer, Julia Evans, Carole Fry, Amanda Gill, Janine Griffiths, Ann E. John, Derith John, Eleri Jones, Jennifer John, Helen Kerton, Felicity Ladbrooke, Donna Lewis, Patricia Miller, Ruth Mitchell, Ruth Nicholas, Bethan Parry, Ann Phillips, Elaine Pike, Margaret Price, Karen Shelby, Pamela Stephens, Jane Thomas, Linda Thomas, Lynne Thomas, Valerie Thomas, Wendy Tong, Deborah Wilcox, Ann Wilkes, Janet Williams, Jayne Wilde.

TENOR
Anthony Crossland, Stephen Crum, Roderick Edmunds, David Dyer, Graham Evans, John Evans, Robert Evans, Hywel Griffiths, Philip Holtam, David M. Howells, Arwyn Jones, Gabriel Jug, Gareth Key, Gareth Lewis, Robert Lewis, Anthony Mathews, Adrian Petheram, Glyn Price, David C. Miller.

BASS
Andrew Badham, Richard Boothby, Huw Owen, Philip Connolly, Arfon I. Davies, Ceri Davies, Ian Davies, Michael Davies, Timothy Dorney-Kingdom, Colin Duffield, Graham Dyer, Anthony Edmunds, John Edwards, Lyndon Edwards, David Emanuel, Gareth Evans, Hywel Evans, Paul Greenway, G. Wynn Griffiths, Wynne Griffiths, Alun Hughes, Stephen M. Jenkins, Gareth Jenkinson, Adrian Jones, Gareth Lewis, Geoffrey Moses, David M. Phillips, Geraint Philp, Ceri Preece, David Rapsey, Huw L. Rogers, Jonathan Wilding, Glyn Williams, Richard J. Williams, John Wilkes.

CHORAL STAFF
Stanley Jones, Gethin Evans, L. Bowen, Brian Parry, Paul Williams, Miss Delor Jones, Mrs. Ann James, Clive Stubbs, Stuart Kale, Kelvin Thomas, Mrs. Angela Mills, Miss Elinor Phillips, Christopher Lewis.

GLAMORGAN YOUTH ORCHESTRA

FIRST VIOLIN
Philip Morgan, Adrian Eales, Peter Jones, Karl Davies, Gareth Jones, Timothy Crossland, Hywel Benjamin, Mark Thomas, Sian Kerslake, Gerald Hopkins, Judith Owen, Denise Phillips, Helen Price, Karen Evans, Richard Lewis, David Emanuel, Gareth Jenkinson, Hugh Tyson, Deborah Jaeger, Hilary Lewis, Richard Wilde, Suzanne Foster.

SECOND VIOLIN
Lynys Morgan, Rhydian Potter, Susan Croot, Hywel Davies, Delyth Evans, Paul Greenway, Ann Gilchrist, Sandra Anstey, Nigel Murray, Elizabeth Standfield, Susan Bell, Jeremy Stubbs, Meryl Jones, Pamela Williams, Colin Murrell, John M. Davies, John Matson, Neil Llewellyn, Catherine Wilde, Robert Douglas, Christopher Simons, Rachel Meredith, Bryan Jones, Lois Davies, Stephen Lloyd, Janet Kallend, Karl Darby, Susan Rees, Alison Williams, Gaynor Hart, Mandy Griffiths.

VIOLA
Edwina Thomas, Geraint Philp, Joan Davidson, Catherine Wilson, Sarah Wilson, Eirlys Gravelle, Corrinne Kent, Julie Watkins, Christopher Ashmead, Rowena Jones, Ruth Nicholas, Robert Evans, Richard Golding, Michelle Butt.

CELLO
Ceri Phillips, Susan Mortimer, Frances Rees, Elaine Watkins, Arwyn Jones, Carol Griffiths, Elizabeth Warlow, Paul Evans, Sian Matthews, Richard Boothby, Christopher Hodges, Philippa Wilson, Andrew Cresci, Sarah Barton, Evelyn Cornelius, Jonathan Lewis, Sarah Thomas.

DOUBLE BASS
Albert Dennis, William Scriven, Jeffrey Ryan, Joy Rowlands, Hilary Williams, Anne Davies, Pauline John, Michael Welsby, Pamela Davies, Robert Ferris.

FLUTE
Ann John, Philip Emanuel, Gruffydd Harries, Ian Davies, Bernadette Drazek, Dyfrig Lloyd Williams, Stephen Ford, Meredydd Harries, Anthony Slade, Barbara Keitch.

OBOE
John Esais, Mark Howells, Graham Dyer, Wayne David, Mary Reynolds, Robert Lewis, Daniel Jones, Simon Gratton.

CLARINET
Janet Griffiths, Ruth James, Elizabeth Murdoch, Stephen Murphy, Jeffrey Williams, Penny Barton, David Pritchard, John Walters, Wynne Griffiths, Mark Ormrod, Deiniol Jones, John Phillip Morgan.

BASSOON
Martin Bowen, Noelyn Bowen, Richard Lane, Ian Belcher, Philip Edwards.

FRENCH HORN
Huw Jenkins, Peter Sheppard, Roger Lewis, Alan Lockyer, Philip Richards, David Rapsy, Paul Lewis, Stephen Price.

TRUMPET
Geraint Davies, Huw James, Andrew Cuff, Dorian Rees, Howard Meade, Ceri Thomas, Alun James.

TENOR TROMBONE
David Saunders, Philip Cowley, Graham Harries, Hywel Williams, Gregory Morgan, Kevin Griffiths, Kim Griffiths.

BASS TROMBONE
Nicholas Paddison, Gareth Key, Peter Hendy.

TUBA
David Langford.

TIMPANI
Philip Thomas, John Evans, Felicity Ladbrooke, Janet Davies, Ian Richards, Michael Evans.

HARP
Amanda Jones, Siwan Jones.

ORCHESTRAL STAFF
Mrs. Pat Hopkins, Bryn Harding, Mrs. C. E. Sheppard, Gordon Mepham, Peter Watts, Alan James, Alan Good, Hugh Phillips, David Hughes, John Jenkins, D. A. Small, Graham Watkins, Mrs. D. Davies, Mrs. Ruth Garnett.

Printed by D. Brown & Sons, Ltd., Cowbridge & Bridgend J9214

As Chief Adviser, Russell Sheppard continued his liaison with the Youth Choir until his retirement in 1979 after exactly thirty years of devoted and committed dedication to music in Glamorgan and Mid Glamorgan. To mark the occasion Shep made his conducting swan-song at three concerts given by Mid Glamorgan. Two more appropriate birds might be cited in substitute for the swan of this allusion. Shep had magnificently swooped down on the musical life of Glamorgan with the all-embracing wing-span of an eagle. With the passing of time and the appreciation and gratitude of generations of singers and players he was to achieve the stature of that fabled bird, the roc of Eastern legend. The cover of the programme of the concerts indicates not only that he was, for the final time, to be solely the Titan at the helm of a cast of singers and players of epic proportions, but that he would take his penultimate curtain call back home where it all began in Mountain Ash.

In the annuls of Welsh choral history there are few who could claim to have achieved so much. Even fewer, despite the honours bestowed upon some of them, could match Russell Sheppard's proud and unparalleled record in raising youth choral standards to well-nigh professional standards whilst providing a platform for a host of soloists of international calibre. As he indicated in the final weeks of his life the ultimate reward was that he "created and managed to tame a choir and orchestra of mammoth proportions". There could have been no more appropriate stage for his adieu than Llandaff Cathedral and no more apposite masterpiece than Verdi's Requiem with which to take his final bow. Throughout its history, the Glamorgan Youth Choir maintained remarkable standards of four-part singing. Like Harri Webbe's "The Singer", Shep evidently realised, that:

A young voice rings
New-minted gold.

Hall of Fame

Beverley Humphreys

Beverley Humphreys

Beverley Humphreys' career has not been confined to the operatic stage, although that is where it all began - as Rosina in "The Barber of Seville" for the WNO. Other roles include Carmen, Santuzza and Amneris. In this country she has graced the Royal Festival Hall, the Wigmore Hall, the Queen Elizabeth Hall and the Royal Albert Hall and she has sung before the Queen and Prince Philip. She has appeared in many venues in Canada and the USA.

In this age of specialism Beverley has dared to be versatile and she is no stranger to Radio 2, 3 and 4 or to television as singer and presenter. She is just as much at home with Stephen Sondheim as Kurt Weill and slips comfortably into the classic standards of the 30's and 40's with the Jazz trio Kaleidoscope.

Beverley has played Gertrude Lawrence in Noel and Gertie and created the role of Vesta Tilley in Carol Gawn's play "You Can All Love Me". Her first straight acting role was in the TV film "Better Days" with Glyn Houston. Beverley became the first woman in the history of Welsh rugby to lead the singing at the National Stadium.

Beverley has written and tours with her one woman shows "Marvellous Party" and "A Tribute to Ivor Novello", and presents her weekly music programme for BBC Radio Wales - "With Melody in Mind". Beverley's "Legendary Ladies" met with great critical acclaim and her latest TV venture was in the culinary arts with Anthony Worrell Thompson in "Sing for your Supper". She is programme associate for the BBC's "Millennium Songs of Praise" and for the Cardiff International Festival of Music Theatre 2002.

Della Jones : Mezzo - Soprano

Della Jones

Della Jones, one of Britain's leading mezzo-sopranos, was born in Neath and studied at the Royal College of Music where she won many prizes including the Kathleen Ferrier Memorial Scholarship. Her wide repertoire ranges from early to contemporary music.

Della has appeared with all the major British opera companies and foreign engagements have included the U.S.A., Russia, Japan, Canada, and Europe. Her vast repertoire includes leading roles in " Ariodante", "Il Barbiere di Siviglia", "La Cenerentola", "Orfeo", "Carmen", "Norma", "Les Troyens", "Don Giovanni", "Salome", "Tristan und Isolde", "Oedipus Rex", "The Rake's Progress", "A Midsummer Night's Dream", "Dido and Aeneas", "Le nozze di Figaro", "Semele", "Boris Godunov" and "The Bartered Bride".

Della Jones is a regular broadcaster at home and abroad. In 1993 she made an acclaimed appearance at the Last Night of the Proms. She is also remembered for her role in "Voices of a Nation" concert for the opening of the Welsh Assembly.

She has recorded prolifically for all the major record companies, including "L'Incontro Improviso", and "Il Ritorno di Tobias" with Dorati, "Alcina", "L' Incoronazione di Poppea", "A Midsummer Night's Dream", "Messiah" and "Stabat Mater" with Hickox, "Tese" with Minkovski, "La Clemeza di Tito" with Hogwood, "Il Barbiere di Siviglia", "Sea Pictures" with Mackerras, "Candide" with Bernstein and works by Peter Maxwell Davies and Hindemith.

Della sang in many choral works with the Glamorgan Youth Choir and also performed a movement of Brahms' Piano Concerto No. 1 in D Minor with the Glam orchestra. Amazingly her wonderful musicianship was also in evidence in her playing of the clarinet and percussion with the orchestra. She writes:

"An extraordinary person Shep had a great vision for Youth in Music and made playing and singing a way of life. When I first went to the Royal College of Music it was the norm to perform with an orchestra and I suddenly realised that for most student singers from other parts of the country this simply had not been possible.

I will always be grateful to Shep for providing this incredible opportunity".

Dennis O ' Neill : Tenor

Dennis O' Neill

Born in Wales of Irish and Welsh parents, Dennis O' Neill is one of the world's leading tenors and a specialist in the works of Verdi. He has enjoyed a long association with the Royal Opera House, Covent Garden where he has sung many roles including "La Boheme", "Madame Butterfly", "Lucia di Lammermoor", "Un Ballo in Maschera", "Attila", "Otello", "Don Carlos" and "Aida".

For the Metropolitan Opera he has appeared in "La Traviata", "La Boheme" and in a new production of "Rigoletto". He has appeared in opera in Chicago, San Francisco, San Diego, Vancouver and Brazil. A frequent visitor to the Bayerische Staatsoper, Munich he has also sung in the opera houses of Vienna, Bonn, Cologne, Nice, Zurich, Paris, Oslo, Brussels, Barcelona, the Arena di Verona and Turin.

His most recent performance in "Cav" and "Pag" with the Welsh National Opera celebrated the company's fiftieth anniversary.

He is a busy concert artist all over the world and his performances of Verdi's "Requiem" have been televised on no less than seven occasions. He has sung with conductors like Muti, Sir Colin Davies, Sinopoli, Sir Simon Rattle, Mehta, Slatkin and Svetlanov.

His own TV series was enormously popular and the accompanying recording went to the top of the classical charts. His many discs include "Der Rosenkavalier" with Solti, "Die Fledermaus" with Dame Kiri Te Kanawa conducted by Domingo, "Macbeth" with Sinopoli and "Mefistofele" from San Francisco. He has recorded Verdi's "Requiem" a solo disc for Chandos and an anthology of Italian songs for Collins Classics.

Dennis O' Neill made his debut as a soloist with the Glamorgan Youth Choir in 1965 and showed his fine musicianship by also playing in the cello section of the Glamorgan Youth Orchestra.

Stuart Kale : Tenor

Stuart Kale

Stuart Kale was educated at Neath Boys' Grammar School where he was a keen sportsman who held the school high jump record. Stuart graduated with first class honours at the Guildhall School of Music and Drama. He also studied with Vilem Tausky and Peter Wishart on the Advanced Vocal Studies and Opera Course.

Early in his career he was a member of the Ambrosian Singers and Opera Chorus and made recordings for Decca and EMI. He also sang leading roles with the London Opera Centre and Sadlers Wells and became a contract principal singer with Welsh National Opera. In addition to singing with choral societies nation-wide, he sang with English National Opera.

Between 1975 and 1987, he became Professor of Singing at the Guildhall School of Music and was a contract Principal singer with English National Opera performing leading tenor roles at London Coliseum and on the ENO American Tour in 1984. At this time he was also a member of the choir of Bromton Oratory.

Stuart has maintained a hectic schedule as an opera principal and specialises in the performance of twentieth century music, especially by Britten and Berg. Plate 29 shows him in the role of Hemptmann in a San Francisco production of "Wozzeck".

In recent years, he has sung principal roles for the ENO, and appeared in opera and on the concert platform in Adelaide, Strasbourg, Nancy, Turin, Parma, Trieste, Bologna, Karlsruhe, Cologne, Stockholme, Toronto, Bordeaux, Tolouse, Venice, Padua, Weisbaden, Dresden, Drottingholm, Montpellier, Rennes, Paris, and Buenos Aires. He has sung in the Accademia di Santa Cecilia, Rome and for Opera North.

Future plans include "Caglia", a return to the Lucerne Festival, Basle and his La Scala debut.

Stuart who sang many solo parts - as a student and member of staff - with the Glamorgan Youth Choir was also a bass player in the Glam and NYOW.

THOSE WERE THE DAYS

Beverley Humphreys

"Each day of our lives we make memories - precious and poignant memories which become corner stones on which we build our existence. Some of the most treasured possessions in my memory store-house were gleaned at the Ogmore Choral courses - laughter after lights-out; daddy long-legs in the toilets; coping with home-sickness, new friendships and old rivalries; the sound of the sea, unsettling in its romanticism; a burgeoning awareness of the opposite sex; and above all, the sensuous rapture of music making. This heady mixture was compressed into those sporadic, idyllic weeks that punctuated my teenage years. They proved to be the stepping stones that guided me, serendipitously, out of my childhood, towards that unknown region known as adulthood.

There is one constant in those mental snap-shots - Russell Sheppard - unique and idiosyncratic, a man with a vision and a dedication that enabled us to discover life and music in the protected microcosm that was Ogmore - taken for granted then, but in retrospect, its essence distilled an unparalleled experience. I do hope he knew that so many of us carry him lovingly in our hearts. Music is life, and like life, inextinguishable".

Stuart Kale : Tenor

"To those of us who were fortunate enough to know him, Shep was a colossus in the development of youth music in Glamorgan.

Without him many of our lives would have been the poorer. It was through his vision and drive that so many encountered many of the great classics. Although I worked with him for almost twenty years as a student, soloist and member of staff, I was always in awe of him. There was something about the man that engendered great respect and eventually warmth and affection. His enthusiasm and determination produced thrilling and stimulating performances from young people despite the odd blemish.

He gave us some amusing moments too. Picture a choral course rehearsal in which he asked a soprano soloist from Tonna, "How far do you go, Mary Davies?" "All the way. Mr.Sheppard," came the reply. Much laughter all round; and Shep peered over the top of his reading glasses with a benign, yet quizzical expression which seemed to say "I'm not such boring old chap after all, am I!"

He gave so much and those of us who were there will always have warm and affectionate memories of him."

Ann James

"Going on my first choral course literally changed my life. On the first morning, after precious little sleep, we met for assembly and I was amazed at the singing of the hymn in four-part harmony. From that moment, I was smitten and realised that this was what I had to do for the rest of my life.

The discipline of good choral singing was instilled into us by Mr. Sheppard - listening to each other's parts, clear diction especially the click of the consonants. Although my father and my grandfather had been sticklers for perfect diction, this was different - it was "official" since it came from Mr. Sheppard.

My first recollection of a major work was Mozart's "Coronation Mass", sung in English by a variety of soloists from each section of the choir. The most thrilling experiences of that time were performances of the Magnificat by Bach. I use the word thrilling because of the intense impact of the Bach trumpets which I had never heard before. This was probably the most influential piece I ever sung with the Glam as it began a life-long love affair with the choral music of Bach.

Many amusing incidents are embedded on my memory. On one occasion, as a young member of the choir, I remember singing to Mary, the Princess Royal at Dyffryn House. When the performance was over and the royal party and county councillors were leaving, one councillor warned the others "Mind the 'arps boys!", just as they were passing the double bass section. Many married couples met while on courses at Ogmore and, indeed, one young newly married couple decided to spend their honeymoon in a tent in a nearby field in order not to miss a choral course.

In 1965 Mr. Sheppard persuaded me to sing in my first opera - the role of Belinda in "Dido and Aeneas" - to be staged in the National Eisteddfod the following year, in my home town of Port Talbot. Accepting the invitation gave me the confidence for many other solo performances. There are fond memories of 1966 - snow drifts at Easter, torrential rain during the Eisteddfod week when the maes (field) was tuned into a quagmire and cars were stuck for hours after the performances.

During my time as a choral tutor with the GYC, I was privileged to visit Bratislava with a small vocal and instrumental group. Performances were given to packed audiences in stunning concert halls with elegant chandeliers and furnishings. Mr. Sheppard's arrangement of "Sospan Fach ", which he prefaced with the opening bars of Dvorak's Symphony No.8 was received with rapturous applause, the audience demanding several encores.

Further memorable occasions are the performances of Verdi's "Requiem". Having previously rehearsed the solos with the other principals, I joined the course totally jet-lagged from a singing tour of Canada and America. Needless to say, the choir was note-perfect and the concerts were superb.

My admiration for Mr. Sheppard grew and grew over the years. Just before Christmas 1998, my husband and I visited Mr. and Mrs. Sheppard. We both thanked him for everything he had done for us but in his quiet, unassuming voice, he replied, "but I was only doing my job". To sum up, I can only parody the words of Winston Churchill:

> *"Never in the field of musical activity has so much been owed by so many to one man".*

Ann James was a singer in the Glamorgan Youth Choir for many years, before becoming a music teacher at Sandfields and Cynffig Comprehensive Schools. Of her many solo appearances with the GYC, Shep recalled with especial affection her outstanding contribution in several performances of Verdi's Requiem.

Alan James

"Like so many other people I was very fortunate to be an orchestral player in the Glam. Tutored on the double bass by the late F.J.Herbert at Neath Boys' Grammar School, I had attended Friday rehearsals under John Richards, Levi Hopkins and others before attending my first Glam course. During one rehearsal at the School for the Blind in Bridgend, my double bass slipped because of the polished floor. Mr. Sheppard stopped rehearsing, turned to me from the rostrum and said "Furniture removing, boy?".

I also remember his first-class sense of pitch. In another rehearsal, a clock chimed during a pause in the music, he turned to a player and said "play Eb please" - he was right. On another occasion I was tuning the bass when Mr. Sheppard arrived, stopped, and said to me, "Bb, Alan." I then realised that he was referring to the drone of an aeroplane which was crossing the Bristol Channel. Following the opening timpani roll in Grieg's Piano Concerto it had been arranged that the orchestra would play an orchestrated version of "Jingle Bells". Although unamused Mr. Sheppard continued conducting. Later, when I was a tutor to the Glam, I remember a series of experiments undertaken by maestro Sheppard.

In the "1812 Overture" Mr. Sheppard insisted on several experiments to achieve the cannon effect. Originally, we had tried shooting George Hannaby's 12 Bore shotgun into a metal drum. George, John Jenkins and I were charged with this experiment at the top of the field above Ogmore Camp - much to the annoyance of the local sheep. Eventually, refusing to pay to hire the cannon charges, Mr. Sheppard settled for members of staff banging energetically on an old metal locker from the dormitories.

Like many others, I am most grateful to Mr. Sheppard for all his musical endeavours. Even now, when I listen to symphonies, concertos, masses and other vocal music, I can say that I performed that with Mr. Sheppard. Had it not been for him, my musical life would have been much the poorer".

Alan James, who had a distinguished career as Head of Music at Cynffig Comprehensive School, played the double bass in the Glam for several years.

He also performed a Handel Organ Concerto with the orchestra and served for many years as a tutor whom Shep greatly respected. Uniquely, he was the double bass teacher of all four future professionals from the town of Neath - Albert Dennis, Mark Jenkins, Rachel Gronow and Julian Walters.

Stanley Jones

" Nearly fifty years ago I was one of forty teachers who attended a music course at Dyffryn House organised by a young man by the name of Russell Sheppard, who had recently been appointed Music Inspector. The first evening session was given by a visiting Monmouthshire teacher whose subject was the teaching of music by way of the recorder. As further tuition by this mentor was not possible, and as I seemed to be the only one in the group with some knowledge of the instrument, I was conscripted to give further lessons. Thus began my long association with Russell Sheppard which involved me not only in the the introduction of the recorder into primary schools, but also with the Glamorgan Youth Orchestra, Brass Band, and Choir and a host of other musical events and organising activities.

Russell Sheppard was a workaholic and a perfectionist and expected all who worked with him to be similarly minded. As an example of his capacity for concentrated work, the Choral work "Deffro Mae'n Ddydd" by David Evans was orchestrated by him as he travelled to London by train and amended on the return journey.

His memory for the names of past and present students was uncanny. One glance around a crowded hall of staff and students and he could detect the non-presence of a culprit.

He was a gifted musician in many ways, and students at the early orchestral courses were privileged to have his brilliant piano playing for their traditional after-supper dance, However, his great love was the organ. Many a time I had the pleasure of an impromptu organ recital whilst on a pre-concert visit to some chapel or church. His gift of perfect pitch did not always prove an asset. Because of a high- pitched chapel organ he endured a miserable, discordant concert as the sound he heard did not agree with the pitch that should have come from the notes on his score.

But his greatest gift was given to thousands upon thousands of children, who, over the years, have benefited from his foresight and dedication in ensuring that every schoolchild was given the opportunity of playing a musical instrument.

This is his legacy to the children of today and, hopefully, tomorrow. If we should seek a memorial to Shep, we only have to look around us and listen to the varied and exciting music heard in our schools. By this we surely will remember him.

Stanley Jones lives in Cwmafan, near Port Talbot. He trained as a teacher and whilst at the Gnoll School, Neath he taught a number of future Glam players including Tony Lewis before they entered Neath Grammar School. Following periods as a deputy and then headteacher, he was appointed as Primary Schools Advisory Teacher to the West Glamorgan LEA. His work as an authority on the teaching of the recorder in schools, led to "Dysgu'r Recorder" which is still widely used. He has conducted choirs and Gymanfa Ganu and has also been an adjudicator on many occasions.

2.

Counter Subject 3 : The Glamorgan Youth Brass Band

§

Bells are polished; valves are free.
Bands like Grimethorpe, Dyke and Cory
Are household names - you'll all agree;
And for a touch of tone and class,
None can be as bold as brass.

Boystrous Brass : John Jenkins

In 1949, South Wales in general and Glamorgan in particular were hot beds of brass band playing. In the Rhondda valley, flourishing brass bands like Cory, Treherbert and Park and Dare, often with links with the mining industry, were potent forces in the national brass band competitive world. To the west, pockets of brass band excellence existed in Pontarddulais, Glynneath, Ystalyfera, Briton Ferry and the Afan valley. In order to ensure their survival, most successful bands had developed their own schemes for training brass players. Beginners were often provided with tuition at the band room and some instruments were available through the bands themselves.

In much the same way as the County Youth Centres provided opportunities for choral and orchestral players, so too a number of these centres were important breeding grounds for brass band playing. As shown in Shep's survey, by 1958 Brass Band Centres existed in the following divisions of the County:

Division	School	Evenings per week	Instructor
West	Cwmllynfell Primary	2	Mr. E.G. Lewis
	Godrergraig Primary	1	Mr.Lewis Williams
	Pontarddulais Secondary	1	Mr.William Skelton
South - East	Gladstone Junior, Barry	1	Mr. I Williams

The mid 1950s was also a period when a few schools, particularly in the Rhondda valley, began engaging talented brass band players and conductors to provide in-house brass instruction on a part-time basis. As will be seen later, the work of staff like Ieuan Morgan in the Rhondda and, at a later stage, Tony Small in the Gowerton/Penclawdd area would produce a rich crop of brass playing talent which would be recognised at a national and international level. The majority of the more enlightened bands were quick to recognise the potential benefits of a close and interactive relationship with the instrumental schemes which Russell Sheppard was pioneering. Whilst a residual introversion and a sense of competitive protectionism continued to be the myopic stance adopted by a small number of bands, Shep worked patiently but with his usual resolve to break down some entrenched attitudes. With the support of a number of influential and enlightened figures in the brass bands of the era, his aspiration to establish a county network of regional and county bands would reach fruition. It would be the remit of the new counties of Mid, South and West Glamorgan to consolidate and further enhance the profile of Glamorgan Youth Bands in the post 1974 period.

The first Glamorgan Youth Band Course (GYB) was held at Dyffryn House in November 1952. As the letter to schools indicates, Shep entrusted the development of the county band to Leonard Davies, the organising secretary of the National Youth Brass Band. Sadly, no records have been discovered of the early courses, but in 1955, two letters from Leonard Davies indicate his grateful acceptance to attend a January course. Mr. Davies had obviously given much thought to the choice of the programme for the course and indicated the preferred time for his arrival.

In a previous letter Leonard Davies had referred to the strength of the Youth Band course held in September 1954 and attended by over one hundred Monmouthshire pupils. Evidently, Shep had acted upon Mr. Davies' recommendation to add Norman Ashcroft to the tutors on the 1955 course. An early photograph illustrates that a band of between forty and fifty players had been established by the mid 1950s, meeting annually at Dyffryn House. In this way Shep had forged a vital link with the National Youth Brass Band Association and gained acceptance and credibility in the banding fraternity of South Wales. Plate 29.

In a report probably dating from 1967 on Brass Band Playing in Schools, Ieuan Morgan wrote :

"Mr. Percy Griffiths M.A., Headmaster of the Upper Rhondda Comprehensive School, Treorchy, was the first Headmaster to form a School Band in Glamorgan with myself, a past pupil, as conductor. This was in 1955 when Mr. Griffiths was the Headmaster of Treorchy Secondary School; the pupils met after school for a rehearsal twice a week, and the band developed into the Treorchy Secondary School Band, the members being past and present pupils of the school.

This band achieved 'A' Class status and became one of the most famous youth bands in the country, broadcasting regularly and appearing many times on television. The band became the first Youth band to compete in the Championship Finals at the Royal Albert Hall, London, competing against band such as Fodens, Black Dyke Mills etc".

Shep recognised Ieuan's exceptional talents as a player, teacher and conductor, and, in 1961, arranged for him to take up full-time employment as a brass teacher in Rhondda valley schools.

In order to provide a nursery for the banding talents nurtured in schools in the 1960s, Shep's next priority was to establish regional centres. These centres mirrored the successful template he had previously established for orchestral centres at Pontypridd, Neath and Bridgend. In the case of the band, two centres were created. The first centre, opened at the College of Further Education at Rhydfelin, near Pontypridd. An extract from the Director of Education's letter dated March 1962, pinpoints Shep's two-pronged vision:

"It is intended that the instruction provided at the rehearsals of this band shall help to raise the standard of performance in existing bands, and, if possible, encourage the establishment of new groups. It is also hoped that the relationship between this band and local bands will be close and mutually beneficial".

With Percy Griffiths as Headmaster and Ieuan Morgan as Conductor, the brass band centre quickly fulfilled Shep's aspirations and central figures from the school and brass band communities of the Rhondda worked shoulder to shoulder to create a base for the enhancement of brass band standards in the East of the County. One of the most influential figures was David Mabey, a woodwork teacher at Maerdy House school. A brass band fanatic, David Mabey would succeed Percy Griffiths as the Head of the East Glamorgan Centre. Invaluable teaching support was provided by Mal Guy of Ynyshir Band, Don Tanner of Cory, Islwyn Williams of Barry Town Band and Tom Jones of Tonyrefail Band.

In the East of the County, the work of Ieuan Morgan in particular would bear fruit. By the mid 1960s, six school bands were successfully established at Bryn Celynnog School, Beddau, Graddfa Boys School, Ystrad Mynach, Maerdy House School, Aberdare, Upper Rhondda School, Treorchy, Llanharry School and Llantwit Major School. Brass band development was undertaken by David Mabey at Maerdy House School, and of course Ieuan Morgan himself at Treorchy/Upper Rhondda School and also at Bryn Celynnog and Graddfa Schools. Two particularly supportive Heads of Music Departments were Graham Barrar at Graddfa and Tony Moore at Bryn Celynog. The latter would bring his boundless enthusiasm and infectious good humour to many brass band courses at Ogmore and in later years to National Youth Orchestra of Wales courses.

Of the importance of brass band work at Graddfa, Graham Barrar commented :

"Being a member of the school band improves a boy's character in so much that he must :

a) attend school regularly,
b) be punctual,
c) accept responsibility ."

Of after-school rehearsals he continued:

"A boy never leaves the band. Boys return in the evenings to rehearse. Some are boys no longer. As young men they are a good influence on the boys who are still at school.

This is teaching without problems of discipline because all concerned realise from the outset that, without discipline a band cannot operate successfully. This is accepted at an early age and continues on".

Having himself been brought up in the Cynon Valley, it must have been especially gratifying for Shep to witness the growth of brass ensembles at Maerdy House, Church of Wales Secondary School, Aberdare. David Mabey's report on the development of the school band recognised the importance of the encouragement of the Headmaster, Mr. Spencer, the support of local brass bands and the local council in providing instruments and the further stimulation of the County's regional band centre and residential courses as potent influences affecting success. Additional factors were the motivation provided by the County Eisteddfod and National Youth Brass Band Championships and the co-operation and involvement of parents. He stressed the motivational aspects of team-work, confidence-building and commented :

"Members of the school staff have been amazed at the progress made by boys from the remedial class, who have been able to read music before they can read English".

By 1971 the kudos which a successful band could bring to the supporting school was recognised by the Headmaster of Graddfa who received a quotation of 1500 books of stamps for a new set of school instruments. Presumably the school and parents had worked exceedingly hard to raise the necessary numbers of books of Green Shield Stamps to fulfil the order.

Established in 1963, the band of Bryn Celynnog School had grown to about thirty players by 1971. Two years earlier the band won first prize at the British Youth Summer Championship at Liverpool repeating this achievement a year later. Of the 60 pupils receiving brass tuition at that time many gained success in the Associated Board examinations and the school report stated that :

"Enthusiasm runs high among brass band members and many have to be dissuaded (sometimes strongly) from remaining any longer than the allotted time at rehearsals thus missing normal time-tabled lessons. Often the same pupils show sporting talents and with the two activities, closely aligned in many respects, they lead a full and active life and are definitely taking full advantage of opportunities that are available to them, but at the same time fulfilling the necessary academic requirements".

Although other school bands achieved great success, the unrivalled standard of the Treorchy Secondary School Brass Band is evident in their honours board :

1959 Won every competition in Class D - 6 Prizes
1960 Won 5 First prizes and 1 Second Prize in Class C
1961 Won 3 First Prizes in Class B
1962 Won 1 First Prize and 1 Second Prize in the Championship section. Competed in the Royal Albert Hall in October 1962 - the only school band to do so in the history of the banding world.

This meteoric rise remains unparalleled in brass band history and earned an M.B.E. for trainer and conductor, Ieuan Morgan, who also led the band to five first prizes and four second prizes in the National Youth Brass Band of Wales competitions. Even more astonishingly, Ieuan would gain ten national Youth

Band titles with the three schools in which he taught.

One of Ieuan's early successes came in the Brass Band Championships held in the Park and Dare Hall, Treorchy on January 30th, 1960 when his Treorchy School band won the Cadwgan Cup and a £10 first prize pipping Lewis Williams' Ystalyfera Youth Band by one point and Coedely - conductor W.D.Priday - and Rhymney Youth Band - conductor R.J.Nash - by two points. The adjudicator was none other than that doyen of the banding world, Harry Mortimer. In the programme notes on this for the concert, Russell Sheppard wrote :

"In congratulating those responsible for organising the Brass Band Championship and Massed Band Concert, I should like to say how pleasant it is to find the spirit of co-operation among the bands so much in evidence. There can be nothing more rewarding for the young players than to participate, as members of one united band, in playing the music previously used as test-pieces during the competition. May this Festival progress from strength to strength and attract still wider support in succeeding years".

The conductors of the massed band and the programme are shown below :

MASS BANDS CONCERT

To commence at 7 p.m.

Conductor - HARRY MORTIMER, Esq.

Associate Conductors :
Ieuan Morgan, Esq. W. J. Priday, Esq.
Lewis Williams, Esq.

Renderings by the Choir
of Tonypandy Grammar School
Conductor : W. R. Lewis, Esq.

PROGRAMME

March	- "The Vanished Army"	-	*Alford*
Fantasia	- "A Summer Day"	-	*Greenwood*
The Choir	- "The Graceful Swaying Wattle"	-	*Bridge*
The Choir	- "All in the April Evening"	-	*Roberton*
Fantasia	- "Melodies of Britain"	-	*Wright*
Euphonium Solo *	"Watching the Wheat"	-	*Geel*
The Choir	- "Noel Nouvelet"	-	16th Century Carol
The Choir	- "Dickory, Dickory, Dock"	-	*Farrar*
Fantasia	- "American Beauties"	-	*Greenwood*

PRESENTATION OF PRIZES

1st Prize—Cadwgan Cup & £10 2nd Prize—£8 3rd Prize—£6
Medal to Best Soloist

Mr. Russell Sheppard, Inspector of Schools
Iorwerth R. Thomas, Esq., M.P., President Treorchy Band
Introduced by Mr. Glyn Morgan, Chairman Parents' Association
Presentation to Mr. I. Morgan—Mr. D. Pugh, Treasurer Parents' Association

March	- "Anchors Aweigh"	-	*Newton*
X Trombone Solo *	- "Angels Guard Thee"		
The Choir	- "Cwsg, Lwli, Cwsg"		*Matthews Williams*
The Choir	- "Laudate Dominum"	-	*Oliver Edwards*
Selection	- "Holiday Sketches"		
Chorus	- "Jerusalem"		

"HEN WLAD FY NHADAU."

* Instrumentalists of Three Bands

In presenting the prizes, guest of honour Russell Sheppard waxed eloquently :

"It gives me much pleasure to preside at your concert for Massed Bands. Throughout the afternoon the bands have been competing in healthy rivalry with one another and now many of the players have joined forces this evening to show that they believe that co-operation is equally important as competition.

The Education Authority has given much support to Youth Brass Bands in the County. During the past eight years, ten residential courses for young players of brass instruments have been held.

I have no doubt that the Authority will continue to give real support to the Brass Band Movement in Glamorgan".

It was also Ieuan Morgan who would provide such invaluable support to Aaron Trotman the conductor of the band from 1960 to 1967. Aaron Trotman photographed next to Shep in Plate 30 was a long -serving Principal Trumpet of the BBC Welsh Orchestra. He also tutored the brass section of the GYO for many years. Staff included in this 1964 picture D. Anthony Small, Ieuan Morgan Mr. Price, Bert Davies, Aaron Trotman, Russell Sheppard, Mrs Price, Islwyn Morgan and David Mabey.

Commenting on the early Ogmore courses, Ieuan Morgan states :

"The starting of Brass Band playing in the Glamorgan schools was the result of much thought and hard work by Mr. Russell Sheppard. It was he who started the Brass Band courses at Ogmore School Camp, attended by pupils from all over Glamorgan. This course was held once a year, but proved so successful that eventually two courses were held. Brass Band playing will, I am sure, increase in the future as more instruments and teachers are made available to the schools".

In the early years, the Senior Band gave its concerts mainly at Ogmore School Camp and generally throughout its early history did not travel to public halls. In many ways, this was a regrettable policy from two standpoints. Firstly, the general public were deprived of the opportunity to hear and applaud the ensemble. Even more importantly a generation of future bandsmen did not gain the thrill of performing in recognised concert halls. This lower profile than that afforded to the County Orchestra and Choir would fortunately be rectified in the early 1970s, when as joint conductors, Ieuan and the author conducted the County Band in concerts held at Ystrad Mynach, Gwaen-cau-Gerwen, Aberdare, Treorchy, Bridgend and Neath. After reorganisation in 1974 bands from Mid (Ieuan Morgan), South (Dewi Jones) and West Glamorgan (under Tony Small) would capture prizes and captivate audiences wherever they performed.

At a Concert held at Dyffryn Gardens on July 11th, 1962, Shep featured the combined banding forces of Treorchy School and Godre'r Graig County Youth Centre who played "The Thunderer March", "Trumpet Voluntary", and several well loved hymn tunes under his conductorship. The Choirs of ten County Youth Centres were also to combine and to contribute individual items :

Aberkenfig	Veronica Rees	Caerau	Veronica Rees
Cymmer Afan	Betty Lewis	Gorseinon	Myra Rees
Kenfig Hill	Alan James	Skewen	Bryan Thomas
Tonnau	Eileen Gethin - Jones	Tongwynlais	John Mabbitt
Victoria (Penarth)	Tegwen Thomas		

The credentials of banding in the county were again put on display in a prestigious concert held at Sophia Gardens, Cardiff on 28th February, 1963. The combined bands of East Glamorgan, Treorchy Secondary School would perform Rimmer's "Holiday Sketches" and Verdi's Overture "The Force of Destiny" under the baton of Ieuan Morgan. Lewis Williams' Godre'r Graig County Youth Centre Band interpreted Weber's "Peter Schmoll" Overture. Godre'r Graig was also strongly featured in solo performances by Alun Evans (Euphonium) and Lewis Williams' son Wynne (Cornet). Like both these players the Loughor String Quartet (Eric Lewis, Vincent Sanger, Roger Thomas and Robert Thomas) had won first prizes at the 1962 Royal National Eisteddfod held at Llanelli. Two other National winners from Glamorgan took the stage. Future opera star Della Jones demonstrated her all-round musicality by performing a movement from the Clarinet Concerto by Tartini, arranged Jacob. Anthony Small, who would soon be appointed brass teacher in the Gowerton area and who later would have such success with the development of the Penclawdd and West Glamorgan Youth Bands, was the outstanding soloist in the Finale from Haydn's Trumpet Concerto.

Under Shep's direction the three previously mentioned bands combined in several community hymns, opening and concluding the concert with Greenwood's "Songs of Wales" and Rimmer's "Men of Harlech" respectively. Youth Centre Choirs representing Aberkenfig, Caerau, Cymmer Afan, Loughor, Kenfig Hill, Pontarddulais, Skewen, Tonnau, Tongwynlais took the stage together with Adran y Llynfi.

In 1965, Shep's letter written in the name of the then Director of Education, Trevor Jenkins, heralded the inauguration of a second Brass Band Centre in the West of the County.

"The Education Committee have decided to encourage the playing of brass wind instruments by the establishment of a Youth Brass Band Centre for the Western part of the administrative County of Glamorgan. The organisation will be similar to that of the East Glamorgan Youth Brass Band which was established for the Eastern part of Glamorgan at Ponypridd in 1962 and which has since grown to 130 players.

A special feature will be a beginners' class for pupils who are not already able to play an instrument".

As conductor of the centre the author had the privilege of working with its Headmaster, Stanley Jones and Anthony Small who since his appointment in the area had already firmly laid the foundation stones for the future successes of brass playing in the area. Remarkably, Tony was to combine brass and woodwind teaching chiefly in the Gowerton schools. Even more surprisingly, in addition to tutoring many fine professional brass players he would also be responsible for the early development of one of the country's finest oboe players, namely John Anderson. He would later mould the West Glamorgan Band into the most formidable Youth Band in the Britain. Having founded the Penclawdd Brass Band shortly after his appointment in Glamorgan, he would take this community band into the Championship Section in next to no time. Tony would also produce many fine professional brass players including his elder son, Gareth. Having performed a concerto with the National Youth Orchestra of Wales and having been Solo Cornet of the National Youth Brass Band of Wales, Gareth is currently a Principal Trumpet of the Halle Orchestra.

As previously stated an important part of the brief of the West Glamorgan Youth Band Centre was the initial training of absolute beginners. An excellent administrator, Stanley Jones splendidly organised the loan of instruments available from the centre. With the author and Tony Small taking responsibility for the senior bands, the task of tutoring the beginners' classes and the C Band fell on the willing shoulders of David Vaughan Jones, the Conductor of the Glynneath Band, Stanley Dodd, conductor of the Seven Sisters Band, with Stanley Jones taking theory classes designed to speed up the progress of members of the beginners' class. Eric James and Idris Rees worked at the centre as it progressed and substantially increased the number of its players.

The table below graphically exemplifies the increase in the number of players from the west who entered the Glamorgan Youth Brass Band from 1964:

DISTRICT	**1962**	**1964**	**1966**	**1968**	**1970**	**1972**
East	53%	74%	69%	70%	58%	49%
West	26%	15%	29%	23%	30%	36%
Mid	21%	11%	2%	16%	12%	15%

The increase in players from the West which rose from 15% to 36% between 1964 and 1972 was due largely to the stirling work of Anthony Small at Gowerton, Penclawdd Llwchwr, and Pontarddulais. Another significant factor was the success of the regional brass band centre at Neath Technical College.

A chart of schools who were the chief providers of players on the GYB's courses is given below. It shows the pre-eminence of Rhondda, Maerdy House and Graddfa schools and the upsurge of talent from schools in the western part of Glamorgan :

DISTRICT	SCHOOL	1962	1964	1966	1968	1970	1972
East	Graddfa Boys Sec.	8	16	10	22	22	13
	Treorchy Sec / Upper Rhondda	6	5	22	17	14	23
	Bryncelynnog	2	6	16	14	20	16
	Maerdy House	1	15	14	12	13	8
	Ferndale GS	6	0	0	0	4	0
West	Penclawdd Sec.	1	0	4	6	10	13
	Pontarddulais Sec.	1	2	2	5	6	12
	Cymmer Afan Sec.	6	1	6	4	2	4
	Llangatwg Sec.	0	0	0	5	5	3
	Neath Boys Grammar	1	0	0	0	5	5
	Llwchwr Sec	0	0	3	0	5	2
	Cwmtawe	0	0	0	0	7	3
Mid	Llanylltyd Fawr Sec.	0	0	0	7	8	8
	Llwynderw (Maesteg)	5	5	0	3	2	3
	Porthcawl Sec.	0	0	0	6	3	3

The above chart records only schools which provided 10 or more players. It is interesting to note the progress of schools such as Llangatwg and Neath Boys' Grammar under the teaching of Idris Rees. In Mid Glamorgan the development of brass band standards resulted from the work of staff at Llanylltyd Fawr, Maesteg and Porthcawl school. Not forgetting the support of the Head of Music and the Headteacher, there is a discernible parallel between the enthusiasm and commitment of the peripatetic teacher of the school and the resultant representation at a county level.

In 1967, Ieuan Morgan succeeded Ron Trotman as the conductor of the GYB. It is important to realise that the Ogmore Brass Band Courses catered for the different musical abilities by providing three graded bands under the same roof. Axiomatically, the influence of pupils in the A Band was important in improving standards. Hearing players many of whom were already members of leading Welsh bands would result in the advancement of less experienced players.Plate 31.

A year later, in an address to the audience assembled to hear the Treorchy Male Choir and the Bryn Celynnog Secondary School Brass Band in a concert at the Parc and Dare Hall, Treorchy, Shep commented :

The tendency today among a great portion of the population is to take pleasures ready-made, so to speak. But there is nothing more satisfying, rewarding intellectually, spiritually and emotionally, than taking an active share in the producing of music - be it as a member of a choir or a brass band.

Taken from the same source, representation in the three structured bands of the time is indicated below :

A Band	46%
B Band	29%
C band	25%

Such was the phenomenal rise in interest of brass playing that two courses were held annually at Ogmore from 1970 onwards. The number of youths and students settled at around 5% during the period. This is a significantly lower figure than that of the Glam Orchestra and Choir and relates directly to the salient fact that a large proportion of its members were drawn from Secondary Modern rather than Grammar Schools. Inevitably, the vast majority of these pupils would leave school at fifteen until 1968 and at sixteen after the introduction of the Raising of the School Leaving Age in the same year. The percentage of girls who were members of the GYB averaged out at approximately 12% during the 1960s. Plate 32.

1969, the year of the Investiture of the Prince of Wales, was also an important one for the County Band. Under the conductorship of Shep, the author and Ieuan Morgan the Band made a lasting impression performing to the young Prince in the grounds of Cardiff Castle. The Prince commented appreciatively on the standard of the band and this platform would create a significant impression on the attending Councillors, resulting in the higher status of the band in the years ahead.

In July 1970 the band captured the attention of the distinguished guests attending a Garden Party given at Dyffryn House and Gardens by the Chairman of the County Council, County Alderman George Adams. Under the batons of Ieuan Morgan and the author, the successful format of combining the best players from the East and the West continued and the band achieved high standards.

The GYB would give opportunities for the many future players to advance to the ranks of top class national bands. Derek Holvey, Alun Williams, Susan Mclean and others would hold principal roles in the leading Welsh Bands. Several like Lloyd Landrey, Wyn Williams and Clive Purnell, from the West, and Anna Hughes, Joanne Dean, Jimmy Davies, Gareth Key, Robert Westacott and Andrew Cheek from the East would take up principal positions in Northern Bands including Besses of the Barn, Brighouse and Rastrick and Black Dyke Mills. The Armed Services Bands would also provide a professional life for a significant number of GYB former members.

Others, like Derek Holvey, Eric James, David James, Andrew George, Jeff Pearce, Alun Williams and Graham Sheppard would later develop their brass band conducting careers in Wales with Gareth Pritchard conducting bands in Norway.

Many future professional orchestral players cut their musical teeth in both the GYB and GYO. In this category, Cornet/Trumpet players David James, Greg

Bowen, Laurence Evans were members in the early years of the GYB who gained success in the profession. Later, Trumpet Principals Gareth Small (Halle Orchestra) and Rhys Owens (Royal Liverpool Philharmonic) head a cast of professional players which also included French Horn player Huw Jenkins, Trumpeters Andrew Cuff from the East, Gareth Rees from Mid Glamorgan and Christopher Turner and Jonathan Mainwaring from the West. Trombonists who showed an equal interest in the band and orchestra included Brian Raby, Phillip Dando, John Hendy, Colin Gummer, Robert Price and Greg Morgan from East Glamorgan and Roger Argente, John Davies and Phillip Dodderidge from West Glamorgan. Another Trombonist from the eastern part of the county was Trevor Herbert who has become a well-known figure in the Open University. Trevor is also well respected as a brass band historian and composer. Tuba player Kevin Morgan (East), together with Andrew Cresci, Andrew Jones, Stephen Follant and Jonathan Rees (West) represent a new generation of top flight professional players who have been engaged by most of the country's professional orchestras. Among future professional percussionists who played in the county bands of Glamorgan and West Glamorgan may be numbered Richard Buckley, Jonathan Morgan, Sean Hooper and Nicholas Ormrod from West Glamorgan and Timothy Wright and Jonathan Morgan from Mid Glamorgan.

Hall of Fame : The New Glamorgans

Rhys Owens : Trumpet

Rhys Owens was born in Abertridwr, near Caerphilly in 1967. He took his first trumpet lessons at the age of eight.

Rhys was educated at St. Cenydd Comprehensive School, Caerphilly and entered Chetham's School of Music, Manchester in 1984.

During this time he became Principal Cornet of the the National Youth Brass band of Wales and Principal Trumpet of the National Youth Orchestra of Wales.

In 1986 he began his studies at the Royal College of Music in London. His tutor was the eminent trumpeter, David Mason.

Rhys Owens

Rhys was appointed Sub-Principal Trumpet of the Royal Liverpool Philharmonic Orchestra, a post he held until 1998. In that year he was promoted to the important position of Principal Trumpet with the orchestra.

Gareth Small : Trumpet

Gareth Small

Gareth Small comes from Penclawdd and gained invaluable experiences with the Penclawdd Brass Band and in all the ensembles of West Glamorgan Youth Music. He studied at the Royal Academy with Laurence Evans, James Watson and John Wallace winning several prestigious awards and prizes including the Sidney Langston and HRH Princess Alice. He also won the Ryan Davies, Mark Jones Awards in addition to a Welsh Arts Council Scholarship and the National Eisteddfod Blue Ribbon. As a result of the 1993 Euro International Trumpeters Guild Competition held in Gothenburg, in 1993 he performed a Recital. He represented the Royal Academy as the first ever winner of the Lasmo Staffa inter-collegiate Music Award.

Whilst at the Academy, Gareth freelanced with the LPO, ENO, the BBC NOW, the Halle, London Sinfonietta, London Mozart Players, Bournemouth Symphony Orchestra, the Welsh Chamber Orchestra and the Asko Ensemble of Amsterdam. Additionally, Gareth played in West End shows and recorded many TV commercials.

In recent years, he has performed with the Philharmonia, Royal Liverpool Philharmonic and the Opera North Orchestras, touring extensively to all parts of the world. He is the only soloist to have performed with both the National Youth Brass Band and the National Youth Orchestra of Wales.

In 1995 he gave the world premiere of Alun Hoddinott's Trumpet Concerto "The Shining Pyramid". Especially written for him, the work was performed at the last Night of the 1995 Welsh Proms by the Halle Orchestra, conducted by Owain Arwel Hughes.

Gareth teaches trumpet at Chethams, the Universities of Salford, Manchester and Keele and has given many master classes. He is at present the Assistant Principal Trumpet of the Halle Orchestra. He is a member of the Halle Brass Quintet and the Orfeo Trumpet Consort with whom he has recorded CD's. He has toured Germany with London Brass.

THOSE WERE THE DAYS

Ieuan Morgan

I first met Russell Sheppard at Treorchy Secondary School when he came along to listen to the school band which had been formed by the late headmaster Mr. Percy Griffiths B.A. Not long afterwards, Mr. Sheppard started the regional brass band sessions on Saturday mornings during term time at the College of Further Education at Rhydfelin. This consisted of a Senior Band, Junior Band and a Beginner's Class, with Mr. Griffiths in charge of administration. David Mabey took over from Percy Griffiths when he retired.

At a later date, Mr. Sheppard set up the Glamorgan Regional Band which rehearsed at Neath Technical College. Stanley Jones was the administrator and John Jenkins the conductor. The Glamorgan County Youth Brass Band was subsequently formed with the amalgamation of the Senior Bands of the East and West Regional Bands, John Jenkins and myself were co-conductors. and concerts were given in Gwaen Cae Gerwen, Treorchy, the Gwyn Hall, Neath and other venues. These achieved much in giving a high profile to the Band.

The standard of the County Brass Band was consistently high and was made up of the best players from the whole of Glamorgan. Numerous prestigious concerts were given, among them a performance for the young Prince of Wales at Cardiff Castle. The Prince spoke enthusiastically about the Band to staff and students alike mentioning that he himself had learned the cello and trumpet whilst at school. Members of the band were thrilled to meet the Prince during his Investiture Year celebrations.

Many other concerts were performed with the County Youth Orchestra and Choir at Parc and Dare Theatre, Treorchy, the Gwyn Hall, Neath and the Bridgend Recreation Centre. Several former players have since become members of Britain's leading orchestras and Brass Bands.

Shep, as he was fondly called, established instrumental and choral music of the highest standard. He was a person of tremendous musical vision, who built an outstanding framework for music in Glamorgan.

I myself, former staff and past students will be forever grateful for his dedicated effort in providing us with the opportunity to make music. He will never be forgotten.

Ieuan Morgan became Principal Euphonium of the Parc and Dare Band at the age of seventeen - a post he held for over sixteen years. Having studied at the Welsh College of Music and Drama he became Head of Brass with the Mid Glamorgan LEA. As conductor of the Mid Glamorgan Youth Brass Band he toured Germany in 1986. Both his sons, Greg and Kevin are professional orchestral brass players. In 1985 he became the first Welshman to receive the Iles Medal from the Worshipful Company of Musicians. In 1994 he received the Masters Dedicated Service Award from the All England Masters Brass Band.

D. Anthony Small

I first came into contact with Russell Sheppard in 1958 when I attended my first orchestral course at Ogmore. Mr. Sheppard was a very well organised, hard-working person with a dry sense of humour. He was very fair-minded and determined, for once he set his mind on something there was no swaying his resolve. He was also a good musician who sought absolute perfection in rehearsals and through his meticulous approach he inspired others to follow his example.

I vividly remember an unforgettable incident on Easter Monday, on the final day of the course. Carried away by the excitement of a game of football and after a hurried lunch, violinist Brian Llewellyn and I were the last out of the showers. We discovered that our friends had played a practical joke on us by removing all our clothes and towels. Checking that there were no girls in A Block, we sprinted naked to Block C to get changed and packed. We sprinted down the hill to find that the coaches had left without us. There was nothing else we could do but to hitch-hike to Neath.

We walked a little way, struggling to carry our suitcases and instruments, before the first vehicle travelling in our direction came along. You can imagine our disbelief when the car stopped and we discovered that the driver was none other than Shep himself. We had a gruelling journey on the old A48 with horrendous traffic jams through Pyle, Port Talbot and Briton Ferry and I had the unenviable task of sitting in the passenger's seat. After much ear-bashing, we convinced our irate driver that the reason we were late for the coach departure was because we had decided to check our dorm and shower room for any property which might have been left behind by our fellow players.

When we arrived at the concert hall our friends displayed great hilarity on hearing of our adventurous journey to Neath. Miraculously, the situation was reversed when Mr. Sheppard took the rostrum and proceeded to admonish the older students. The nearest person to him, principal cellist Wayne Warlow, took the brunt of Shep's outrage for not delaying one coach until we had completed our thoughtful, public-spirited deed.

Like many others, I was fortunate to have been given the opportunity to work in music education by Mr. Russell Sheppard. My love of music and the additional experiences gained in the Glam proved most invaluable to my career. He also encouraged me to take up woodwind instruments in addition to trumpet studies at the Royal Academy of Music. He was also indirectly responsible for the formation of the successful Penclawdd Brass Band which, under my direction developed largely from my school based work to win the Championship Section Welsh Regional Title in 1986.

Future authorities largely modelled their activities on his blue-print. Mr. Sheppard was unique as the pioneer of a plan for music making based on a strong team of dedicated instrumental teachers and residential courses which inspired so many young musicians. His legacy is there for all to see.

A native of Penclawdd, D. Anthony Small continued the family tradition of influential brass band players and conductors. A student at Cardiff University, Tony has successfully combined a teaching career with performance as a trumpeter with many professional orchestras, Theatre Orchestra, Jazz and Big Bands. His outstanding work with the Penclawdd and West Glamorgan Youth Brass Band and Big Band is widely recognised. Formerly Principal Advisory Teacher for West Glamorgan, he is also an examiner and mentor teacher for the Guildhall and Associated Board of Music respectively. He was one of the founder members of the National Youth Brass Band of Wales. His sons Gareth and Ian have developed successful careers in music and business.

Plate 31 - Glamorgan Youth Band Course 1972 - Conductor Ieuan Morgan and Bert Davies, Headmaster of Ogmore, are seated to the left and right of the course board respectively

Plate 32 - Shep inspects a cornet belonging to Glamorgan Youth Band members. Also pictured are Jeffrey Francis, Ieuan Morgan and John Jenkins

Plate 35 - Mid Glamorgan Youth Orchestra - Conductor: Jeffrey Francis

Plate 36 - Mid Glamorgan Youth Brass Band - Conductor: Ieuan Morgan

Plate 37 - Mid Glamorgan Youth Choir - Conductor: Jeffrey Francis

Plate 38 - South Glamorgan Youth Orchestra - Conductor: Jeffrey Lloyd

Plate 39 - South Glamorgan Youth Brass Band - Conductor Dewi Morris

Plate 40 - South Glamorgan Youth Choir - Conductor Helena Braithwaite

Plate 41 - West Glamorgan Youth Orchestra - Conductor John Jenkins

Plate 42 - West Glamorgan Youth Brass Band - Conductor: D. Anthony Small

Plate 43 - West Glamorgan Youth Choir - Conductor John Jenkins

Plate 44 - West Glamorgan Youth Arts Company - Director Godfrey Evans; Conductor: John Jenkins

Plate 47 - Four Counties Youth Orchestra: 1995

Plate 48 - Cardiff County and the Vale Youth Orchestra

Plate 49 - West Glamorgan String Youth Orchestra and Wind Band

4.

Trios 1974 - 1996

§

We stand now
On the threshold of a new age,
When everything is possible,
When many voices call
To be heard and echoed among us,
Many instruments to be tried and tested
Until they become commonplace and comfortable.

The Hall of Song : Harri Webb.

1. Music in Mid Glamorgan

§

by

Jeffrey Francis

The concert presented by the Glamorgan Youth Orchestra and Choir at the Gwyn Hall, Neath on Friday January 4th, 1974 was the last time that these two bodies of young musicians combined to make music. Many who attended the concert must have thought that they would never again hear youth music making of such high standard. Each of the newly created counties - Mid, South and West Glamorgan - would have much smaller populations, might lack the will to develop this branch of their pupils' education or might not be able to financially support the structure necessary to produce such an orchestra or choir.

Fortunately for the pupils and students of Mid Glamorgan, the county council adopted the practices of the Glamorgan County Council in promoting instrumental music tuition in schools, extending the provision of instruments and in encouraging weekend music centre and residential instrumental and vocal provision.

Of fundamental importance was the development of a team of Visiting Teachers of Instrumental Music - VTIM. There were considerable deficiencies in school provision in each of the six districts of Mid Glamorgan. Rigidly controlled by the limited funds available to provide staffing and instruments, a team of 54 full time teachers of instrumental music was eventually established to provide each of the 42 comprehensive schools with free tuition on the majority of orchestral and brass band instruments. Until the early 1990's only violin tuition was available in primary schools. From that date, cellos were purchased and, in some schools in the Rhymney Valley, specialist cello and brass tuition was introduced. Additional harp tuition was provided in the ever increasing number of schools where pupils were taught through the medium of Welsh.

The authority's commitment to music was evident in the extension of the instrumental teaching team and in providing free tuition and free loan of an instrument for a period of up to twelve months.

Staffed mainly by VTIM, district orchestras were formed for secondary school pupils. Rehearsals continued to be held at Coedylan Comprehensive School, Pontypridd and had a membership of some 250 pupils. About 240 pupils also attended the Bridgend district orchestra held at Penybont Primary School. At a later date, Friday evening rehearsals were held at Merthyr Tydfil Technical College. When it became obvious that the county was to be divided into four County Boroughs, a district orchestra was formed in Caerphilly. Until the mid 1980's the main emphasis at each of the four centres was the development of orchestral playing. The expansion of the peripatetic service and an increase in the numbers of pupils learning woodwind instruments led to the development of wind bands at the centres.

Weekly Saturday morning rehearsals for pupils learning brass instruments continued to be held at Pontypridd Technical College. Staffed predominantly by tutors who earned their livelihoods outside teaching, classes were held for pupils as young as 7 or 8 years of age for, at this time, tuition on brass instruments was only available at the centre. Some fifteen years later rehearsals were transferred to the University of Glamorgan. Concerts for parents were a feature of all the centres.

Pupils living within the authority had the great advantage of subsidised access to a wide range of residential courses held at Ogmore Residential Centre (formerly Ogmore school Camp). The physical condition of this facility had greatly improved since the early days of the Glamorgan Youth Orchestra and excellent facilities were available for pupils and staff. The following music courses were included in the centre's crowded timetable :

Recorder for primary school pupils(2), recorder for secondary school pupils(1), for pupils learning brass instruments(2), Junior Orchestra(2), Transitional Orchestra(2), Senior Orchestra(3) and the Youth Choir(2). From 1982 there was an annual course for wind band and a few years later, two courses per year were introduced for primary string players. Members of the County Youth Orchestra and Choir were chosen by audition and for all other courses, acceptances were based on nominations submitted by schools on the advice of VTIM.

In 1980, the county suddenly decided that, because of insufficient funds, it was no longer able to finance the district orchestras. This brought a sharp reaction from parents who formed the Friends of Mid Glamorgan Youth Music. The Friends developed all sorts of ideas for fund raising and brought pressure to bear on the politicians who soon decided to allow the resumption of rehearsals on a restricted basis.

From 1992 Senior instrumental staff of the authority were :

John Varney	Upper Strings
Diana Thomas	Lower Strings & Harp
Michael Griffiths	Woodwind
Ieuan Morgan	Brass

Due to the financial problems of the authority, savings were also made relating to transport and meals on concert days. The Youth Orchestra gave one end of course concert instead of two and the County Band no longer held a summer concert but joined the choir and orchestra in the concert held each January. Thanks to the considerable amount of money raised by the "Friends", music and expensive instruments were able to be purchased. They also raised funds to assist the senior orchestra, choir and brass band to make visits to Germany and Eire. Thanks to the existence of the "Friends" and the on-going support of the County Council, the provision for instrumental music in children's general education continued. The support of various Chief Advisers and Directors of Education was an essential factor.

On the first Mid Glamorgan Youth Orchestral Course, held in Ogmore during April 1974, there were about 63 members of the former GYO and 33 pupils drawn from schools in the county who were attending their first senior course. The first concert was held in the Assembly Hall at Ogmore.The programme began with Schubert's "Rosamunde Overture" and finished with the "New World Symphony". The former MEP Wayne David played the oboe on this course. Over the following few years, the orchestra grew from 96 to a maximum of 161 players. The average number of players was 120-125 with the average age being about seventeen years and six months.

With the increasing size of the orchestra, the number of suitable venues was considerably reduced. This situation eased over the years with the building of more Sports Centres. The orchestra played in the National Museum of Wales, in Urdd Eisteddfodau at Tonyrefail and Rhymney and in St.David's Hall to mark the city's association with Voroshilograd. In 1983 the Orchestra, Choir and Band performed at St. David's Hall, Cardiff and the annual Mid Glamorgan Gala Concert was held at this venue up to and including January 1996. Plate 35.

For many years, the wind players of the orchestra had formed their own informal wind band, and, in 1986 they played several items in the Gala Concert. Such was their success that in 1987, and in subsequent years, The Mid Glamorgan Wind Band presented a twenty minute programme in the Gala Concert.

Over the years, several BBC recordings were made of the choir and orchestra and in 1996 a CD was made of the whole of the Gala Concert.

In April 1988 the Youth Orchestra, by arrangement with Cadw, held a concert in Llandaff Cathedral, presenting a programme which was, in the main, to be performed on the visit to Nurtingen in West Germany the following August. The soloist in concerts at Filderstad and in the Stadthalle in Nurtingen was trumpeter Rhys Owens, who is now Principal Trumpet with the Royal Liverpool Philharmonic Orchestra.

For the Orchestra's visit to Ulm in 1992 the soloist in Mozart's Flute Concerto in D was Susan Thomas. Music for a dinner at County Hall, Cardiff in honour of George Thomas, the Speaker of the House of Commons, was one of many appearances of small ensembles from the Orchestra at special functions. Several years later a small orchestra of 15 players performed for HRH Diana Princess of Wales at the University of Pontypridd.

Over the years a large number of Youth Orchestra players gained invaluable concerto experience, and of the thirty five or so instrumentalists who later entered professional orchestras, Carl Darby played violin concertos by Tchaikovsky and Bruch, Elunid Pritchard played works by Beethoven, Svendsen, Vaughan Williams and Massenet and Elin Edwards played a movement of Lalo's "Symphonie Espagnole". Andrew Cuff and Rhys Owens were the trumpet soloists in concertos by Hummel and Arutunian respectively, Timothy Wright (percussion) performed Monti's "Czardas" and Simon Morgan was featured in Strauss' Horn Concerto No.1.

Other concerto soloists included Gerald Hopkin, Peter Jones, Juliet Leighton Jones, Bethan Richards (Violin), Anita Gratland (Viola), Julia Tucket (Cello), Graham Dyer (Oboe), Peter Sheppard (Horn), Harpists Rebeca Jones, Katherine Thomas and Deian Rowlands and Pianists Gerald Hopkin, Christopher Davies, Timothy Rhys Jones and Stewart Roberts.

The orchestra provided an average of twenty players for the National Youth Orchestra of Wales and performed a wide range of works including symphonies by Dvorak, Brahms, Borodin, Britten, Schubert, Mahler and Schumann. The orchestra gave several first performances of works by Mark Burrows, Mervyn Burtch, Kevin Adams, Neil Day and Neville John and guest artists Alun Francis and Stuart Burrows.

The county's Youth Brass Band numbered some eighty players. Initially, many of its members were pupils from a small number of schools where outstanding brass bands had been developed. Eventually, as with the orchestra and choir, many other schools contributed pupils to this band and former members joined Service and Works Band whilst others became valued members of local bands.

In 1977 the Mid Glamorgan Brass Band played in Caerphilly Castle before Her Majesty the Queen and a year later the band played in the presence of Princess Alexandra. The band also played in an Urdd Eisteddfod concert at Merthyr Tydfil. As well as giving local concerts, the band made highly successful visits to Ludwigsburg in 1986 and 1990 and, in 1987, played at the first ever School Proms Wales. Plate 36.

Over the years some of the band's outstanding players were Alun Williams, Gregory Morgan, Kevin Morgan, Nigel Guy, Robert Westacott, Nigel John, Angela Gay, Gareth Rees, Andrew Gardner, Stephen Howell and Lynne Croft. The county was represented on all of the National Youth Brass Band of Wales courses.

The Mid Glamorgan Youth Choir of about 105 Choristers met twice a year in Bridgend either at Ysgol Cefn Glâs or at The School for the Visually

Handicapped until, eventually, they resided at Ogmore. The programme for the January course often contained more popular music and the choir shared the concert programme with the County Orchestra and Bands. The music studied during the summer course was usually a very demanding major work of a religious nature. Accompanied by about fifty of the more experienced Youth Orchestra players, two summer concerts were held, usually in the appropriate ambience of a church.

In 1989, the “Friends” arranged for the Choir to visit Kilkenny in Eire. Rapturous applause was received for the performances at St. John’s R.C.Church and at the Anglican Cathedral. The impromptu rendition in the cellar of the Guiness brewery was perhaps the most unusual setting for any of the performances. Earlier that year, part of the Youth Choir represented Mid Glamorgan at a civic event held in Ulm.

As well as engaging professional singers, the Youth Choir gave invaluable concert experience to members from its ranks including Ceris Deverill, Josephine Jones, David Gwestyn Smith, Eldrydd Cynan Jones, Jeffrey Lloyd Roberts, Darren Jones, Ellen Pritchard, Ruth Kavanagh and Joanne Thomas. Several of these singers have become professionals.

The choir tackled many works from the major repertoire including Bach’s “Magnificat”, Brahms “Song of Destiny”, Handel’s “Messiah” and “Samson”, Haydn’s Creation, Orff’s “Carmina Burana”, Mendelssohn’s “Elijah” and Mozart and Verdi’s “Requiem”. Works by Beethoven, Mozart,Walton, Elgar, Rutter, Holst and Vaughan Williams and several works by Welsh composers were sung in churches and concert halls throughout the county. The Choir regularly provided members of the National Youth Choir of Wales. Plate 37.

In order to maintain instruments and re-hair bows, in the early 1980’s, the Education Committee financed the establishment of the Welsh School of Instrument Making and Repair. This developed into a centre of excellence where students from all over the world were taught how to make and repair stringed instruments, pianos and harps.

During 1976-1977, the Mid Glamorgan County Council were holders of the National Music Council of Great Britain Local Authority Award. Chosen from over seventy competitors, the Authority received this award for its contribution to music in the wider field.

Jeffrey Francis hails from Port Talbot and was a member of the first Glamorgan Youth Orchestra Course in 1949. For almost fifty years he has maintained a virtually unbroken connection with youth music in Glamorganshire - as a student, orchestra leader, tutor and Music Adviser. From 1974 to 1996 he was Music Adviser in Mid Glamorgan, a post he retained after reorganisation to his recent retirement.

Jeffrey is a JP and has given outstanding service to music at Margam Abbey. As Head of Music at Sandfields Comprehensive School, he created an outstanding music department. He graduated from Aberystwyth University and played a prominent role in the Welsh Music Advisers Association and many national bodies.

2. Music in South Glamorgan

§

by

Helena Braithwaite

As a beneficiary of the excellent peripatetic and orchestral system established by Russell Sheppard in Glamorgan, from the time of my appointment as Music Adviser in 1979, I was eager to develop music in South Glamorgan in a similar way. All those who played in the Glamorgan Youth Orchestra had a tremendous pride in the County and a huge loyalty to the Youth Orchestra which inculcated in the students a confidence and belief in themselves. My long term aim was to encourage and develop within the students of South Glamorgan a similar pride in the musical achievements of the County and new confidence in themselves. This proved to be a very difficult task. Before reorganisation in 1974, instrumental music in the City of Cardiff was underdeveloped, with only two full-time peripatetic teachers, one string and one brass and a mass of part-timers, some of whom taught for one hour a week. The two orchestras, A and B, were of a fairly low standard and there was no choral structure.

Dewi Jones was appointed as a brass peripatetic in 1972 and in seven years developed a Youth and Schools Brass Band and a Saturday morning brass school. His work was so successful that in 1979 the Youth Band won an Outstanding Performance Award at the National Festival of Music for Youth. He formed parents' associations for all the bands which proved to be an excellent support and model that was followed later by all County ensembles and choirs.

At the time of reorganisation in 1974 it was realised that the A orchestra was not of a sufficiently high standard for a County ensemble. Therefore, an arrangement was made with the Welsh College of Music and Drama. Pupils paid £1 and officially became students of the College. The orchestra was conducted by College lecturers, firstly Walter Gerhardt and then Frank Kelleher. College instruments and music from the library were used by the orchestra. As the orchestra had made such good progress under Frank Kelleher I decided not to take it over but to bring it back under County control when a new Head of strings could be appointed.

The inclusion of Barry and Penarth in the County of South Glamorgan in 1974 meant that their two string teachers joined the Cardiff staff. In 1979 it was obvious that instrumental teaching needed urgent reorganisation, redressing the balance between full and part-time teaching. An hierarchical structure was established whereby teachers could progress from Scale 1 to Scale 3 (Head of Section), Dewi Jones being the first Head of Brass. The number of part-time staff was drastically reduced and full-time peripatetics appointed. Instrumental teachers were given in-service training and lower string, brass and woodwind teaching was extended from secondary to primary schools. As well as supplying instruments to schools, the more expensive instruments were bought centrally by the County and a County Library of orchestral, band and choral music was established.

The orchestral provision was enlarged to include four orchestras, from the County Junior Schools Orchestra through Transitional and Schools orchestras to the Youth Orchestra. In 1982 Jeffrey Lloyd was appointed as Head of Strings. As well as directing the Youth Orchestra from 1984, Jeff also established an extremely successful Youth Chamber Orchestra. Previously the string body at youth level was under strength. The Chamber Orchestra included pupils who had yet to be accepted into the main Youth Orchestra, but, nevertheless, had tremendous potential. The repertoire of the Chamber Orchestra encompassed Baroque, Classical and Contemporary music, which allowed the Head of Strings to emphasise the development of string technique. Able to call on a larger body of strings the Youth Orchestra expanded its repertoire to embrace large-scale orchestral works including many of the Mahler Symphonies. Another innovation introduced by the Head of Strings provided a concert platform - often proceeded by a master-class given by international conductors - for students who displayed latent conducting talent. The high standard of playing within the Orchestra now meant that it was possible to select soloists from within the Orchestra itself for virtually all the main concerts. International soloists engaged included Sir Geraint Evans, Emma Johnson, Felix Schmit, Martin Jones. The development of the Youth Orchestra owed much to the work of Frank Kelleher and Jeff Lloyd. The later appointment of Eric Phillips as deputy conductor preceded his becoming conductor upon Jeff Lloyd's early retirement. The Youth and Chamber Orchestras both won outstanding performance awards in the Festival of Music for Youth and played in the Schools' Proms in London, Manchester and Cardiff. Plate 38

Dewi Jones continued to develop brass teaching to the extent that the County had five brass bands. Numbers in the Saturday brass school grew to four hundred. The Youth Band continued its success and in the 1980's moved from Class D to Class A in adult competition - one of few bands to achieve this feat. Plate 39. In the 1970's Bill Salaman, a lecturer in Cardiff University, established a Wind Band. This was brought under County direction in 1979 as the County Youth and Schools Bands were established. A Head of Woodwind was appointed in the late 1980's and provision was extended to include a double reed ensemble and a flute and clarinet ensemble for those younger players who were not quite ready to enter the Wind Bands. The Youth Wind band won a silver award at the National Concert Band Festival and as a result represented Wales in the European Wind Band Festival.

In 1940 Walford Davies established a Schools' Music Festival in Cardiff. Area Junior Schools' choirs, recorder groups and the City's A and B Orchestras took part in the Festival which ran for a number of evenings in the Sophia Gardens Pavilion, Cardiff. In the late 1970's it became difficult to sustain the Festival financially and it was felt that the breadth of the music curriculum was being neglected in some primary schools in order to prepare for a one-off event. With the approval of the teachers, it was decided to cancel the Festival and, instead, to build a structured choral system and concerts in more prestigious venues, such as City Hall and Llandaff Cathedral. In 1979 the County Youth Choir was formed, followed by the Junior Schools Choir in 1980 and, a few years later the choral system was completed with the formation of the County High Schools' Choir. I directed the Youth Choir for fourteen years. Beginning with forty choristers the choir grew to over a hundred members during the 1980's. In 1988 they won the coveted first prize at the Youth Choral competition at the Llangollen International Eisteddfod. The choir was awarded the outstanding performance award at the Festival of Music for Youth in 1990 and, in the same year, they also won the Choir of the Year Award in the British Open Competition. The choir as well as appearing regularly with the Youth Orchestra, also performed with the National Orchestra of Wales, the Royal Philharmonic, London Symphony and the Halle Orchestras. They sang in a number of major festivals and represented Great Britain in the "Zimrya", the World Assembly of Youth Choirs in Jerusalem. The choir was in demand for radio and television broadcasts, one of the most interesting being the premier of "Jazz Messiah" for BBC television. The High Schools' Choir, too, sang in many prestigious events, including singing with the British Children's Orchestra and in the presence of Princess Diana. Plate 40.

Jazz was not neglected in the County. Jazz College, Stan Barker and Digby Fairweather worked in the County's schools developing jazz improvisation and performance skills over a number of years in the 1980's. This led to the formation of "Jazz News", the County's Jazz Ensemble. They were Wales and the West winners of the Daily Telegraph Jazz Competition in 1988, 1989 and 1990. A number of youngsters went on to study Jazz at a more advanced level. Jonathan Thomas (Bass Guitar) and Osian Roberts(Saxophone) both studied at the Royal College of Music and Osian, now a professional player will feature at the 1999 Brecon Jazz Festival.

Another keen student of jazz, Ceri Torjusson gained the highest first class degree at York University before winning a Fullbright Scholarship to study composition at the University of Southern California, Los Angeles. Among a number of outstanding instrumentalists from around the world and two or three composers he was chosen in 1999 to study composition for big band and film at the Henry Mancini Institute in America. The Vale of Glamorgan Festival intends to commission a work from Ceri to be played by the BBC NOW in the 2000 festival.

As Cardiff is the home of the Welsh National Opera and as many orchestras perform at St. David's Hall, schools were encouraged to participate in master classes with the WNO and visiting orchestras, Many of these projects were based on world music, including African drumming and Gamelan playing. My last innovation was the purchase of Steel Pans. An expert was placed in Fitzalan High School - a multicultural school - and its feeder Primaries. This development is still successful and the Band played in Llandaff Cathedral on the day of the opening of the Welsh Assembly in June 1999.

In 1979 the ensembles were housed in various schools throughout the City. In 1982 all County groups moved into purpose-built rehearsal rooms in the Friary building which was centrally situated for pupils from all over the County. Regular weekend courses were organised for County ensembles and the opening of St. David's Hall gave them a wonderful performing home. Every year to the present each of the various levels of ensembles have given a Festival in the hall. The Youth Choir and Orchestra have performed some of the greatest choral and orchestral works there including "Elijah", the Verdi and Faure Requiems, Bernstein's "Chichester Psalms" and Poulenc's "Gloria". A number of first performances include the first television performance in 1991 of "Jonah" by William Mathias with the County Youth and High School Choirs, the Youth Orchestra, young dancers and actors from the County. Another major premier was the performance at the Cardiff Festival of Music in 1985 of "Bells of Paradise" by Alun Hoddinott, which was later recorded.

Foreign tours have been a central focus of the County's activities. From my appointment I felt that this activity broadened pupils' awareness of musical standards world-wide and of the comparison of standards of music making in South Glamorgan.

County groups have travelled to America and Canada on numerous occasions and have also visited Russia, the Ukraine, Hungary, Israel, Malta, Germany, Austria, Belgium, Switzerland and France. The outstanding groups in this field have been the County Brass Bands, who between 1978 and 1993 raised over £100,000 for various charities. This effort culminated in a group from the Youth Brass Band travelling to Kiev at Christmas 1990 to deliver £35,000 of medical supplies and thousands of presents to children suffering from radiation induced cancers, following the Chernobyl disaster.

In 1979 five hundred young people took part in County activities. This number grew to 1,600 in 1983 and 3,000 in 1990. Representation at National level grew too. Only 6 instrumentalists represented South Glamorgan in the NYOW in 1979. By the mid 1980's and into the early 1990's between 20 to 25 South Glamorgan students were chosen each year. A number of pupils played in the British Youth and British Children's Orchestra and in 1984 three of the five Welsh musicians attending the European Youth Orchestra were from South Glamorgan. Choristers from the county formed nearly half the National Youth Choir of Wales at its formation in 1983 and this large number continued through to the early 1990's. Dewi Jones, Head of Brass put forward the idea of a National Youth Brass band of Wales and asked Edward Gregson to direct it. The Arts Council agreed to administer and fund the band and it is now firmly established.

From 1979 onward South Glamorgan funded 80 scholarships, both vocal and instrumental to the Welsh College of Music and Drama. These helped some excellent musicians. Outstanding among many instrumentalists now playing professionally are Eluned Owen, violin, leader of the Paris-based Ludvig Quartet, Christopher Cowey, Co-principal Oboe in the Philharmonia and Professor in the Royal College, Nichole Wilson, violinist with the Philharmonia Orchestra, Nicholas Barr, freelance viola player including the Academy of St. Martin's in the Field, Christopher Thomas, percussionist in the LSO, Rachel Thomas, harpist with the Bournemouth Symphony Orchestra, and Huw Davies, cellist with the BBC Concert Orchestra. Clare Salaman works as a free-lance Baroque violinist. She has led most of the leading British early instrument orchestras and the European Union Baroque Orchestra on two major European tours.

Over twenty ex-Youth Choir members are now singing professionally. Many sing in Britain's opera companies as well as doing free-lance work. These include Rosemary Joshua (ENO) and international opera houses, Catrin Davies (WNO), Wynne Pencarreg (Glyndebourne), Anthony Stuart Lloyd (ex- WNO now singing in a German Opera House), Susanna Tudor Thomas and Geraint Roberts (ENO), Stephen Mullan (Florence Opera) and Dyfed Evans (English Touring Opera). Many more are free-lancing. Jeremy Williams was the Welsh representative in the Singer of the World competition, and Nicola Humphries was a finalist in the Young Welsh Singer competition. Elen ap Robert, Iona Jones also perform professionally and Kate Woolveridge was the winner of the NFMS Alfreda Hodgson Award. Iona Jones, Kate Woolveridge and Dyfed Evans are tutors with the National Youth Choir of Wales.

The achievements of music in South Glamorgan were recognised by the British Association of County Councils and Local Authorities on many occasions. This association presents an award each year for the British County that shows the best provision for music. South Glamorgan entered six times from 1985 to 1993 and was awarded the Premier Award four times and was one of four merit award winners twice.

The work of Russell Sheppard was not confined to Glamorgan. He has inspired his proteges, wherever they have had the opportunity, to inspire new generations of young people with enthusiasm for music and the qualities of loyalty and confidence that he created. His influence will long continue.

Helena Braithwaite MBE was born in Pontarddulais and educated at Gowerton Girls' Grammar School. She was a cellist with both the Glamorgan and National Youth Orchestras. Helena graduated from University College,Cardiff with an MA in Twentieth Century Music. Following posts as Head of Music at Cowbridge and Cardiff High Schools she became Lecturer in charge of the Post Graduate Certificate studies at University College, Cardiff. Helena served on the supervisory panel of the National Foundation for Education Research and the Schools' Council.

As Music Adviser to the South Glamorgan LEA, she won many prestigious awards including the John Edwards Memorial Award. Helena held high office on several national educational bodies and has received national recognition for her work as the first Education and Community Officer to the BBC NOW. Her work as the conductor of the internationally renowned Cardiff Ardwyn Singers has taken her all over the world. Currently she is an External Examiner for the MA in Music Education at Trinity College, London and serves on the Vale of Glamorgan Festival Committee. In 1999, Helena was awarded the MBE for services to Welsh music.

3.

Music in West Glamorgan

§

by

John Jenkins

Described by the "Western Mail" as "the County probably most committed to providing creative outlets for young people in the Arts", the development of schools and youth music in West Glamorgan was firmly rooted on the models which Russell Sheppard had established in Glamorgan. Indeed, when an HMI report on music in West Glamorgan confirmed the "general excellence" of the LEA music provision, highlighting "its impressive programme of courses and centres and the rich variety of opportunities" available, they were in many ways confirming not only the achievements of the new county but also those of its predecessor.

In terms of instrumental music, the broad philosophy of the county was :

* to provide an equal opportunity to all children able to benefit from instrumental tuition and willing to put in the necessary practice.
* to provide special facilities (such as weekend centres and residential courses) appropriate to the talent thus discovered.
* expressly to add variety to the possible range of activities at any given school through group music work.

Although string and some wind teaching was a feature of comprehensive schools in Glamorgan, the schools in the former Swansea area (Districts 1 and 2) were impoverished in this regard. The enlightened approach of the new authority facilitated a dramatic expansion of instrumental provision :

District	Schools	Violin		Cello/Bass		Woodwind		Brass	
		1974	1977	1974	1977	1974	1977	1974	1977
1	5	2	5	1	5	1	5	2	5
2	7	2	7	0	7	0	7	1	7
3	1	1	3	1	3	1	3	1	3
4	4	4	4	1	4	2	4	4	4
5	4	4	4	1	4	2	4	2	4
6	5	5	5	0	5	0	5	5	5
Totals	**26**	**16**	**26**	**4**	**26**	**6**	**26**	**15**	**26**

Piano and harp teaching was introduced into a number of schools and by 1997 over 1400 orchestral and band instruments were purchased. This together, with a policy of instrument repair, resulted in a massive increase of pupils learning at school. By March of that year, 2100 string, 400 woodwind and 560 brass players were being taught by the county's instrumental team. Significantly, the LEA appointed Aneurin Edwards(later Kenneth Watkin) and D. Anthony Small as Supervisory Teachers for Strings and Wind respectively.

In curricular terms the appointment of Stanley Jones (later John Butler) as Primary Advisory Teacher would have a powerful impact on the school-based, in-service and residential course activities of the county. Within a few years, the authority pioneered the development of music programmes in its Special Schools where Janet Burgess' innovative work was very successful. The Adviser, working with John Butler and Janet Burgess, promoted the extension of work with physically and mentally disadvantaged pupils. In this regard, a strong liaison with Claus Bang in Denmark culminated in an International Conference which also involved the percussionist Evelyn Glennie. The LEA developed strong links with the Schools Council and for many years hosted a National Dissemination Centre for Music. At a later date Technics Keyboard Music Academies were geographically introduced with the Adviser becoming much involved in developing the successful introduction of a BTec Rock and Pop Module organised at Neath Tertiary College.

Weekend Centre activities were dramatically expanded with the former provision of a Friday orchestral centre and Saturday brass band centre mushrooming into two secondary orchestral and band centres based at Neath and Swansea respectively. A network of as many as 7 primary and choral centres was eventually established. By 1977 over 1300 pupils attended - a number which, in succeeding years continued to grow. In this regard, the contribution of the instrumental service and of local teachers was highly significant.

By 1977 an annual pattern of almost 30 residential courses had been established. In that year 2250 primary and secondary school pupils attended residential courses held at Dan y Coed residential Centre and the West Glamorgan Institute of Higher Education. Courses were organised for the Youth Orchestra,Chamber Orchestra, Youth Choir and Chorale, Youth Brass, Big, and Wind Bands attracted large numbers of schools and youth musicians. Junior and Transitional Orchestral and Band Courses, and a range of string and recorder courses for primary and junior secondary pupils provided a recognised line of progression through to the county's youth ensembles.

The late 1970's and 1980's was an exciting period which saw the development of an arts for all policy including a Smaller Community and the Arts Programme and the foundation of the Margam Festival. Based at the beautiful Orangery, Margam Park, the Festival attracted major artists and ensembles and embraced not only music but also the visual, dramatic and cinematic arts. Ably supported by administrator Wayne Carpenter and senior staff the festival ensured a summer platform for all the county's music groups. National competitions for young composers ensured that the performance of new music was regularly premiered by county ensembles. These dimensions of the County's provision featured strongly in West Glamorgan winning four National Music Council of Great Britain Diplomas of Merit and a Major Award for its overall excellence of music provision.

Established in the Summer of 1974, the West Glamorgan Youth Orchestra quickly gained a national reputation. It was particularly delightful to be able to be part of the future development of so many fine young players, a significant proportion of whom became principal players and soloists with the National Youth Orchestra of Wales. Timothy Crossland, David Emanuel and later Sali Wyn Ryan led the NYOW and Mark Howells and Phillip Thomas performed solo works with the orchestra. Katie Clarke (now with the BBC Symphony Orchestra) became leader of the National Youth Orchestra of Great Britain. Amongst a long list of other string players who entered the playing profession are violinists, Robert Tonkin, Susan Croot, Alan Titherington, viola players Simon Aspell (Vanbrugh Quartet), Steven Burnard (Principal: BBC NOW), and Andrew Beazley (BBC Symphony Orchestra), cellists David Watkin, Judith Rees and Gethyn Jones and bass players Albert Dennis, Mark Jenkins and Julian Walters. Sian Jones has been principal harpist of the Gothenburg Opera Orchestra for several years and Rachel Davies appears regularly with leading orchestras. Oboists Mark Howells (BBC Symphony Orchestra) and Sian Davies, and bassoonist Martin Bowen head a distinguished cast of former West Glamorgan woodwind principals. Several outstanding brass players who played in the county orchestra and bands, have become respected professionals. These include Gareth Small, Jonathan Mainwaring, Robert Samuel and Christopher Turner(trumpet), Roger Argente, and Phillip Dodderidge(trombone), and tuba players Andrew Cresci, Stephen Follant, Andrew Jones and Jonathan Rees. Richard Buckley and Nicholas Ormrod are well-respected percussionists.

Three other outstanding founder members of the West Glamorgan Youth Orchestra have developed international careers in music. A review of violinist Mark Thomas's international work as a composer has already been featured in the book. As an accompanist, Phillip Thomas - who, in addition to being a fine percussionist, performed Rachmaninov's Second Piano Concerto with the WGYO in its inaugural concert - combines his outstanding career in opera with being an accompanist to the Cardiff Singer of the World Competition and such eminent artists as Lesley Garrett. Having performed piano concertos and played in the viola section of the orchestra, Gareth Jones has developed an outstanding conducting career, particularly with Welsh National Opera. Mention should also be made of the conducting contributions of pianist-percussionist, Eric Phillips in Youth Orchestral conducting and Michael Bell(bass) who has done so much to establish the reputation of the Cardiff Philharmonic Orchestra. Plate 41.

The Orchestra began a long and continuing association with the National Festival of Music for Youth with appearances in the Schools Proms and at the Silver Jubilee Concert at the Royal Festival Hall in 1977. Honorary patrons include Andre Previn and Owain Arwel Hughes and the orchestra has undertaken successful tours of Germany, Denmark and the USA as well as giving frequent broadcasts on radio and TV. Notable artists who have performed with the WGYO include Sir Geraint Evans, Nigel Kennedy, Yitkin Seow, Jack Brymer and Julian Lloyd Webber and many concerto opportunities have continued to be given to orchestral members over the years. From the mid 1980's Kenneth Watkin and Phillip Emanuel played a crucial role in the development of the WGYO.

The West Glamorgan Youth Band was founded by the Music Adviser in 1974 and gave its first performances under the joint conductorship of John Jenkins and D.Anthony Small. It was under the latter's baton that the Band was to become the most successful youth brass band of the 1980's. The development of brass playing in the county's schools and the formation of a Centre of Excellence at Dynevor School Swansea resulted in the band's winning the National Youth Championships of Wales on many occasions. Plate 42.

Under the direction of Tony Small, the band became the first from Wales to win the coveted National Youth title at the National Championships in 1984. additionally two members of the band won the supreme accolade of Best Soloist of the Championships - Gurnos Rees (Soprano Cornet) in 1984 and Gareth Small (Cornet) in 1987. Winning major prizes every year from 1984 to 1990 the band's marvellous record is demonstrated in their becoming the Youth Champions of Great Britain in 1984, 1986, and 1989. Such was the outstanding standard of playing that the West Glamorgan Youth Brass Band won second prize in the European Youth Band Championships of 1991 and were the highest placed Youth Band in the World Festival of Bands held in Brisbane in 1988.

Foreign tours by the Band were made to Switzerland in 1987 and to Denmark and Sweden in 1985. Under the conductorship of Andrew George the County Youth Band were Champion Band of Great Britain (Advanced Class) in 1995 and earned excellent reviews for its performance in the 1996 Schools Music Association Concert held at the Royal Festival Hall. The band has also toured France and given many broadcast concerts and produced a record of "Boycestrous Brass" with their patron Max Boyce. Many brass celebrities have appeared with the band including Jim Sheppard, Maurice Murphy, Gordon Higginbotham and Robert and Nicholas Childs.

West Glamorgan developed an acknowledged excellence in the field of Big Band and Wind Orchestral playing. Established in 1981, under the direction of Tony Small, the Big Band undertook a tour of Germany in 1992. Regular performers at the Margam Festival the band appeared with Danny Moss, Humphrey Lyttleton, Kenny Baker, George Chisholm, Don Lusher and Marian Montgomery. Derek Fox also played an important part in the development of Big Band and Wind Band music. The Wind Orchestra owes a great deal to the work of Phillip Emanuel who succeeded me as Head of the West Glamorgan Music Service in 1992. Considerable support was given by David Rees, Derek Fox, Hugh Phillips and others. The Wind Orchestra undertook a Scottish tour in 1995 and gained considerable success in National Music for Youth Festival also performing at St. David's Hall on several occasions.

In the development of the West Glamorgan Youth Choir and Chamber Choir it was a privilege to work closely with Chorus Masters, Haydn James, John Hugh Thomas, Jason Shute, Clive John, John Mills and Lesley Ryan. Other dedicated staff worked tirelessly to prepare the choir for performances of major choral works by Bach to Bernstein and Britten, from Mozart to Verdi and from Purcell to Poulenc. Stanley Jones and later, John Butler made hugely influential contributions to the organisation of the Choir. Honorary Patrons Sir Geraint Evans, Della Jones and Sir Harry Secombe also contributed significantly to the successful future of the choir until the late 1980's. In the development of the Schools Choral Centre the work of Moira and Peter Greeney has been very important.

Soloists in major oratorio performances include Penelope Ryan, Diane Fuge, Euthwen Harrhy, Paul Harrhy, Christopher Jones, Jason Shute and Della Jones Several outstanding future professional emerged from the ranks of the WGYC, including Karl Daymond, Rebecca Evans, Ros Evans, Christopher Evans, Paul Harrhy, Vaughan Howells, Catrin Ley, Geraint Miles, Huw Priday, Geraint Roberts and Karen Shelby. Helen John (Mills), Elizabeth Johnson(Phillips) and Paul Brophy were among other students who sang solo roles with the Choir. Plate 43.

As well as performing in major concert halls, several broadcasts were made and the choir visited Denmark, Belgium and Normandy. At a concert in 1977, I was privileged to receive from the HRH Prince of Wales, three Silver Jubilee Awards for the Best County Youth Orchestra, Choir and County overall. A year later the John Edwards Memorial Award was presented by the Guild for the Promotion of Welsh Music to the Glamorgan Youth Choir and Orchestra and their conductor John Jenkins in recognition of their services to music in Wales.

In July 1975, the County Youth Orchestra and Choir combined with a group of dancers from the County Youth Theatre Company in a performance of Borodin's Polovtsienne Dances. From this highly successful collaboration Adviser Godfrey Evans and I developed the idea for the production of "West Side Story" which received critical acclaim in 1976. A production of Purcell's "Faerie Queen" broke new ground a year later in a setting which captured the atmosphere of a seventeenth century private performance at the Orangery, Margam Park. Over three hundred singers, dancers, actors, production team members and orchestral players took part in productions of the monumental "Mass" by Leonard Bernstein, firstly at the Brangwyn Hall, Swansea, and in September 1979 at the Wembley Conference Centre. The taxing role of the Celebrant was brilliantly interpreted by John Quirk who has subsequently developed a successful career as conductor, composer and arranger. In October, 1981 the Company presented Vaughan Williams' "Job : A Masque for Dancing" in the presence of their Royal Highnesses the Prince and Princess of Wales. Plate 44.

From the cast of these Youth Arts Productions several leading actors-producers would emerge. Director of the film "Twin Town", Kevin Allen played the part of A-Rab in the production of West Side Story which also featured future professional actors like Derek Hutchinson, Gareth Snook, Francine Morgan and Caroline

Berry. It is also interesting to note that the lead part of Tony was sung by clarinettist Mark Ormrod who is now Professor of Medieval History at York University. In performances of "Mass", Martyn John and Christopher Evans have appeared professionally in the West End. John Dummer, a principal in "Mass" and Assistant Stage Manager : Sound for "West Side Story", has, under the stage name Jay Alexander, become Musical Director in many successful London shows and has conducted several TV programmes, most recently as MD to Peter Karrie.

Throughout the period 1974-1996, the Friends of West Glamorgan Youth Music provided wonderfully generous support to the County's young musicians. Their emphasis on the provision of regular master classes by leading musicians has been particularly beneficial in maintaining and developing high standards.

Hall of Fame

Rebecca Evans : Soprano

A native of Neath, Rebecca Evans was hailed by the press as the "Operatic discovery of the year" in 1991. She has appeared in Britain as Susanna at the Royal Opera House and in the roles of Ilia, Cendrillon, Marzelina, Norina, Gretel and Susanna with Welsh National Opera and in the title role in "Cunning Little Vixen" for Scottish Opera. Abroad she has sung principal roles with the Bayerische Staatsoper, Netherlands Opera, Opera de Lausanne, De Vlaamse Opera, Santa Fe Opera, San Francisco Opera, Metropolitan Opera and on a European tour as Nanetta in "Falstaff" conducted by John Eliot Gardener.

Rebecca Evans

She has made many concert appearances with Pavarotti, at the Edinburgh Festival, and the Proms and has toured Europe in Haydn's "Creation". In America she has performed with Michael Tilson Thomas and the San Francisco Symphony, Jeffrey Tate and the Boston Symphony and also with the Indianapolis Symphony Orchestra. In 1996 she made her Australian debut and has given recitals at the Wigmore Hall and in Spain, Ravinia and Belfast. Recently Rebecca sang at the opening of the Welsh Assembly, and in Japan and Australia.

She sang Belinda in the BBC film of "Dido and Aeneas" and this CD forms part of a highly impressive discography. In the near future principal opera roles she will sing at the Met., Chicago, San Francisco and with Bayerische Staatsoper.

Rebecca was a member of the West Glamorgan Youth Choir and Chamber Choir and made several appearances with West Glamorgan Youth Ensembles.

Gail Pearson: Soprano

Gail Pearson

Gail Pearson was born in Neath and studied at University College, Cardiff and the Royal Northern College of Music. Awards include third prize in the prestigious Kathleen Ferrier Scholarship, the Towyn Roberts Scholarship at the National Eisteddfod and the Gwilym Gwalchmai Jones Award at the Royal College of Music.

Gail made her professional debut in Verdi's "Rigoletto" for Welsh National Opera were she later sang principal roles in "Cosi fan Tutti", "Hansel and Gretel", "La Cenerentola". She has sung principal roles for Zurich Opera, Glyndebourne Festival, Royal Opera House, Covent Garden, Scottish Opera, several roles for English National Opera, the Buxton Festival, English Touring Opera, The Opera Company, Mid Wales Opera and South Wales Opera. Her impressive and versatile operatic repertoire includes Gretel, Musetta, Ninetta, Susanna, Mimi and Carmen.

Concert Performances include operatic Galas with WNO conducted by Carlo Rizzi, the Bournemouth Symphony and the Bournemouth Sinfonietta. She has made solo appearances at the Aix-en-Provence, Cardiff and Fishguard Festivals. Gail has also given recitals at the Wigmore Hall (which was recorded by HTV) and the Fairfield Halls, London.

Future plans include Oberto in "Alcina" for English National Opera, a series of outdoor concerts with the Bournemouth Symphony and Anna Truelove in a concert performance of the "Rake's Progress" at the Endellion festival.

A frequent soloist with West Glamorgan Ensembles, Gail played the violin in the County Orchestra and was member of the Youth Choir and Chamber Choir with whom she toured Denmark.

THOSE WERE THE DAYS

The following statements from a former West Glamorgan singer and brothers who played in the Youth Orchestra encapsulate the feelings of many players and singers who were members of Mid, South and West Glamorgan ensembles.

Gail Pearson: Soprano

Gail recalls that Mahler 4, the Mozart Requiem, Elijah, the "Chichester Psalms" and "Messiah" were the favourite works she performed. She writes :

"The courses were a wonderful way in which to spend the holidays.They were instructive and great fun and saw us develop both musically and socially. I have many happy memories of the courses which helped to lay the foundations for a sound musical education through practical music making and we embraced it with huge enthusiasm".

Nicholas Ormrod : Percussion

"Musically, the courses gave an invaluable opportunity for learning repertoire and the chance to play in outstanding venues like the Royal Festival Hall - where I clearly remember performing "The Pines of Rome" - and in the Brangwyn Hall. It was a period when we appreciated the fun of music making in a serious context. Educationally, it gave us life-changing opportunities".

As a professional percussionist and timpanist, Nicholas has worked with most of the country's major orchestras including the RPO, BBC NOW, ECO, BBC Symphony, the Bournemouth Symphony and the Philharmonia. His interest in period performance has included performances with the Hanover Band and the Orchestra of the Age of Enlightenment. He has played with the Royal Opera House, English National Opera, the RSC and appeared in many West End Shows. He teaches at Dartington and the Royal College and has published several articles on percussion playing.

Mark Ormrod : Clarinettist/Singer

"As a keen player and singer but not having the ambition to pursue a career in music, I benefited enormously from course activities in both cultural and social terms, deriving an abiding appreciation of the classical repertoire, an understanding of how to perform in public - which has been very useful in my current career - and a capacity for building strong friendships on the basis of shared work and interests. As time passes and the resources available to young people seem to become more and more restricted, I realise how fortunate and privileged we were to participate in the great days of the Glam and West Glam".

Dr. Mark Ormrod, who sang the leading role of Tony in West Side Story with the West Glamorgan Youth Arts Company and played the clarinet in the WGYO, graduated from London University before taking a doctorate at Oxford. He taught at Sheffield and Queen's University, Belfast before becoming a research fellow at St Catharine's College, Cambridge. In 1995 he became Professor of Medieval History at York University, where he is also Director of the Centre for Medieval Studies. In addition to his teaching and research, Mark has published several books on the history of medieval England.

5.

Variations on a Theme 1996 - the present

§

Whatever the future brings us, the past has brought us gold,
For this land was a land of singing in the stirring days of old.

Gold : Idris Davies

Until the end of his life, Russell Sheppard maintained a healthy, inquiring interest in the activities and achievements of the young musicians of the present generation. He confessed that whilst he was puzzled by and concerned about the effect of the 1996 local government reorganisation on music provision and its impact of the establishment of a myriad Mini-Glams, he was also confident that a continued emphasis on achieving high standards would be the number-one priority for those at the helm of future youth music-making policy. One can understand the reason for this optimism in as much as five out of seven of those who are currently able to dictate music policy had experienced the tradition and achievement of the Glam :

Kevin Adams	Violin	Music Adviser : Adviser for Music : ESIS
Mostyn Davies	Violin	Music Service : Cardiff County and the Vale
Phillip Emanuel	Flute	Manager of the West Glamorgan Music Service
David Hughes	Horn	Music Co-ordinator: Bridgend
Christopher Jones	Cello	Music Adviser : Cardiff

Shep's principal concern centred around the apparent decline in some areas of the opportunities for young musicians to experience singing the master works of the mixed voice choral repertoire. He was also anxious that pupils should continue to have free access to instrumental tuition and access to an instrument - free at the point of entry. Much heartened by the achievements of the Ogmore Centre Trust, his belief in the underlying socio-musical value of the residential experience remained a pivotal point of his educational philosophy. The diminution in this facet of music provision in the former Glamorgan area remained a disappointment to which he frequently referred until his death.

In April 1996, Mid Glamorgan was replaced by four County Boroughs each of which retained its own instrumental service and developed its own Youth Orchestras. Because no single authority had adequate finances to maintain Ogmore Residential Centre plans were made to mothball the centre which had been the base for youth music for forty-five years. What was thought to be the final course for the renamed Glamorgan Valleys' Youth Orchestra took place in July 1996. Due to the pressures of the Ogmore Centre Trust, courses were eventually restored and it is interesting to note that Roger Lewis, author of a leading article of this book acts as Chairman of the Trust.

The new Unitary authorities are :

Bridgend County Borough Council	representing most of the former Ogwr district.
Rhondda-Cynon-Taff CBC	the former districts of Rhondda, Cynon Valley and Taff-Ely
Merthyr CBC	the former Merthyr Tydfil district
Caerphilly CBC	the former Rhymney Valley district with the addition of part of the former Gwent

The music service at Bridgend is led by Music Co-ordinator David Hughes - a former principal horn player with the Glam. A team of peripatetic teachers provides instrumental tuition in primary and secondary schools, and the county has orchestras, wind bands and a choir which all meet weekly. The service has recently expanded its provision in primary schools to include woodwind and brass tuition.

Rhondda-Cynon-Taff's Head of Music Service is Simon Thomas. The county has a team of peripatetic teachers providing instrumental tuition in all instruments taught previously with the addition of percussion, keyboard and guitar. Both primary and secondary schools are included in this provision. County orchestras and bands rehearse on a weekly basis at Pontypridd.

Merthyr Tydfil CBC, not having had its own Head of Music Service, utilises the services of the Adviser for Music at ESIS (the Education Support and Inspection Service for the four counties. The present Adviser for Music is Kevin Adams - a former violinist with the Glam. He co-ordinates the work of the peripatetic teachers in primary and secondary schools and also the weekly rehearsals of the choir, orchestras, wind band and brass band.

Caerphilly Music service is organised by Principal Music Officer, Keith Ellerington. A broad range of music provision is available for all the county's primary and secondary schools. The service has recently expanded to include tuition in percussion, keyboard, guitar and voice. There is also a music co-ordinator for primary curriculum support. The county choir, orchestras and bands rehearse weekly.

The four authorities work together to maintain the Four Counties ensembles. These generally rehearse on residential courses held at the Ogmore Centre and are jointly organised by the heads of music services of the four boroughs. At senior level, there is at present a Choir, Symphony Orchestra, Chamber Orchestra, and Wind Band. A show-case concert featuring all these ensembles is held annually in January. The ensembles also give separate concerts at other times of the year. Recently, the Choir and Orchestra took part in Schools' Prom Wales organised by Music for Youth at St. David's Hall, Cardiff. Residential courses are also facilitated - some on a Four Counties basis and others by two or three counties in collaboration.

In addition to the large numbers of former members who have become professional musicians, there are numerous present members who are studying at various colleges of music. For many more, the various ensembles provide a valuable leisure pursuit as they prepare for, and undertake careers in other fields. Plate 47.

Following reorganisation, the pattern of instrumental provision for South Glamorgan by the Cardiff County and Vale of Glamorgan Music Service remained under the organising remit of former Glam violinist, Mostyn Davies. Any anticipated decline in music provision was quickly dispelled and, in reality, the music service has continued to grow. At present 65 peripatetic teachers are employed teaching in primary and secondary schools. Instrumental teaching hours have virtually doubled in recent times and the service offers an ever expanding range of provision which encompasses the traditional spectrum of orchestral and band instruments together with keyboard, guitar, vocal and ethnic instruments. The Music Adviser for the City of Cardiff is another Glam old boy, Christopher Jones.

In total, 28 different ensembles are represented including :

4 Orchestras
10 Brass Bands
Wind Bands and Ensembles
3 Choirs

Over 2000 pupils participate and flourishing Parents Associations continue to give essential support to all activities. Regular foreign tours have been made, more recently to Norway, Austria, France and Canada together with very successful orchestral performances at the Edinburgh Festival. Jazz and Caribbean music also exemplify the broad range of provision.

The link with the Glam continues with Eric Phillips - a former pupil of the author at Neath Boys Grammar School - conducting the Youth Orchestra and former soloist with the Glamorgan Youth Choir, Kelvin Davies, taking charge of the Youth Choir. The bands are in the capable hands of Keith Griffin and Peter Knight.

The Friary is busier than ever as the focal point for musical activity and it is encouraging to record that residential courses have recently been arranged at Ogmore. Successful concerts of all types - including several at St. David's Hall - are regularly held and the proud record of South Glamorgan in the area of fund-raising continues to be a fundamental feature of the activities of Cardiff County and Vale of Glamorgan pupils and staff.

Ensembles have featured prominently in the Festival of Music for Youth and most recently the Youth Orchestra distinguished itself at an international festival in Vienna where it gained second prize to a more senior ensemble from a South African University. Plate 48

Despite the fact that the former West Glamorgan Authority was split into two County Boroughs, the wise decision was made to preserve arrangements for music organisation under one umbrella organisation. Sensibly arrangements for all music provision in the Neath Port Talbot County Borough and the City and

County of Swansea Borough Council remained under the auspices of the West Glamorgan Music Service and its Manager Phillip Emanuel.

Of this arrangement Vivian Thomas, Director of Education for Neath Port Talbot, recently commented :

"We are delighted to continue and build upon the excellent reputation that was created by pupils in the former West Glamorgan area, who for many years performed with great skill and pride as members of various West Glamorgan County Orchestras".

This sentiment was echoed in the same concert programme by the Director of Education for Swansea, Richard Parry :

"We are very pleased that the long tradition of the West Glamorgan Music Service has been allowed to continue. The list of successes proves that the investment has certainly been justified and augurs well for the future".

During the life of the music service the size and scope of instrumental music in schools has increased to include instruction in percussion, guitar and wind band playing. Moreover, the service now offers a wide range of school based curriculum support.

Of the recent successes of West Glamorgan musicians, Phillip Emanuel writes :

"High standards of school performances are upheld and the Service co-ordinates a wide range of instrumental and vocal activity at the County Primary, Transitional Orchestras, Training and Senior Brass Bands, Youth Symphony and String Orchestras, Wind Orchestra and Choir. In 1998-1999 five ensembles were particularly successful - the County Brass Ensemble, Saxophone Quartet, Brass Band, Wind Orchestra (winning highly commended Award) and the String Orchestra(winning an Outstanding Performance Award) - invited to perform at Symphony Hall, Birmingham, at the National Festival of Music for Youth. More recently, the Wind Ensemble were presented with a highly commended Award at the Royal Festival Hall".

According to a report in the "Times Educational Supplement", the excellent West Glamorgan Youth String Orchestra performed to great acclaim at the Schools Prom in the Albert Hall.

The music staff of West Glamorgan Youth Music are highly committed to instrumental work and the various ensembles are directed by :

Brass Band	Andrew George
Big Band	Derek Fox
Wind Ensemble	David Rees
String Orchestra	Julie Emanuel
Choir	Moira Greeney

The Friends of West Glamorgan Youth Music continues its outstanding work in support of young musicians. They provide regular support at the music centres and concerts and are justifiably proud of their achievement in offering financial assistance for musical ventures over the last three years. The catalogue of their corporate ventures includes tours to Salzburg (1997), Paris (1998), Scotland (1998) by the Choir, Brass Band and String/Wind Orchestras respectively. This support has also been readily forthcoming for the Brass Band in visits to the National Championships between 1996 and the present and in the appearance of various ensembles in the National Festival of Music for Youth over the years.

They have promoted the purchase of specialist instruments, music and equipment and have enabled West Glamorgan to continue its strong tradition of facilitating regular master classes. Appearances have been held in the International Masterclass Series by such eminent musicians as Gordon Back (Piano), Emma Johnson (Clarinet), Dong-Suk Kang, Jojo Hattori and Mathew Trusler (Violin), John Anderson (Oboe), Julian Lloyd Webber and Nina Katova (Cello), Della Jones (Mezzo-Soprano), William Bennett (Flute) and Gareth Small (Trumpet). 1999 saw the inaugural concert of the Gordon Back Young Recitalists at the Brangwyn Hall. Eight young recitalists were given the opportunity to perform sonata and concerto movements, accompanied by Gordon Back. This represents a very appropriate link between youth music of the present day and the Glamorgan Youth Orchestra with which Gordon performed many concertos. Plate 49.

6.

Intermezzo

§

General Educational Role

When my family sent me to college,
I looked at those spires tall
And my head was buzzing with bits of advice,
I couldn't remember them all;
But my uncle's advice I shall never forget,
More precious than rubies to me;
"A supporter or two on the Council
Is better than any degree".

The Way Up : Idwal Jones

Readers will recall from Chapter 3 that music was only a small part of Russell Sheppard's wide span of local government, national negotiating and professional association responsibilities. In point of fact, until the appointment of Jeffrey Francis as Music Adviser in 1972, his incredibly varied portfolio and the degree of his total commitment was never fully appreciated or, indeed, known to those who encountered him in his specific musical role. It took a report of 1970 to highlight "an overwhelmingly strong case for the appointment of an Assistant Music Organiser".

In February 1970 and again in March 1971 Russell Sheppard wrote to the LEA concerning financial recognition for the exceptional responsibilities of certain County Organisers including himself. He reminded the Authority that :

"Successive Burnham improvements for heads of schools (for which he had himself negotiated) have not been matched with comparable Soulbury improvements for inspectors until the Tenth Report in 1970, where local authorities were provided the means of restoring relatives which had been eroded over the years".

Continuing this justification he cited the example of a comprehensive school which came under his jurisdiction. The account provides an interesting insight into the time-consuming and often frustrating aspects of his more general purview :

"From the time of its establishment as a new secondary school it has been beset with difficulties. On a number of occasions I was asked to exercise continuous oversight because of local sensitivity and professional unrest within the school. Some years ago I arranged that a full inspection should be held. Improvements

which were made led to a more settled period. But the Headmaster, now retired, leaned heavily on officers, such as myself, for help and advice in difficult professional situations. I found, however, that his salary, which had been lower than mine in earlier years had rapidly made substantial increases as the size of the school increased. At maximum his salary is now £600 higher than mine".

In his letter of 1970 Russell provided a specific and detailed resume of his general duties :

"Throughout the period, I have occupied the post, I have constantly kept the conditions of my appointment in mind. I therefore have given approximately equal time to the general and specialist sides of my work. Whenever a possible conflict of interest has arisen I have always given priority to my duties as a general inspector. As a result of this I usually find that I give a greater part of the school week to general work, much of which is a direct result of the official requests for my opinion or professional judgment of the work of schools and teachers. Immediate educational needs,e.g. in connection with school reorganisation or the assessment of probationer teachers in the primary and secondary schools or staffing of schools, take up a quite significant proportion of my time.

The result is that I give a smaller slice of the school week to the needs of music but I tend to compensate for this by putting in extra time at weekends and certain other evenings in order to promote the development of music in Glamorgan".

The same missive highlighted the areas of inspection, short routine visits and follow-up activities, acting as an arbiter in disputes between schools and parents, responsibility for about thirty to forty probationers annually, and special oversight of schools experiencing particular difficulty. His involvement in educational developments, heads of department meetings and reorganisational matters was also time-consuming. In addition to this, he held responsibility in two Districts for collaborating with other officers. He gave the following examples :

a) I visit and consult with the Divisional Education Officers, providing administrative support.

b) I have been co-opted as a member of the management panel of the Coedparc Teachers' Centre and attend meetings to offer professional help and advice.

c) I attend such meetings as necessary with the educational psychologist in connection with remedial education in my two divisional areas.

d) I am involved in detailed approval of plans for new schools, school extensions and minor projects in my areas, as well as assessing priorities with the DEO.

Additionally, he was expected to assess the staffing of schools in these districts and to advise on the In-Service training needs of teachers.

How he was able to undertake all the course and music centre duties referred to in the previous chapter, and at the same time manage the complexities of an ever growing peripatetic teaching team is, in every sense of the word, astonishing.

Yet, almost from the start of his post in Glamorgan, Russell Sheppard championed the cause of improved remuneration and enhanced status for teachers, inspectors and advisers. It was he who successfully pioneered a more appropriate and universally recognised pay scheme for unqualified teachers of instrumental music in Glamorgan. From 1950 he consolidated the teacher association experience gained in Holyhead by supporting teachers' rights via the new Burnham pay agreements. His impact on the National Association of Inspectors and Education Officers was immediate and in 1953 he received a letter from the NAIEO Honorary General Secretary which indicated that he had become an influential figure in the Glamorgan Inspection service.

Dear Mr. Sheppard,

I want to congratulate you on the proposals put forward by the Glamorgan members. I shall have great pleasure in putting the matter on the agenda for the Executive Committee in November.

"Up with the Welsh" says my wife.

Yours sincerely,

Henry Cole.

By 1962, as his letter to Sir Ronald Blooming indicates he had become confident and unequivocal in his language to the top brass of the Burnham Committee :

Dear Sir Ronald,

Thank you for your letter of 15th June.

The Executive Committee of the National Association of Inspectors and Education Officers does not agree with your statement that "until the position with regard to the Burnham Committee is clarified by a special conference of the union, no useful purpose would be served by having a meeting of the Officer's Panel of the Soulbury Committee".

For many years he was the Honorary Secretary of the Professional Committee and Chairman of the Salaries, and Policy Sub Committee of the association which would become better known as the National Association of Inspectors and Educational Advisers (NAIEA). In the latter capacity he negotiated not only on the government's Soulbury Committee but was in contact on a regular basis with Chief Education Officers nation-wide. Of several letters from these CEO's, which complimented Russell Sheppard on the innovative structures he had introduced in Glamorgan, an extract from the response received from the CEO for Leeds in 1964 encapsulates the respect in which he was held nationally :

"Thank you very much for your very interesting comments on the minimum establishment for Inspectors and Organisers. I feel that your scheme is worthy

of much deep consideration and would go far to rationalise our position in the scheme of things".

As a NAIEA negotiator, Russell Sheppard was uncompromising in his dealings with his own Glamorgan employers. Despite the potential tensions of his having to serve two demanding masters in the pattern of annual discussions and occasional disputes, his resolve is transparently evident in telling sentences taken from three of many letters written by Russell Sheppard to Directors of Education and Chairmen of various committees over the years :

1956 "In Glamorgan we have recently considered our present Soulbury Scales, and are naturally dissatisfied with the present position whereby a number of headteachers are paid considerably more than the Inspectors of the Authority".

To Emlyn Stephens : Director of Education

1964 "We ask that the Committee should favourably consider increasing the salaries of our posts under the provisions of Paragraph 3 of the Soulbury Report by an amount equal to the grade under the scales for general inspectors. This would do much to redress the progressive deterioration which has occurred in our positions compared with those of headteachers whose schools we inspect, and those of senior officers of the Authority whose posts have been regraded".

To Trevor Jenkins : Director of Education

1970 "On 23rd July of this year the Director of Education received a deputation representing 33 Glamorgan Inspectors, Educational Organisers and School Meals Organisers. They presented the Director with a letter bearing all their signatures, expressing deep dissatisfaction with the implementation of the Tenth Soulbury Report. The chairman advised us to write to you as Chairman of the Establishments Sub-Committee.

The basis of the case is that Inspectors and Organisers have, as a result of the Committee's implementation of the Report, lost ground in status and salary compared with other officers in the education service, both locally and nationally".

To County Alderman Phillip Squire, O.B.E.

Despite these non-conciliatory statements, the national acclaim for his work in music and the obvious experience and credibility which Russell Sheppard had earned for his general educational work, would make it impossible for his political masters to overlook his obvious and undeniable credentials for the post of Chief Adviser of Glamorgan to which he was appointed in 1972. When a disagreement related to his salary developed with the Mid Glamorgan LEA, he eventually pursued his own Statement of Appeal through NAIEA channels. This lengthy and occasionally acrimonious litigation began after reorganisation in 1974 and lasted until 1980. In 1974 Russell Sheppard's principal political protagonist, Lord Heycock transferred his allegiance to the new county of West Glamorgan and it is unlikely that Russell Sheppard's continued political and personal challenges would have made him exactly popular with Mid Glamorgan Authority's County Councillors. Be this as it may, when his retirement came in 1979, could it be possible that the memories of his then more elevated political masters might have militated against his receiving the national honours which those who worked with him seemed so passionately to have believed he deserved?

Not withstanding this conundrum, NAIEA, the association which he served with such distinction throughout his years as an inspector had earlier, in 1961 paid Russell Sheppard its ultimate and most prestigious honour - that of its Presidency. His presidential address - "Music in Education, Present Day Problems", was delivered at the Connaught Rooms in London.

Maxwell Evans a Glamorgan Advisory College who also worked closely in harness with Russell Sheppard in NAIEA and Mid Glamorgan has provided the following tribute :

The close liaison and understanding I had with Russell Sheppard came about in the first instance through his work for NAIEA. Russell was firmly embedded as one of the undisputed leaders of the Association having obviously made an ingression in that direction early on. In 1969, I found myself attending the national conference and in no time joining him on Executive Committee and at regional conferences. I have always been grateful to him for this additional dimension that he brought to my career.

From the time of his appointment as Chief Adviser, it became obvious that the emphasis would be on team work. From this there grew a valuable new approach when members from different sections would arrange to visit schools together. In addition to this new reports on primary and secondary education were thoroughly studied and analysed so that any worthwhile suggestions could be put into practice effectively. Russell was tireless. He would never be away from his work for long periods but enjoyed flying on short breaks with Karen to catch some winter sunshine.

His support for all his team was outstanding and he would never dodge the responsibility of reprimanding any member of the team whenever he considered this necessary; always in a discreet manner and avoiding any public embarrassment.

Regarding Russell Sheppard's views on music education, a separate book could be written based on the research of the many papers, lecture notes and addresses to public bodies and other organisations which he generated over the years. However, a synopsis of extracts from a few of these papers reveals a number of key facets and dimensions of his achievement, work, and overall philosophy.

His paper, "A Summary of Instrumental Music in Glamorganshire Schools", dated May 1949, indicates that he lost no time in making immediate contact with the authority's schools. Between February 14th and May 19th in the first year of employment as a Glamorgan Inspector he managed to visit no fewer than 31 Grammar Schools and 33 Modern Secondary Schools. His summary indicated that no instruction was being provided in primary schools, that teaching in the secondary schools was under-remunerated with teachers of strings receiving £10 per term for their services, that few instruments existed, many of which were in urgent need of repair or replacement and that tuition in the Modern Secondary Schools was inadequate.

Recognising, in the main, the importance of the LEA's commitment to a provision which had been sustained since the scheme came into being in 1926, Russell Sheppard took exception to the statement in the 1926 minute which read :

"That pupils on entering the school should be given the opportunity of learning during school hours, provided that they are willing to purchase instruments".

He argued vehemently that :

"No child should be deprived of this activity through inability to provide his own instrument".

Over the years he ensured that a range of instrumental tuition - wherever possible provided by full-time teachers or instructors - was available to all secondary schools and introduced string tuition in many primary schools. Large numbers of instruments were purchased for schools. By 1966, Russell Sheppard reported that about 3,000 pupils were receiving instrumental tuition in schools. By the time of this report, entitled "Music", all grammar and non-selective secondary schools were taking advantage of the County's Instrumental Scheme.

The same report indicates the importance which he gave to improving the situation with regard to pianos in schools :

"Music equipment has been provided to all schools which could benefit from it. Before 1949 the only schools which had been provided with pianos were a small number of new secondary schools. At all other schools the pianos had been obtained by a variety of means and the large majority of such pianos were second-hand when bought and very old. A survey made in 1949 revealed that 62 departments were without a piano of any kind while only 20% of those in the schools were stated to be in good condition".

Some of the replies to the questionnaire make interesting reading :

"Second hand. One leg missing. Worm-eaten.

Practically useless since pulled over by a cleaner.

Tuner states that it cannot be tuned.

No piano - only one harmonium of ancient vintage, about 1860.

Completely unserviceable - remains leant against the wall of the classroom as it cannot stand".

During the seven year period form 1949 to 1956, no less than 263 new or reconditioned pianos were supplied to schools and for a further ten year period about 20 pianos were supplied annually. His paper proudly reported that since 1953 only new pianos were supplied. The hall of each new secondary school was provided with a grand piano of medium size and an upright piano for the music room. Thus the status and credibility of school music was much enhanced by the progressive scheme of piano replacement he pioneered.

The many tracts written by Russell Sheppard embrace the complete spectrum of school and youth music. Lectures, conference addresses and council papers such as "Music in the Infant School" . "Music in the Junior Schools", "Music in Education in Glamorgan" and "Music in the Schools of Wales" had an unquestionable influence on educational thinking in the field of music in Glamorgan. At secondary level "Music in the Grammar School" and "Music in the General Education of the Sixth Form Pupil" were written in a progressive style which made abundantly clear his philosophy that the essentially practical nature of music education would be successful only if this performance experience was anchored to the pupils' progressive understanding and knowledge of the rudiments of music and music appreciation.

Several papers indicate that he was never shy of being at the sharp end of current debate on contentious aspects of music education. In October 1962 his response to a "Times Educational Supplement" article entitled "In Key", and based on The Schools Music Association Survey of music teaching in secondary schools, provides evidence of his determination and resolve to further the cause and credibility of music's place on the curriculum of schools. Arguing vehemently against the view that music might be best viewed as an "out of hours activity", he stated :

"Since the adoption of attitudes, informed or otherwise, by those who help to control the content and quality of education provided in our schools influences so vitally the treatment accorded to a subject - music in the case under consideration - it is necessary that differing viewpoints should receive adequate publicity and I sincerely trust that you will allow this".

His argument was consolidated by the following observation ;

"Many enlightened headmasters would argue eloquently concerning the intellectual, academic, aesthetic and social benefits to be derived from the inclusion of music as an integral part of the curriculum of a secondary school".

Russell Sheppard continued :

"It is highly debatable whether any subject can be successfully developed solely after school hours. Surely the rather precious attitude that the enjoyment of music would be killed by being taught to all pupils as a subject in the timetable would apply in the case of other worthwhile subjects. By enforcing this principle in similar situations we might find ourselves, slowly, but surely, in the position of recommending that the teaching of every subject to its own band of adherents

should take place after school hours in order that enjoyment should not suffer! What an absurd situation this would be, even if highly hypothetical".

The same argument would have been equally applicable thirty or so years later in the struggle to secure parity for music and art within the National Curriculum - an argument tragically lost in the case of drama.

This fundamentally egalitarian stance is a focal feature of his writing on the subject of music. It was perhaps most patently prevalent in the debate regarding giftedness and the appropriateness of Specialist Music Schools which followed the publication of the Gulbenkian Report : "Making Musicians". In response to an article, "Music and the Gifted" by Harold Sylvester, published in "Education" on 27th June 1969, and in reply to a request from Trevor Jenkins, Director of Education, Russell Sheppard penned one of his most individualistic and well - reasoned paper. He began :

"Proposals for developing Music Schools have emanated from interested bodies during the past few years for various reasons, most of which are not necessarily concerned with the needs of all children, but with a selected few to be educated in accordance with age, aptitude and ability".

Using the Plowden Report in support of his contrary stance, Russell Sheppard argued :

"In my view, the way to develop special aptitudes and abilities is to give special attention, as required by needs and circumstances, within the framework of general education in the pupil's own district".

He continued by quoting Page 366 of the Gittens report in support of his rationale :

"In the normal run of events we would prefer to see gifted children educated with other children, following enriched and accelerated programmes rather than being segregated".

Within Glamorgan he contended that :

"The musical development which has taken place has been achieved by giving special attention for children within their general education. This system can be improved, in my opinion, but not by the segregation of such children in residential schools far from their home environment".

Citing the complete range of centre and course activity as appropriate nurseries for the many professional musicians produced via the Glamorgan system he made reference to research he had undertaken that year, which indicated that of the 54% of the Glamorgan Youth Orchestra who wished to take up a career in music only 9% wished to become professional performers. In any case, he argues :

"It does not follow that because a child is musically gifted he or she will wish to take up a career in the profession of music either as a performer or teacher. Very often those who are musically gifted have general intelligence of a very high

order and choose careers, invariably more lucrative than music. Recently, a gifted oboist who had been trained through the Glamorgan Youth Orchestra took a first class degree in Physics at Cambridge. He could have done well in music, but chose another avenue for his career".

That same oboist, David Rayner Jones - a product of Neath Boys' Grammar School - did manage to combine a distinguished career as a university fellow and lecturer, with becoming a specialist in Baroque instrument making, and performing. David performed in many professional early music concerts and recordings.

As far as Shep was concerned QED!

Other papers discovered in research, although undated, were evidently written for In-Service courses for teachers in the Authority. They include "The Percussion Band", "The Teaching of Rhythm", "Teaching the Pianoforte to Classes", "Pianoforte Accompaniment" : "Introductory Lecture", "Music in the Junior School", "Music in the Youth Service", "Moods in Music" and "Music in Leisure : Youth". In the lecture on "Conducting", Shep gave a whole range of helpful hints for the intending conductor including the very practical axiom, "What is required is simplicity, economy of effort and, above all, clarity".

In the previously mentioned paper, "Music in the Grammar School", Russell Sheppard's creed concerning the less esoteric, but nevertheless kernel significance of music in education was nowhere better exemplified :

"Possibly the idea of educating for living and leisure has become hackneyed - but is still true. After all, the professional element in any sphere is comparatively small, but the amateur element quite large.

The social importance of music cannot be over-estimated. A school which cultivates its music seriously always displays good "tone". It is also true to say, I feel, that the school which gives serious attention to music invariably does well in the academic world also.The general "refining" influence of music upon those who partake is not always appreciated - it can pervade a school and affect other subjects favourably".

The Raising of the School Leaving Age to sixteen brought an instant response from Russell Sheppard, who, in a paper on the significance of music to a new generation of older pupils, provided a further insight into his mission statement for music education :

"The course should endeavour to equip pupils to appreciate music of all kinds. It should provide opportunities for those who want to make their own music to learn to play an instrument; the reading of music becomes an important aim of such a scheme. The more practical the approach the greater is the possibility of ensuring that music reading is seriously tackled. The child who has learnt to read his music immediately becomes self-sufficient and independent of the help of others (including teachers) when learning new work. He can then make his own musical discoveries and will become literate. The well-worn adage that there can

be no true appreciation without participation is certainly true in the teaching of music at all ability levels in the secondary school".

The visionary dimensions of his musical tenets anticipated Robert Witkin's influential book of the 1970s - "The Intelligence of Feeling". Russell Sheppard was fond of quoting two sentences from the "Education Handbook of Suggestions for Teachers" published in 1927, which reads :

"Music has, at all stages, a justification in itself because it allows children to give disciplined expression to feelings that are common to the groups of which they are members. The sense of unity which they express deepens the feelings and increases their delight in expressing them,".

In a single sentence, Russell Sheppard encapsulated much of the post-Paynter philosophies which would exercise a seminal influence on the declaration of the central importance of the creative dimensions of the arts curriculum embedded in the National Curriculum vis a vis music :

"Music is probably the most intensely emotional of all the arts and can, therefore, fulfil a deep human need".

Not for him the mindless machinations of some representatives of a later generation of avant-garde music educators who would attempt to throw out the baby in the form of the performance-led successes of many more traditional schools with the over-emphasised compositional bath water. Russell Sheppard's credo, based as it was on a deep sense of the achievable and founded on an unfathomable depth of practical experience, without doubt instilled into the vast majority of Glamorgan music teachers - over three decades - a feeling of forward-looking confidence.

Plate 50 - Orchestra comes of Age, 21st Anniversary
Ivy Morgan, a long serving member of course staff congratulates Russell Sheppard. Also in the picture are (from left to right) Bert and Ceinwen Davies, George (Tex) Hannaby, Jeffrey Francis, Alan James and Karen Sheppard

Plate 51 - Leader of the NYOW, Wendy Sheppard in conversation with Clarence Raybould
Other NYOW members are Alun Francis, Jonathan Williams, Trevor Herbert and Elizabeth Davies

Plate 52 - Leader of the NYOW, Patricia Sheppard shares a smile with Clarence Raybould

Plate 53 - Show me the way to go home!
A young Peter Sheppard ponders the best route home with his parents

Plate 54 - Design in Music - Karen Sheppard with one of her school orchestras - Leader: David Emanuel Also in the picture are Tex Hannaby, John Arthur Davies and Graham Watkins

Plate 55 - Portrait of a Family Man

7.

Recapitulation

§

1. The Family Man

§

And what is Heaven but a house, like every other one,
Where the homing man finds harbour and the hundred roads are done.

The Ballad of the Homing Man : Ernest Rees :

Upon his retirement in 1979, Russell Sheppard could not only look back on an abundantly successful career but also reflect, with a sense of pride, on the achievements of his wife and three children, all of whom, in their distinctive and different ways would also achieve success in their professional lives.

1979 was a year in which, during a period of industrial action, dustbins were left overflowing and hospitals turned away patients. Margaret Thatcher replaced James Callaghan as Prime Minister. As his retirement began, Russell Sheppard would have read of the terrorist bombs that killed both Airey Neave, Margaret Thatcher's senior aide and Earl Mountbatten. Whether or not he voted for a form of devolution for Wales in the referendum held in March is unknown, but it is likely that he would have read with great interest of the elevation of a former Bass singer in the Glamorgan Youth Choir, Neil Kinnock, to the position of Shadow Education Spokesman.

Russell Sheppard would almost certainly have been more interested in the West End premiere of Peter Schaffer's "Amadeus" than in the fact that amongst the "hits" from films of the year were "Bright Eyes " and the theme music from "The Deer Hunter" starring Robert Di Nero. The pictures sent back from Voyager 1 showing Jupiter's Rings, and news of the death of John Wayne and Sir Barnes Wallace would without doubt have been read with greater enthusiasm as he gradually - but not always contentedly - became accustomed to the new experience of leisure time - than the sporting headlines reporting Manchester United's 3-2 victory over Arsenal in the FA Cup final and the victories of Martina Navratilova and Seve Ballesteros at Wimbledon and the Open Golf Championships respectively. Plate 50

Penllwyn, a large, imposing house in Merthyr Mawr Road, Bridgend was home for the Sheppard family from Easter 1957. It was here that Wendy, Patricia and Peter grew up. Both girls made their early tentative attempts at violin and piano playing within its walls and Peter developed as a french horn player - all under the watchful eye of Russell and Karen. All became principal players in the Glam. There are few families who would produce such a trio of NYOW players.

Wendy led the NYOW in under the baton of Clarence Raybould in 1963. Plate 51.

Of Pat's leadership, three years later, Clarence Raybould wrote, in a letter to Russell Sheppard :

"I must write you a little note to tell you how entirely delighted I have been at our recent course at Swansea with the splendid work of your daughter Patricia. I found her always keen and intent and, in fact she proved herself a model leader.

You can be very proud and glad. May she have as happy a life as she deserves". Plate 52

A principal horn in both the Glam and the NYOW, Peter was a fine horn player who became a very close friend of Huw Jenkins and Roger Lewis. Roger's success in the media is featured in his foreword to this volume. Huw would become a leading professional horn player who, following a substantial period with the Philharmonia, has had an outstanding freelance career.

By a remarkable coincidence all three children studied in the north of England. Wendy qualified in music education at Bretton Hall College, and Pat and Peter also studied music in Yorkshire - at Hull University. For a period, their father was an external examiner at the nearby Teachers' Training College in Hull.

All three children have subsequently developed successful teaching careers. Wendy still teaches violin in Neath schools and was an Advisory Teacher for Strings. Both her children pursue music as a career. Karin Jenkins, who holds an MBA, has worked in the media and is currently a violin teacher in the Swansea area. She led the West Glamorgan Youth Orchestra and the Second Violin section of the NYOW. Also a principal of the West Glamorgan Orchestra and member of the NYOW, Mark is currently a double bass player in the National Symphony Orchestra of Ireland and is a tutor in the Royal Irish Academy of Music.

Pat is a very well respected Head of Music at Beverley High School, where her department has gained much critical acclaim both for the excellence of its academic work and for its outstanding orchestra and choirs. For many years she has also been leader of the Hull Philharmonic and the Beverley Chamber Orchestras. Pat is married to Robert Mitchell, a Head of Instrumental Services, who formed the Beverley Chamber Orchestra, conducts the East Riding Youth Orchestra and is a horn player. Both their children are violinists. Ceri, a music graduate is an Instrumental Teacher married to Gordon Peterson, another qualified musician. Siân is a principal player in the East Riding Youth Orchestra and, like the rest of her family, is a member of the Hull Philharmonic Orchestra.

Peter has continued the Sheppard tradition of marrying a musician/teacher, Janie. Both are successful teachers and live in Ystrad Mynach. Peter combines his duties as Head of Music with a career in broadcasting. He is a familiar voice reading the BBC Radio news and specialises as a bilingual sports' commentator. His authoritative commentaries on rugby are enjoyed every Saturday afternoon on the sports programme. Peter established and conducted the City of Cardiff Symphony Orchestra. Their young sons are developing successfully as instrumentalists. Gareth, like his cousin Mark, plays the double bass and Owen is learning percussion and the cello. Plate 53.

Those who mourned at the funerals of Karen and - three months later - Russell Sheppard would have been moved by the playing of Pachelbel's "Canon" by Karin, Ceri, Siân, Gareth and Mark. Several comments were made to the effect that both grandparents would have been extremely proud of their performances.

In his introduction to this volume, David Emanuel spoke eloquently of the inspiring nature of Karen Sheppard's work as a violin teacher. In the early years of her teaching role in Glamorgan she was a familiar figure in the Bridgend and Porthcawl area as she drove around in her bubble car. As Plate 54 indicates she developed several fine school ensembles and was a popular and admired teacher both at school and on the courses she attended as a tutor. In the later years of his life she lovingly looked after her nonagenarian, former sea captain father. Until the ravages of Parkinson's disease took their insidious toll in the final few years of her life, she ensured that the family maintained a close dialogue with her sister Betty and Russell's family - including Austen's wife Joan and her son Richard, and also with Beatrice, her husband Albert and their children John and Cynthia.

Old friendships were maintained especially with Bert and Ceinwen Davies from Ogmore School Camp and with several colleagues from Glamorgan and NAIEA. Their retirement enabled them to take holidays abroad and to enjoy extended visits to their children. Although he readily accepted invitations to attend concerts in the new Glamorgans and maintained, for a while, his examining role at Hull Training College, life would revolve more and more around the upkeep of Penllwyn and its gardens. Not the tidiest of men Russell Sheppard was an inveterate hoarder. Fortunately, his reluctance to throw virtually anything away has provided the author - who, incidentally, took many days to clear his study and to catalogue important compositions and documents - with a rich source of research material.

Throughout almost all of his period of retirement Russell Sheppard maintained strong connections with Tabernacle Chapel, Bridgend. He and his wife were regular members of the congregation and for many years he served the church loyally and with outstanding musicianship as its organist. He also made a vital contribution to plans to restore and refurbish the chapel organ and wrote several church compositions for the instrument. His love for composing pieces for family occasions is particularly in evidence in the "Ceremonial Marches" written for the weddings of his children. The arrangement of "Away in a Manger" - quoted overpage - was written late in 1985 when Russell and Karen stayed in Beverley. Known as "Taid" - the North Wales word for grandfather - Russell spent many happy hours encouraging his three and a half year old grand daughter, Siân to sing "Away in a Manger". This lovely arrangement for the Beverley High School Chamber Choir was the happy outcome.

Away in a Manger

For Sian

arranged for Beverley High School Chamber Choir

Russell Sheppard

49
S.
(pp)
care, And fit us for Hea - ven, to - live with thee there. Ah
S.
(pp)
care, And fit us for Hea - ven, to live with thee there. Ah
A.
care, And fit us for Hea - ven to live with thee
A.
care, And fit us for Heav'n, to live with thee
54
S.
Ah Hm
S.
Ah Hm
A.
(pp)
there. Ah Ah Hm Hm
A.
(pp)
there. Ah Ah Hm Hm
59
S.
rall. a tempo calando
Hm Hm
S.
rall. a tempo calando
Hm Hm
A.
rall. a tempo calando
Hm Hm
A.
rall. a tempo calando
Hm Hm Hm

The celebration to mark Russell and Karen's Golden Wedding was a happy and joyful occasion for the couple who also became great - grandparents to Chloe a little more than a year before their demise. Plate 55.

The author's fondest recollection of a man who was not always prepared to allow his natural good humour to come to the fore is taken from an extract of a certain father of the bride's speech made in 1965 :

"In due course, it was hinted to me that he intended to approach the conductor of the orchestra to suggest that he, as leader of the trumpet section, might be allowed to play a duet with the leader of the first violin section. I thought this was a bit odd, but I then remembered that he had already played solo with the orchestra in Purcell's "Trumpet Voluntary", and so I assumed that he wanted to play a duo so as to have some company. I wasn't far wrong as it turned out. But at the time I thought it rather unusual to have a trumpet playing a duet with a violin. You need a lot of violins to balance one trumpet - a dozen would be reasonable enough. But then I realised that anything would be a change from Haydn's Trumpet Concerto which all trumpet players play to death for want of something better.

What was to be the key of the the work they had in mind. Major without a doubt, the earlier part in Bb (probably a Wagner march) and the second also in the major key of C (possibly by Mendelssohn).

Nor did he want any cadenzas where each player could show off technical prowess because it might lead to bad blood between the duettists. The duet would be long, continuous and never ending.

And then it became as clear as daylight what sort of duet he had been talking about - a wedding of course but not with the hackneyed nuptial marches of Wagner and Mendelssohn. I'd simply have to write my own - con amore".

2. The Colleague

§

Now thirty - one years is a very long time
To put into words in five minutes,
To mention the hundreds of people you've known -
Musicians and songsters like linnets.
DEO's, AEO's - we've no notion
Of the number you've watched as they've scrambled to climb
Up the ladder of speedy promotion.

Poem on RJS's retirement
as Chief Educational Adviser : Maxwell Evans

Of the many tributes received from Russell Sheppard's collegues, two, in particular, seem to encapsulate the respect and admiration felt by those who worked with him in the educational and artistic arena.

The Reverend Maxwell Evans, who spoke so tellingly at the funerals of both Russell Sheppard and his wife Karen, has penned a poignant, and yet realistic, portrait of his colleague's educational overview :

"When Russell Sheppard retired in September 1979 he had served the Glamorgan LEA, and, from 1974, the Mid Glamorgan Authority for over thirty years as the Organiser for Music, Inspector and finally Chief Adviser.

It was my privilege to work with Russell for over eleven years and although my immediate superior as a Welsh Organiser was Mr. Lewis Angel, I soon found myself in close association and understanding with Russell Sheppard. He was tireless in his work and completely dedicated in his service to the Local Educational Authorities. Others will tell of his tremendous contribution to the success of music in the Authority. The quality of the concerts staged will never be forgotten.

Even before his appointment as Chief Adviser, Russell's relationship with colleagues was unique. Many benefited from a chat with him, knowing full well that any confidence would never be betrayed and whether his advice was accepted or not, in the final instance he would always be at hand to lend a friendly ear.

As Chief Adviser, Russell was always available to discuss any problems or ideas and many of us affectionately remember late night, midnight and early morning calls! His strong personality was further enriched by his gentlemanly sense of humour.

I know I can speak confidently for all my colleagues when I say that it was an honour to have known and worked with Russell Sheppard".

Maxwell Evans was appointed as a Welsh and Bilingual Organiser in 1968, becoming Senior Adviser for Languages and Religious Education after the 1974 reorganisation. In this role he successfully pioneered Welsh Medium Education and the establishment of two Welsh Medium Comprehensive Schools. President of the Welsh Branch of NAIEA and Press and Publicity Officer of the Association nationwide, he returned to church work following his retirement. He was made an honorary member of the Gorsedd of Bards for his contribution to Welsh Education and Culture.

Another artistic and educational friend and colleague of Russell Sheppard, Godfrey Evans, became a very widely revered figure in the dance and drama education world. Following eleven years of teaching, he was appointed County Adviser in Drama and Dance for West Glamorgan where, amongst his other duties in schools, colleges and the community, he directed the County Youth Theatre and County Youth Dance Companies. In the mid 1970's he worked with the author on a number of highly acclaimed West Glamorgan Youth Arts Company productions. His work as a theatre director has ranged from Shakespeare to Brecht, Pinter, Opera and Musicals. He has lectured for the University of Wales, the Welsh College of Music and Drama, Gorseinon College and for the Welsh Office and has been a member of the Welsh Arts Council's Drama, Dance and Regional Committees. He now works as an education consultant, lecturer and theatre director.

That Godfrey Evans struck up a close professional association with Russell Sheppard is evident in a tribute made after the latter's death :

"Early in 1966 I was invited to direct that summer's National Eisteddfod schools' performance. I accepted : what twenty - five year old would turn down the opportunity to work with professional singers, a cast of five hundred, a substantial production budget, and the BBC Welsh Orchestra? The choice of production had already been made - Purcell's "Dido ac Aeneas" - and whilst this was never stated, it was clear that the choice had been made by the conductor, Russell Sheppard. So there I was, a very junior teacher, partnered with one of Wales' most experienced musicians, educationalists and administrators.

Our first meeting was at Ogmore where Russell Sheppard was leading an orchestral course. Over tea and biscuits - for which I was expected to pay - we mapped out our work. I don't remember the meeting as being particularly one - sided; from the start, it was clear that whilst he was the senior partner, he wasn't going to pull rank. At the same time he was generous with his advice and went to the heart of the challenge that would face me in co-ordinating the work of many older and more experienced teachers, designers and Eisteddfod personnel - "Godfrey", he said, "you must practice the art of professional distance". It was sound advice which I tried to digest as I fumbled my way through the Byzantine, but usually genuine, sensitivities of the varied colleagues with whom I would work over the next six months.

At an artistic level I was worried that "Dido ac Aeneas" was not, at first glance, suited to the performance scale of the Eisteddfod pavilion or the vast chorus of primary and secondary pupils. I suggested re-thinking the opera in a Greek theatre style. Russell Sheppard accepted the idea with enthusiasm and this led to us exploring ways of expanding the performance length so that it would fill a whole evening.

Could we devise a dance prologue which would contextualise, for a modern audience, Virgil's tale of the Greek Prince and Princess of Carthage? Russell Sheppard fell on this idea with energy and immediately suggested using Britten's Peter Grimes Sea Interludes" as the music for the dance work. It was a brilliant idea; we were using Britten's version of Purcell's opera and "Sea Interludes" were a most exciting stimulus for the choreography of our prologue to be danced by the boys of Sandfields Comprehensive School.

The way the prologue was evolved characterised the way Russell Sheppard and I were to work over the next months - ideas bounced from one to the other and underpinning the creative work his vast experience and pragmatism helped me to get from idea to rehearsal and then to performance. He relentlessly insisted on thinking through the implementation of each production idea - what would it mean in rehearsal terms, would it encourage the maximum involvement of pupils and teachers? The quality of children's experience had to be our first priority, he rightly insisted.

This principle was summed up in one other piece of advice Russell Sheppard gave to me - "never ask anyone to do anything unless you are ninety per cent certain he is going to say Yes". At first glance, this might seem to be a management ploy; maybe it is, but in focusing on the likely response it places the individual at the heart of all decisions. Russell Sheppard knew that good teams are made up of motivated, positive and fulfilled players and that they are led by integrity and kindness.

"Dido ac Aeneas" was a success though I never worked as closely with Russell Sheppard again. "You know" he told my mother when they met after the performance, "Godfrey and I never had a cross word". He seemed surprised. We kept in regular contact over the years. He supported my work from a distance and attended many of the performances I directed. The personal message on his 1998 Christmas card reads, in retrospect, like a goodbye as he remembered 1966 and our "hands on" work together : "practical methods", he wrote, were the basis of excellence. Russell Sheppard found the balance between art and administration, between consistency and flexibility, saying "yes" in January 1966 changed my life".

8.
Coda
§

O spirit of music and wonder and passion
Flood with thy rapture our derelict valleys,
And give unto men the motion to action,
The impulse to build what is worthy of man.

Capel Hebron : Idris Davies

Because of the author's family relationship to Shep it seemed more appropriate and objective to cite the more detached eulogies written by others who respected his musicianship and organising panache. These are written by his former lecturer, a leading conductor, by probably his closest working colleague and musical standard-bearer and by two Glam members - who later became collegues and whose lives and careers ran in tandem with his tenure in Glamorgan.

Firstly, writing in March 1966 Professor Joseph Morgan commented :

"I have known Mr. Sheppard since his undergraduate days and have followed his career with interest and admiration. The Departmental records remind me that he was clearly the best student of his year. His subsequent year in the Teacher Training Department was also unusually successful and he got a First Class in the Tests of Practical Skill, a rare achievement.

In 1948 he was appointed to a responsible post under the Glamorgan Education Authority and, since then, I have been able to observe the results of his enthusiasm and energetic (but diplomatic) approach to the many and varied tasks attached to the post. Most importantly, he has brought about the position in which every grammar, secondary and comprehensive school in his area has at least one fully qualified teacher of music on its staff, and a complete range of peripatetic teachers providing instrumental instruction.

He has organised regular residential courses and presented choral and instrumental works in public concerts of a very high standard.

Many of the pupils trained in the Glamorgan schools have come on to this University College and I can testify to the fact that, they have achieved much success in both theoretical and practical work".

The conductor of the National Youth Orchestra of Wales, Clarence Raybould, who created, moulded and honed the orchestra - the first of its type in the world - summarised his respect and admiration in a letter, dated 26th March 1966 :

"I know of no-one more fitted for the job, for without your wise guidance and help in your post as Inspector of Schools in Glamorgan, it would have been quite impossible for the NYOW to carry on in the way it has done. Wales should be very grateful for the invaluable work you have so long been doing for the youth of Glamorgan in the building-up, over nearly twenty years, of the great revival of Welsh instrumental music".

The outstanding contribution of Stanley Jones to Glamorgan (not forgetting West Glamorgan) Youth music was featured in Chapter 3. In Stanley's view :

"Russell Sheppard created and directed the Glamorgan Youth Choir and for most of his conductorship I was honoured to have been given the opportunity to work at his side. Always concerned that every detail of course and concert preparation should be meticulously accomplished he was an inspiration to staff and students alike.

The repertoire of the choir was second to none and he encouraged many young singing talents. Students like Della Jones, Stuart Kale, Dennis O' Neill, Beverley Humphreys and many more sang early solos in ambitious choral works with the Glam before developing outstanding opera careers. For his work in youth music and in the development of a whole range of schools' music - including the use of the recorder in schools - he will always be remembered".

Jeffrey Francis pinpoints the significant influence of Shep's heritage on the new Glamorgans : "Mr. Sheppard's influence on my work as Music Adviser in Mid Glamorgan - as it was for Helena Braithwaite and John Jenkins in South and West Glamorgan respectively - was inestimable".

Jeffrey Francis' indebtedness was further crystallised in the letter he sent on September 30th, 1979 to mark Shep's retirement from the post of Chief Adviser:

Dear Mr. Sheppard,

I feel it would be very remiss of me not to express in writing the very great debt I owe you.

Looking back over the years, it is obvious that my life was greatly influenced by the formation of the Glamorgan Youth Orchestra in 1949, for, like many others, the regular opportunities to play orchestral music resulted in my choice of career associated with music.

Later being a tutor with the senior orchestra and the regional orchestra at Neath gave me invaluable experience which was of immediate use in my early days of teaching. Little did I realise at the time how useful all this "inside" information would be some years later.

Since my present appointment I know that I had your unfailing support and guidance. Despite your own very heavy work load, you have always found time to discuss any problems which have arisen and invariably you have been able to provide a solution.

I would like you to know how very grateful I am for all your help and kindness over the last seven years in particular.

I also wish to thank Mrs. Sheppard for always giving me such a warm welcome whenever I have visited your home.

Wishing you a happy and active retirement.

Very sincerely,

Jeffrey

Finally, former Glam and NYOW leader, Jeffrey Lloyd, who later conducted both the South Glamorgan Youth Orchestra and the Rhondda Symphony Orchestra, has captured the feelings of generations of young musicians who came under Shep's musical spell. He has also crystallised the incredulous amazement of many who remain perpetually puzzled by the staggering omission of Russell Sheppard from any form of national recognition :

"Russell Sheppard was, without doubt, a most formidable champion in the field of music education throughout Wales. His pioneering work in the field of instrumental tuition throughout the schools of the old administrative county of Glamorgan sent audible shock waves through the county which are still reverberating to the present day.

He was an educational luminary whose vision of music as a homogeneous element in the overall educational scheme enriched the lives of thousands of young people. The county youth orchestra bestowed upon youngsters throughout the county the privilege of performing the works of the great composers. These were largely ordinary kids from ordinary homes; the odious and socially divisive label of elitism simply did not apply.

Each orchestral course was eagerly awaited and became an integral part in life's pattern. Such was the impact of these courses that on the mournful morrow of departure, a touching torrent of tears was released as heady, new-born courtships were temporarily suspended, and many of the overtly enthusiastic Glam devotees simply would not let the course evaporate. Bridgend bus station, the anguish point of dispersal, suddenly erupted with impromptu jam sessions as the brass players entertained queues of unsuspecting passengers to a free concert. As I lived but a few miles north of Bridgend, my ever resourceful mother regularly expected, and received a motley gang of Ogmore refugees. Invariably the names of Mark Roberts, Picc Axtell, Tony Randall, Benj Thomas,Vivian E. Davies and many others were on the guest list at our humble Sarn council house. We lads simply could not sever that umbilical cord which still tenaciously connected us to our beloved Ogmore.

As a young raw recruit I regarded Mr.Sheppard (even now I am unable to address him less formally) with an almost tangible degree of awesome fear; but, over the years, I began to relax more in his presence. And whilst he constantly strove to maintain the stiff upper lip of propriety, the mask did once slip.The occasion was a rehearsal of "Lo, Hear the Gentle Lark" for soprano and virtuoso flute obligato. As the dulcet tones of the superb soloist Sylvia Thomas began to falter, the ever alert Mr.Sheppard looked up to behold the most bizarre spectacle of flautist and zany comedian, Michael Axtell playing brilliantly but with the mouthpiece of his flute precariously positioned directly under his nose! Totally bereft of his innate reserve, Mr.Sheppard dissolved freely into paroxysms of pure laughter.

A man of utmost honesty and integrity who would never compromise on the high professional standards he set for himself, Russell Sheppard could be quite adroit when he perceived shoddiness and lack of commitment in others. This may well have invited the opprobrium of a few lofty dignitaries, but it earned him the eternal respect of his friends and colleagues. His conspicuous absence from any inclusion in an Honours List defies belief. Thankfully, however, this dignified gentleman, who never sought for himself the limelight and plaudits yearned for (and frequently received) by lesser men, has left an incredible legacy which cannot be equalled. And there can be no finer honour".

Never fully accepted or appreciated by the representatives of the Welsh musical establishment, Russell Sheppard thought little and cared even less about official acknowledgement. This was confirmed in several conversations in the final weeks of his life. Asked whether or not he was disappointed at not having received the plaudits of officialdom, he retorted with a wry smile, "Don't you think that the honour of being able to conduct such wonderful young people was honour enough?"

Touché! There could be no other reply to that simple, yet sincere question. It befalls few people in the world of music education to be offered the challenge of creating an institution. It befits even fewer to so richly fulfil that ambition and to become a revered legend for so many musicians. Undeniably, the dream lives on in the youth music making of a now much segmented Glamorgan. Unequivocally, even though the present generation of players and singers may not even know his name, Shep's vision is vibrantly alive in schools and music centres across South Wales. Although it remains a tragedy that much of the structure of residential education which he held so dear has evaporated like the sea mists over Ogmore bay, the spirit of Russell Sheppard's inspirational creation lives on. I, like countless others can still, in my mind's eye, see Shep rehearsing and directing his ensembles. An indescribable inner ear still resounds to the chords and climactic cadences of the Glam - fresh and fantastic today as they have been over half a century. Like Idris Davies all who played and sang in the Glam must surely feel that :

The theatre shall never be empty.
For in the auditorium the echoes linger
And never completely die away.

The Glam

Key Dates

1949 First course by the Glamorgan Youth Orchestra Duffryn House (39 players). Concert held at Glamorgan Training College on Friday 23rd September.

1952 First Brass course, held at Duffryn House - tutor Leonard Davies,Manchester

1953 Coronation Concert held on July 8th at Duffryn House
First appearance of a "full" symphony orchestra; concert at Town Hall, Maesteg.

1958 July 9th : Festival of Wales Concert at Gwyn Hall, Neath.
July 29th : Concert for the Duke of Edinburgh at County Hall, Cardiff - Commonwealth Games.
Qualiton recording of works performed.

1959 Tenth Anniversary Concerts - Penarth, Aberdare, Bargoed, Bridgend.

1960 First Youth Choir courses :-
September 12th - St. Martin' Church Caerphilly - County Grammar Schools Choir
- "Hiawatha's Wedding Feast"
December 30th - Title Glamorgan Youth Choir used for the first time.

1962 May 15th - Duffryn House concert in the presence of HRH the Princess Royal.
Formation of the East Glamorgan Section : Youth Brass Band.
September 5th - first concert by Youth Choir at Russell Sheppard's own church - St.Margaret's Mountain Ash.

1963 February 28th : Combined Bands perform at the St. David's Festival - Sophia Gardens, Cardiff.
April 16th : BBC Recording of Youth Choir and Orchestra from LLandaff Cathedral.

1965 September 3rd : Performance of "Toward The Unknown Region" by Vaughan Williams at St.Elvan's Church. Russell Sheppard studied the organ at this church as a boy and, in 1930, heard Vaughan Williams conduct the work at nearby Cwmaman.
September 5th : "Songs of Praise" TV recording of Choir and Orchestra from St.Margaret's Parish Church, Mountain Ash.
Formation of the West Glamorgan Section : Brass Band.

1966 September 1st -15th - Youth Orchestral tour of Western Slovakia. Soloists Della Jones (Soprano), Stuart Kale (Tenor) and Gordon Back(Piano).

1967 August/September : Concert tour of Wales by the Bratislava Conservatory Orchestra.
September 11th - 22nd : Tour of Western Slovakia by the a section of the County Choir.

1969 September 4th - Investiture Celebration Concert at Sandfields Comprehensive School.
County Band Performs at Cardiff Castle.

1970 July 20th and 21st : First performances of the Verdi "Requiem"
September 4th and 5th : 21st Birthday Concerts at Ystrad Mynach and Sandfields School.

1971 March 26th : Orchestra and Choir perform at a concert organised by the Schools Music Association at the Royal Festival Hall, London.

1972 January 4th : Russell Sheppard 's final concert as sole conductor of the Choir and Orchestra.

1974 January 4th :Final concert given by the Glamorgan Youth Choir and Orchestra : Gwyn Hall, Neath.

The Glam - A Few examples of the achievements former members

1. National "Personalities"

David Emanuel	Choir	International Fashion Designer/Couturier and TV presenter
Ioan Gruffudd(SG)	Orchestra	Actor
Edwina Hart (Thomas)	Orchestra	Politics : Welsh Assembly : Finance Director
Neil Kinnock	Choir	Former Leader of the Labour Party: European Commissioner
Tony Lewis	Orchestra	Captain of Glamorgan, England Cricket Teams,Broadcaster, Chairman : Wales Tourist Board etc
Cerys Mathews(WG)	Orchestra	Singer, Composer : Catatonia
Mary Hopkin	Choir	Singer
JPR Williams	Orchestra	International Rugby Player/Coach. Doctor

2. Media, etc.

Jay Alexander(WG)	Arts.Co.	Musical Director-West End Shows, TV.
Kevin Allen (WG)	Arts.Co.	Director " Twin Town", "The Big Tease"etc.
Lisa Barsi(MG)	Choir	TV Broadcaster
Mansel Bebb	Orchestra	Orchestral Manager : Philharmonia
Helena Braithwaite	Orchestra	Formerly Education and Community Officer BBC NOW
Raymond Bowden	Orchestra	Stockbroker, Chairman of the Wine Club
Huw Chiswell(WG)	Orchestra	Commissioner for Light Entertainment S4C
Brian Clarke	Orchestra	Lecturer
Andrew Connelly	Orchestra	Orchestral Manager : RPO
Hywel Davies	Orchestra	AVS Records
Wayne David	Orchestra	Former MEP
Prof. Bleddyn Davies	Orchestra	LSE
Mari Emlyn(MG)	Orchestra	Actress
John Evans	Orchestra	Head of Radio 3
Kenfin Evans	Orchestra	Formerly Educational Computer Software Services
Adrian Evett	Orchestra	Orchestral Manager : BBC Concert Orchestra
Kenneth George	Orchestra	Lecturer LSE
Siwan Geraint(MG)	Orchestra	TV Production
Griff Harris	Orchestra	Orchestral Manager :National Chamber Orchestra of Wales
Alun Hughes	Choir	BBC Producer
Alun Hughes	Orchestra	Music Retail : Boosey and Hawkes
Menai Williams	Orchestra	Broadcaster
Beverley Humphreys	Orch/Choir	Broadcaster
Mari Griffiths	Orchestra	Broadcaster
Ffion Jenkins(SG)	Orchestra	Wife of William Hague (Leader of the Opposition)
Carolyn Hitt(MG)	Choir	Reporter TV: Presenter
Ian M. James	Orchestra	Consultant : British Performing Arts Trust
Martin Jenkins	Orchestra	Businessman
Alun John	Choir	BBC Producer
Kevin Johns(WG)	Choir	Broadcaster, Comedian, Actor.
Steven John	Orchestra	Librarian BBC NOW
David Rayner Jones	Orchestra	Lecturer Cantab; Specialist in Baroque Oboes
Siwan Jones	Orchestra	TV Presenter
Roger Lewis	Orchestra	Formerly Head President of Decca, Managing Director and Programme Controller Classic FM
Paul Loveluck	Choir	Formerly Chief Executive Wales Tourist Board Chief Executive, Countryside Council for Wales
Alan Milosovic	Orchestra	Businessman
Andrew O'Neil(WG)	Orchestra	Broadcaster
Jonathan Ormrod(WG)	Orchestra	Manager : Birmingham Royal Ballet
Nicholas Ormrod(WG)	Orch/Choir	Professor of Medieval History : York University
Penelope Ryan	Choir	College Principal
Susanne Smith	Choir	Former Headteacher : PR Consultant
Emyr Walters	Orchestra	Capital Radio
Sara Thomas(MG)	Orchestra	Librarian WNO
Robert Suff(WG)	Orchestra	Record Producer
Prof. Malcolm Williams	Orchestra	ENT Specialist - Kingston, Ontario

3. Composers

Karl Jenkins	John Mills(WG)	Christopher Painter(WG)	John Quirk(WG)
Anthony Randall	John Ray	Rhian Samuel	Hilary Tann
Wayne Warlow	Gareth Wood	Mark Thomas	Ceri Torjusson(S

4. HMI : Music

Gareth Adams	Orchestra
Haydn Davies	Orchestra
Robert Swain	Orchestra

5. Music Advisers

Kevin Adams	Orchestra	ESIS
Helena Braithwaite	Orchestra	South Glamorgan
Haydn Davies	Orchestra	Gwynedd
Ioan Davies	Orchestra	Wiltshire
Jeffrey Francis	Orchestra	Mid Glamorgan
D.James	Orchestra	Winchester
John Jenkins	Orchestra	West Glamorgan
Christopher Jones(WG)	Orchestra	Cardiff
Eric Jones	Orchestra	Montgomeryshire
Alun Williams	Orchestra	Monmouthshire

6. Advisory Teachers : Music - Heads of Instrumental Services

Kevin Adams	Orchestra	Merthyr Tydfil
Mostyn Davies	Orchestra	Cardiff and The Vale
Graham Dyer	Orchestra	Caerphilly
Phillip Emanuel(WG)	Orchestra	C.C Swansea/Neath and Port Talbot CBC
John Esaias	Orchestra	Oxfordshire
Gillian Harrison(Jones)	Orchestra	Neath-Port Talbot CBC : Arts Advisory Teacher
David Hughes	Orchestra	Bridgend County Borough
Wendy Jenkins(Sheppard)	Orchestra	West Glamorgan
Jeffrey Lloyd	Orchestra	South Glamorgan
D.A.Small	Orchestra	West Glamorgan
Leigh Thomas	Orchestra	
Alun Thomas	Alun F.Williams	Martyn Owen(WG)

7. Opera Singers

Principals with Welsh National Opera

1970 - 1985		Number of roles
Susan Dennis	Choir	1
Marion Davies	Choir	1
Mary Davies	Choir	15
Ryland Davies	Choir	2
Meryl Drower	Choir	3
Jean Evans	Choir	5
Helen Field	Choir	19
Maureen Guy	Choir	3
Beverley Humphreys	Choir/Orch	1
Gillian Humphreys	Choir	1
Della Jones	Choir/Orch	1
Stuart Kale	Choir/Orch	8
Geoffrey Moses	Choir/Orch	9
Dennis O'Neill	Choir/Orch	5
Kelvin Thomas	Choir	1

1985 -

Catrin David(SG)
Dianne Fuge(WG)
Gail Pearson(WG)
Rebecca Evans(WG)
Vaughan Howells(WG)
Geraint Roberts(WG)
Ros Evans(WG)
Anthony Stuart Lloyd(SG)

Other Opera Principals/Professional Singers

Karl Daymond(WG)
Ceris Deverill(MG)
Paul Harrhy(WG)
Darren Jones(MG)
Josephine Jones(MG)
Kenneth Lewis(MG)
Anthony Stuart Lloyd(SG)
Tim Morgan(MG)
Wyn Pencarreg(SG)
Elen ap Roberts(SG)
Lesley Roberts
Susanna Tudor Thomas(SG)
Valerie Heath Davies
Christopher Evans(WG)
Nicola Humphries(SG)
Eldrydd Cynan Jones(MG)
Rosemary Joshua(SG)
Catrin Ley (WG)
Peter Lodwig
Stephen Mullen(SG)
Penny Munden
Geraint Roberts(WG)
Jeffrey Lloyd Roberts(MG)
Jeremy Williams(SG)
Catrin Davies(SG)
Dyfed Evans(SG)
David Gwestyn Jones(MG)
Iona Jones(SG)
Jean Lewis
Mark Luther(MG)
Geraint Miles(WG)
Gill Nalder(WG)
Huw Priday(WG)
Carys Lloyd Roberts (SG)
Sylvia Thomas
Kate Woolveridge(SG)

8.Professional Conductors/Musical Directors

Jay Alexander (WG)
Wyn Davies
Gareth Jones(WG)
Anthony Randall
Geoffrey Arnold
Iwan Evans(SG)
Grant Llewellyn(MG)) -Student Cond.
Wayne Warlow
Nick Davies(MG)
Alun Francis
John Quirk(WG)

9. Professional Players/Accompanists (all Orchestra)

Violin

Phillip Aird(MG)
Robert Bird (MG)
Katie Clarke(WG)
Timothy Crossland(WG)
Clive Dobbins
David Emanuel
Helen Griffith (MG)
Leonard James
Peter Jones(MG)
Jeffrey Lloyd
Sian Owens (MG)
Frances Richards(MG)
Eifion Price (Folk Music)
Hilary Squire
Clive Thomas
Robert Tonkin(WG)
Sharon Williams (WG)
Denise Bassett
Helen Brown (MG)
Susan Croot(WG)
Carl Darby
Adrian Eales(MG)
Selyf Edwards(Folk Music)(WG)
Cicely Holliday
Catherine Hughes - Jones
Peter Leighton Jones(MG)
Patricia Mitchell(Sheppard)
Eluned Owens (SG)
Edward Roberts
David Protheroe
Geraint Tellem(MG)
David Thomas
Alan Titherington(WG)
Mansell Bebb
John Canter
Huw Davies(SG)
Hywel Davies
Elin Edwards(MG)
Dale Evans(MG)
Gerald Hopkin(MG)
Juliet Leighton Jones(MG)
Bethan Leach(MG)
Phillip Morgan
Martin Patterson
Nigel Rowlands(MG)
Clare Salaman(SG)
Alun Thomas(MG)
Mark Thomas(WG)
Richard Wilde(MG)

Viola

Christopher Ashmead
Andrew Beasley(WG)
Stephen Burnard(WG)
Eirlys Gravell(WG)
Richard Mainwaring(WG)
Alison Phillips(WG)
Susan Salter
Simon Aspell(WG)
Stephen Begley(MG)
Karen Demmell(WG)
Enid Griffiths
David McKelvay(MG)
Wynford Potter(WG)
Brian Thomas
Nicholas Barr(SG)
Stephen Broom
David Emanuel(WG)
Stephen Lloyd (WG)
Gordon Mepham
Nigel Rowlands(MG)

Cello

Hilary Boothby(MG)
Catrin Davies (SG)
Geraint John
Judith Rees (WG)
David Watkin (WG)
Brian Clarke
Huw Davies(SG)
Gethyn Jones(WG)
Julia Tucker(MG)
Dewi Watkins
Elizabeth Davies
Christopher Hodges(MG)
Claire Lacy(MG)
Richard Weigold(MG)
Meirion Williams

Bass

Albert Dennis(WG)
Robert Ferris
David Parr
Michael Welsby(MG)
Gareth Wood
Rachel Gronow(WG)
Ashley Frampton
Alan Shimell
Alun Williams
Jonathan Francis(MG)
Mark Jenkins(WG)
Julian Walters(WG)
Stephen Williams(MG)

Flute

Michael Axtell
Paul Griffiths
Delyth John(MG)
Griff Harries
Susan Buckland (Higgens) (WG)
Neil Harries
Hilary Jones(MG)
Phillip Emanuel
Christopher Harding(MG)
Susan Thomas(MG)

Oboe

John Anderson
Graham Dyer
Karl Jenkins
Christopher Cowey(SG)
John Esaias
Sian Davies(WG)
Mark Howells(WG)

Clarinet

John Hempenstall
Janet Griffiths
Alun Williams(WG)
Carolyn Hier(MG)
James Mainwaring(WG)
Verity Fielding (SG)
Paul Price(WG)

Bassoon

Martin Bowen(WG)
Peter Morgan
Adrian Evett
David Rees
Martin Locke(WG)

Saxophone

Griff Harries(WG)
James Mainwaring(WG)
Lisa Hill (WG)
Osian Roberts(SG)
Karl Jenkins
David Pritchard

Horn

Vivian E. Davies
Robert Evans(SG)
Duncan Gwyther (WG)
Huw Jenkins(WG)
David Lewis (WG)
David Pritchard
Stephanie Rees(WG)
Jonathan Dempster (WG)
Alun Francis
Nigel Hiscock(WG)
Terence Johns
Richard Martin (G)
Anthony Randall
Huw Evans(WG)
Simon Griffiths (MG)
David Hughes
John V. Jones
Simon Morgan(MG)
Alun Rees(WG)

Trumpet

Andrew Cuff
Laurence Evans
David James
Gareth Rees(MG)
D.A.Small
Lawrence Davies
Martin Evans(SG)
Jonathan Mainwaring(WG)
Robert Samuel(WG)
Christopher Turner(WG)
Michael Downing(WG)
Andrew George(WG)
Rhys Owens (MG)
Gareth Small(WG)

Trombone

Roger Argente(WG)
Phillip Dando
Phillip Dodderidge(WG)
John Davies(WG)
Jeffrey Evans
Colin Gummer
Daniel Hannaby
John Hendy
Greg Morgan
Bryan Raby
Jeff Pearce
Robert Price(MG)

Tuba

Andrew Cresci(WG)
Stephen Follant(WG)
Huw Jones
Andrew Jones(WG)
Kevin Morgan(MG)
Jonathan Rees(WG)

Other Leading Brass Band Players

Andrew Cheek
Joanne Dean
Jimmy Davies
Dereck Holvey
Anna Hughes
Gareth Key
Loyd Landry
Clive Purnell
Robert Westacott
Wyn Williams

Harp

Rachel Davies (WG)
Ann Griffiths
Rachel Jones (SG)
Shân Jones(WG)
Margaret Rees
Katherine Thomas(MG)

Percussion

Helen Bool(MG)
Richard Buckley(WG)
Christopher Evans(WG)
David Griffiths(SG)
Sean Hooper
John Jeffreys
Jonathan Morgan (MG)
Nicholas Ormrod(WG)
Christopher Thomas(SG)
Timothy Wright(MG)

Guitar/Lute

Stephen Goss(WG)
David Miller

Full - time professional pianists/accompanists

Gordon Back
Cynthia Coombes
Arnold Draper
Geoff Eales
Heather James(Lewis)
Phillip Thomas(WG)

Keyboards

Patrick Seymor :Eurythmics (WG)Geoff Eales

10 Authors

John Cross(SG)
David Emanuel(Orch/Choir)
John Evans(Orch)
Adrian Evett (Orch)
Diana Griffiths(Orch)
Trevor Herbert (Orch)
Tony Lewis (Orch)
Neil Kinnock (Choir)

11. Conductors of Amateur Ensembles

Amateur Operatic Societies

Barry OAS	Mark Roberts	
Footlights	Norman Harries	
Maesteg OAS	Alun Jones	
Melyncrythan OAS	Mair Lewis	
Mid Rhondda OAS	Paul Williams	Diana Llewellyn
Neath OAS	Rhian Evans(WG)	
Neath Opera Group	Edward John(WG)	
Cadoxton OAS	Alan James	Christopher Jones John Jenkins

Brass Bands

Briton Ferry	Jeffrey Pierce		
Glynneath	Eric James		
Penclawdd	D.A.Small		
Parc and Dare	Ieuan Morgan		

Male Choirs

Aberafan	Huw Morgan	Phillip Juliff(MG)	
Caernarfon	Haydn Davies		
Côr Meibion De Cymru	Alun John		
Dowlais	John Samuel		
Dublin Welsh	Jonathan Williams		
Dynfant	Arwyn Jones		
Ferodo	Haydn Davies		
Glynneath	Enfys Brown(Davies)		
Hong Kong	Brian Clarke		
London Welsh	Haydn James		
Past Ogmore Choir	Glyn Price		
Pontarddulais	Noel Davies		
Pontypridd Male Voice Choir	Jonathan Gulliford(MG)		
Rhos Cwmtawe	Glyn Williams	John Jenkins	
Treorchy	John Cynan Jones	John Jenkins	Andrew Badham

Other Choirs

Aberystwyth	Haydn Davies		
Ardwyn Singers	Helena Braithwaite		
Barry Choral Society	Peter Rees		
Cowbridge Choral Society	David Cynan Jones		
Neath Municipal Choir	John Jenkins		
Bro Nedd	Terence Lloyd		
Bro Ogwr	Alun John		
Trebanos Mixed Choir	Lawrence Bowen		

Amateur/Semi Professional Orchestras

**** denotes founder***

Cardiff Symphony Orchestra	Peter Sheppard*		
Cardiff Philharmonic	Michael Bell(WG)*		
Gower Orchestra	Hugh Morris Jones		
Neath Symphony	John Jenkins*	Alan Good	Alan Lockyer
Rhondda Symphony	Jeffrey Lloyd*	Kevin Adams	
Pontypridd Choral/Orchestra Soc	Haydn Davies	Jeffrey Ryan(MG)	
South Glamorgan YO	Jeffrey Lloyd*	Eric Phillips(WG)	
Swansea Sound Sinfonia	John Jenkins*		
Welsh Philharmonic	Michael Bell Alan Good Jeffrey Lloyd	Wyn Davies Timothy Jones	Phillip Emanuel John Jenkins
Mid Glamorgan YO	Jeffrey Francis*		
South Glamorgan YO	Jeffrey Lloyd*	Eric Phillips(WG)	
West Glamorgan YO	John Jenkins*	Phillip Emanuel	
Mid Glam Youth Choir	Jeffrey Francis*		
South Glam Youth Choir	Helena Braithwaite*		
West Glam Youth Choir	John Jenkins*		
West Glam Youth Band	John Jenkins*	D.A.Small*	Andrew George

12. Higher Education Lecturers : Music/Music Education

John Anderson(Royal Coll.of Music)
Gordon Back(Guildhall)
Helena Braithwaite(Cardiff)
John Cross(SG)
Dr. Huw Davies(OU)
Ryland Davies(RNCM)
Dr. John Evans
Trevor Herbert (OU)
John Jenkins(Swansea)
Mark Jenkins (WG) Royal Irish Academy
Timothy Rhys Jones(MG)
Stuart Kale(Guildhall)
Jeffery Lewis(Bangor)
Cyril Lloyd(RAM)
Dr.Keith Morris(Swansea)
Andrew Phillips(WG)
Aldon Rees(Carmarthen)
Rhian Samuel(City Uni)
Gareth Small(WG)Various Colls.
Christopher Charles Davies(MG)(Atlantic College)

13. Soloists with the NYOW

John Anderson(Oboe)
Carl Darby(Violin)
Clive Dobbins(Violin)
Leonard James(Violin)
Geraint John (Cello)
Kenneth George(Flute)
Mark Howellls(WG)(Oboe)
Phillip Morgan(Violin)
Elunid Owen(MG)(Violin)
Anthony Randall(Horn)
Gareth Small (WG)(Trumpet)
Alan Thomas(SG)(Violin)
Phillip Thomas(WG)(Piano)

14.Leaders/Principals

Glamorgan Youth Orchestra

1949 Cecily Holliday
1951 Leonard James
1952 Betty Evans
1953 Cecily Holliday
1953 Hilary Squire
1954 Leonard James
1955 Denise Bassett
1956 Jeffrey Francis
1957 Mark Roberts
1958 Mansell Bebb
1959 Victor Chamberlain
1960 Jeffrey Lloyd
1962 Barbara Perry
1963 Wendy Sheppard
1966 Emyr Walters
1968 Edward Roberts
1970 Bryn Harding
1972 Phillip Morgan

National Youth Orchestra of Wales Leaders

Denise Bassett
Leonard James
Cecily Holliday
Hilary Squires
Victor Chamberlain
Jeffrey Lloyd
Wendy Sheppard
Patricia Sheppard
Edward Roberts
Phillip Morgan
Timothy Crossland(WG)
Carl Darby(MG)
David Emanuel
Elenid Owen(SG)
Alan Thomas(SG)
Sali Wyn Ryan(WG)

National Youth Brass Band of Wales : Principal Cornet

Edward John(WG)
Gareth Small(WG) (Soloist)
Rhys Owens(MG)
Chrisopher Turner(WG)
Ryan Mathews(WG)

Footnote

Every effort has been made to ensure the accuracy of the above catalogue of musicians. The author apologises for any omissions or errors.

The Glam : Appendix 1

Concert Repertoire - 1949 - 1974

Concertos, Concert Solos with Orchestra; Chamber Music

1949	Handel	Concerto Grosso in G(Also 1950)	
1950	Bach	Piano Concerto in F	Jeffrey Arnold
	Bach	Brandenburg Concerto No.3	
	Nardini	Violin Concerto in E Minor	Leonard James
	Mozart	Clarinet Quintet (movements)	
	Haydn	Trumpet Concerto	James Hargreaves
	Bach	Violin Concerto in A Minor	
1951	Mozart	Violin Concerto in G	Leonard James
	Handel	Organ Concerto No.2 in B Flat	John Cynan Jones
	Cimarosa	Clarinet in C	John Hempenstall
	Haydn	Concerto in Eb	James Hargreaves
1952	Handel	Concerto Grosso in F	Cecily Holliday, Jeffrey Francis, Ioan Davies, Marion Lloyd, Haydn Davies
	Handel	Concerto Grosso in Bb	Soloists above - Graham Jones replaced Ioan Davies
	Mozart	Horn Concerto in Eb	Haydn Davies
	Mendelssohn	Octet	
	Grieg	Piano Concerto in A MInor (1s Movt)	Geoffrey Arnold
	Vaughan Williams	The Lark Ascending	Leonard James
	Prokofiev	Overture sur Themes Juifs	John Hempenstall, Clive Thomas, Joel Clompus, Valerie Davies Geoffrey Arnold
	Debussy	Danse Sacre	Ann Griffiths
	Mendelssohn	Violin Concerto in E Minor (Movt 2)	Leonard James
1953	Handel	Concerto Grosso Op3.No.2	Denise Bassett, Jeffrey Francis, Valerie Davies
	Mozart	String Quartet in D Major	
	Beethoven	Piano Concerto No.4	Geoffrey Arnold
	Bach	Brandenburg Concerto No.5	Cecily Holliday, Kenneth George, Keith Morris
	Mozart	Clarinet Concerto in A	John Hempenstall
	Vaughan Williams	String Quartet	
	Beethoven	Piano Concerto No4 (1st Movement)	Cynthia Coombs
	Mozart	Concerto in F for Two Pianos	Carwen Rees and Keith Morris
1954	Schumann	Piano Concerto in A Minor(1st Mov)	Cynthia Coombs
	Mozart	Flute Quartet in F	
	Haydn	Trumpet Concerto in Eb	Laurence Evans
	Bach	Brandenburg Concerto No.6 in Bb	
	Wieniawsky	Violin Concerto No 2 in D	Leonard James
1955	Stainer	Quintet for Wind Instruments	
	Rachmaninov	Piano Concerto No.2(1st Movement)	Kieth Morris(Twice); Peter Rees
	Beethoven	Piano Concerto No.5 in Eb(1st Mov)	Cynthia Coombs
1956	Grieg	Piano Concerto in A Minor	Keith Morris
	Beethoven	Romance in F	Denise Bassett
	Rachmaninov	Rhapsody on a Theme of Paganini	Keith Morris(Also 1957)

1957	Handel	Organ Concerto in Bb	Alan James
	Beethoven	Wind Octet	
	Mozart	Horn Concerto No.3 in Eb	Anthony Randall
	Mozart	Flute Concerto No. 2 in D	Kenneth George
	Mozart	Piano Concerto in A (1st Movement)	Heather Lewis
1958	Mozart	Piano Concerto in A	Heather Lewis
	Mozart	Piano Concerto in A(1st Movement)	Aldon Rees
	Svendsen	Romance in G	Victor Chamberlain(Twice)
	Lizst	Fantasy on Hungarian Folk Tunes	Keith Morris(Also 1959)
1959	Mendelssohn	Piano concerto No 1 in G	Arnold Draper
	Handel	Viola Concerto in B Minor	Susan Salter
	Rachmaninov	Piano Concerto no.2 (Movts 2/3)	Keith Morris
	Mozart	Piano Concerto No 15 in Bb	Arnold Draper
	Purcell	Trumpet Voluntary	David Ayres
	Rachmaninov	Piano Concerto No 2 in C Minor	Keith Morris
1960	Franck	Variations Symphoniques	Arnold Draper
	Bruch	Kol Nidrei	Helena Davies
	Beethoven	Piano Concerto No4 in G	Peter Rees
	Bach	Violin Concerto in E (Movement 2)	Jeffrey Lloyd (Twice)
1961	Mozart	Flute Concerto No.2 in D	Michael Axtell
	Beethoven	Piano Concerto in Bb	Arnold Draper
	Beethoven	Piano Concerto in C	Peter Rees
	Bach	Arioso	Wayne Warlow(Twice)
	C.P.E.Bach	Sonata for Wind	
	Mozart	Concerto for Flute and Harp	Paul Broom/John Weeks Margaret Rees (Twice)
	Saint Saens	Concerto No 2 in G Minor	Arnold Draper
1962	Faure	Berceuse	Wayne Warlow(Twice)
	Hoffmeister	Concerto in D (Allegro - Rondo)	Gordon Mepham
	Mozart	Piano Concerto in A K488	Michael Beynon
	Beethoven	Romance in F	Jeffrey Lloyd
	Weber	Konzerstuck	Arnold Draper
	Grieg	Piano Concerto in A minor	Arnold Draper(Twice)
	Vivaldi	Concerto for Two Trumpets	John Jenkins & D.A. Small (Twice)
1963	Beethoven	Piano Concerto No.3 in C Minor	Peter Rees
	Vivaldi	Concerto for Two Trumpets	John Jenkins & D.A.Small (Twice)
	Mozart	Piano Concerto in D Minor K466	Michael Beynon
1964	Bach	Brandenburg Concerto No 5 in D	Wendy Sheppard, John Weeks Paul Broom, Peter Rees
	Handel	The Trumpet Shall Sound	Anthony Davy & John Jenkins (Twice)
	Lizst	Piano Concerto No 1 in Eb	Arnold Draper(Twice)
1965	Rachmaninov	Piano Concerto No3 in D Minor	Arnold Draper(Twice)
	Tchaikovsky	Piano Concerto No.1 in Bb Minor	Geoffrey Hopkins
	Chopin	Piano Concerto No.1 in E Minor	Arnold Draper(Twice)
	Bach	Violin Concerto in E Major	Wendy Sheppard(3 Times)
1966	Brahms	Piano Concerto No.1 in D Minor	Della Jones
	Beethoven	Piano Concerto No.5 in Eb(1st Mov)	Michael Jenkins(3 Times)
	Bach	Violin Concerto in A Minor	Emyr Walters
	Schubert	Octet	
1967	Rachmaninov	Piano Concerto No. 2 (1st Movement)	Gordon Back
	Bach	Brandenburg Concerto No.2 in F	Patricia Sheppard, David Richards, Alan Good, Christopher Weeks (3Times)
	Rachmaninov	Piano Concerto No 2 in C Minor	Gordon Back
1968	Grieg	Piano Concerto in A Minor	Gordon Back
	Beethoven	Piano Concerto No 5 in Eb (1st Mov)	Marion Williams
	Wieniawski	Concerto No 2 in D Minor (Romance)	Edward Roberts(Twice)

	Strauss	Horn Concerto No1 in Eb	David Hughes
1969	Mozart	Piano Concerto in Bb	Gordon Back(Twice)
	Gershwin	Rhapsody in Blue	Geoffrey Eales
	Addison	Trumpet Concerto (1st Movement)	Kenvin Evans(Twice)
	Bach	Suite No2 (I)	David Richards
	Mozart	Piano Concerto in Eb K499	Marilyn Phillips
1970	Tchaikovsky	Piano Concerto in Bb Minor(1st Movt)	Gordon Back
	Lizst	Hungarian Fantasia	Gordon Back
1971	Bach	Concerto for Two Violins	Bryn Harding & Phillip Morgan
	Grieg	Concerto in A Minor	Phillip Thomas(Twice)
1972	Strauss	Oboe Concerto(Andante)	John Anderson
	Shostakovich	Piano Concerto No.2	Gordon Back
1973	Franck	Symphonic Variations	Phillip Thomas

Symphonies

Beethoven	No.2 in D (I) 1958	No5 in C Minor 1957/1958
Brahms	No.1 in C Minor1954/1960/1961	No.2 in D 1970
	No 3	No 4 in F 1973
Bruckner	No.4 in Eb "Romantic" 1972	
Dvorak	No 7 in D Minor 1960/1961/1973	No.8 in G 1959/1960
	No.9 "The New World" 1956/1962/1958	
Haydn	Toy Symphony 1951/1953/1954	No.104(I) 1952
	G Minor (1) 1953	D Major (III) 1954
Mozart	Jupiter Symphony (Minuet) 1950	Eb (II & III) 1962
Rachmaninov	No.2 in E Minor (III and IV) 1961	
Schubert	No.1 in D 1953/1963	No.8 in Bb Minor
	No.9 in C Major 1961/1962	
Schumann	No 3 in Eb 1964	
Sibelius	No.1 in E Minor (I) 1965	
Tchaikovsky	No. 4 in F Minor 1957/1969	No.5 in E Minor 1955/1963
	No.6 "Pathetique" 1959/1967	

Major Choral Works

Bach	Arr. Walton Suite : "The Wise Virgins:" 1961	
	Magnificat 1966	
	Cantata No.28 "O Praise The Lord" (1964)	
Borodin	Polovtsienne Dances 1964	
Brahms	Song of Destiny 1965	Requiem 1968
Coleridge - Taylor	Hiawatha's Wedding Feast(1959)	
Dvorak	Stabat Mater 1972	
Evans(David)	Deffro Mae' n DDydd 1970	
Handel	Dettingen Te Deum 1962	Sixth Chandos Anthem 1965
	Zadok the Priest 1965	
Haydn	Sixteenth Mass 1967	
Holst	Festival Te Deum 1960	
Hughes(Arwel)	Gweddi 1965	
Mendelssohn	Lauda Sion 1961	Festgesang 1971
Mozart	First Mass in C 1960	Requiem Mass 1970
Thiman	Gloria in Excelsis Deo 1968	
Thomas(Vincent)	Y Bumed Gerdd 1965	
Vaughan Williams	Toward the Unknown Region 1963	Serenade to Music 1968
Verdi	Requiem 1970, 1972, 1974	
Walton	Coronation Te Deum 1964	

The Glam : Appendix 2

Performances of Twentieth Century Works

1949	Thiman	Gloria in Excelsis Deo
1950	Fletcher	Fiddle Dance
	W.S. Gwyn Williams	Vocal Arrangements
	Vaughan Williams	Fantasia on "Greensleeves"
1952	Britten	Ceremony of Carols
	Debussy	Danse Sacre (Harp:Ann Griffiths)
	Vaughan Williams	The Lark Ascending (Solo Violin : Leonard James)
	Debussy	Prelude a L' Apres Midi D'Un Faune
1953	Vaughan Williams	Overture "The Wasps"
	Barber	Adagio
1954	Coleridge Taylor	La Caprice de Nanette
	Delius	The Walk to the Paradise Garden
1955	Holst	Planets : Mars, Venus, Jupiter
1957	Jacob	Passacaglia on a Well Known Theme
1959	Vaughan Williams	Fantasia on a Theme by Thomas Tallis
1960	Holst	Festival Te Deum
1961	Vaughan Williams	Prelude on Rosymedre
	Walton	The Wise Virgins
		Fantasia for Orchestra
1962	Ravel	Bolero
	Hoddinott	Two Welsh Nursery Tunes
	Burch	Rumba
	Khatchaturian	Sabre Dance - Lullaby in 1969 1964
	Vaughan Williams	Toward the Unknown Region
		(First of many performances)
		Part songs by Holst, Elgar and Charles Wood
	Elgar	Enigma Variations
1965	Grace Williams	Fantasia on Welsh Nursery Tunes
	De Falla	Ritual Fire Dance
	Vincent Thomas	Y Bumedd Gerdd
1966	Arwel Hughes	Gweddi
1967	Walton	Coronation Te Deum
1968	Elgar	Serenade to Music
1969	Shostakovich	Festival Overture
	Coates	Knightsbridge March
	Arnold	Little Suite
	Addison	Trumpet Concerto (1st Movement) Kenfin Evans
	David Evans	Deffro Mae'n Ddydd
1970	David Wynne	Cymric Rhapsody No.2 Also 1971
	Bernard Rands	Agenda
1971	Britten	Young Person's Guide to the Orchestra
1972	Gareth Wood	Suite for Orchestra
	Strauss	Oboe Concerto (John Anderson)

Several performances of Rachmaninov No.2 : Piano Concerto and Symphony No.2

The Glam : Appendix 3

Russell Sheppard Collection

Compositions and Arrangements
1. Published Works

1.1. Hymns and Services for Secondary Schools in Wales
Emynau a Gwasanaethau i Ysgolion Uwchradd Cymru
Oxford University Press, 1965
(The greatest number of Hymns/Arrangements by a single composer)

i)	**Original Hymns**	
37	Disgyliaf O'r Mynyddoedd Draw	Pen - Llwyn
127	Praise Ye The Lord	
145	Courage Brother Do Not Stumble	Merthyr Mawr
189	O Brother Man	Oldcastle
318	Psalm XLVI	
ii)	**Harmonisations, Adaptations, Arrangements of Hymn Tunes:-**	
121	Mae Hen Wlad Fy Nhadau	James James
129	A Gladsome Hymn of Praise We Sing (Deganwy)	Benjamin Williams
134	Be Thou My Vision, O Lord Of My Heart	Irish Traditional
135	Blest Are The Pure in Heart (Franconia)	Konig's Choralbuch
143	Come Ye Thankful People Come (St.George's Windsor)	George Elvey
175	Let Us With A Gladsome Mind (Monkland)	Prob. John Antes
181	Love Divine, All Loves Excelling (Bonn)	Beethoven
196	O worship The King (Hanover)	Ascribed : Croft
210	The Heavens Declare (Creation's Hymn)	Beethoven
230	As With Gladness men of Old (Dix)	Konrad Kocher
/231	Am Brydferthwch Daear Lawr	Konrad Kocher
248	O Saviour, Precious Saviour (Brahms)	Brahms
/249	Gyfrannwr Pob Bendithion	Brahms
284	Good Christian Men Rejoice (In Dulci Jubilo)	Early German Melody
289	The First Nowell	Old English Carol

1.2. Other Publications
The Gwyn Publishing Co. Langollen,1954
Arrangement for SSA
"Creation" — Haydn

2. Unpublished Works : Original Compositions

2.1. Choir and Orchestra

1935	Exercise for B.Mus degree	SSATB Orchestra
	1) The Nativity : MIlton "Ode and Hymn on the Morning of Christ's Nativity"	Chorus and String Orchestra
	2) The Passion	Tenor Solo, Ch and Orch
	3) On time	Quartet - SATB A Capella
	4) Fugue/Paradise Lost	Chorus and Orchestra
1946	Cymru Fu, Cymru Fydd : Sir John Morris SSAATTBB, - Jones Prize Winning National Eisteddfod Piece : pseudonym "Hyder"	Tenor Solo,Full Orchestra
1949	Mawl Gân : Molwch Yr Arglwydd	SATB Chorus and Orch (Piano part only extant)
	Old Castle	SATB Hymn & Orch
1981	Fanfare on C & D : God Bless The Prince of Wales Visit of HRH's to Swansea	SATB Chorus, Orchestra

2.2. Orchestra

1968 Fanfare for a Royal Occasion
1970 Celebration Fanfare : Glamorgan YO 21st Celebrations

2.3. Chamber Music

1950	Myfyrdod (Meditation)	Violin, Cello, Piano

Performed by the London Harpsichord Ensemble at the Royal National Eisteddfod of Wales : Chamber Music Concerts, Van Road Congregational Church, Caerphilly, August 9th and also on Youth Choir's Tour to West Slovakia, 1967.

2.4. Organ Music

Fantasia on An Unknown Christmas Theme
Fantasia On An Easter Hymn (Emyn Pasg)
Ceremonial March

2.4. Opera for Schools

1939	The Vagabond Student : Libretto : W. Alex Jones	Soloists, Chorus & Orch
	Performed Holyhead Town Hall, March 7th and 8th	Music Score Missing
	Parts for Vln 1, Vln 2, Viola, Cello, Tr.1-3, Perc, Piano Score	
	Holyhead CS School Operatic Society and the Holyhead Orchestral Society	

2.5. Songs

Cân Ysgol	: Geiriau : G. Prys Jones	Unison /Piano
Ein Hysgol Ni	: Geiriau : G. Prys Jones	Unison /Piano

2.6. Part Songs

Sanctaidd Faban	: Karen Sheppard	SATB A Capella
Trearthur	:	SATB Hymn

2.6. Part Songs (Continued)

Song Cycle

Daffodil	: D.Hooson	SA/Piano
Ai Damwain Yw?	: R.H.Jones	
Yr Ehedydd	: Wyn Williams	
Cwn Y Gwynt	: J.Morris Jones	

3. Unpublished Works : Arrangements/Orchestrations

3.1. Part Songs

Bugeilio'r Gwenith Gwyn	Jane Williams	SSAA; also SATB
Y Gwcw Fach		SATB
Rew Di Ranno		SATB
Away in a Manger for Beverley High School Chamber Choir		SSAA

3.2. Orchestrations of Vocal Works

Yr Utgorn	W.Mathews Williams	SATB ;FO
Cymru Annwyl	Osborne Roberts	SATB ;FO
Drosom Ni	Afan Thomas	SA;FO
Ffarwel Y Wenol	Tawe Jones	Orch Parts Only
Alawon Y Bryniau	E.T.Davies	Orch Parts Only
Codiad Yr Ehedydd	Folk Song	SATB; FO
Deffro, Mae'n DDydd	David Evans	SATB ;FO
Paradwys Y Bardd	J.Morgan Lloyd	SA; FO
Cymru Fach	David Richards	SA B Stg .& Timps
Cân Yr Arad Goch	Strings.	
Arise Sweet Messenger	Arne	2 Fl.,St.
Tra Bo Dau	Trad.	SA; Stg.
Brightly Dawns Our Wedding Day	Sullivan	Incomplete Score
Hymn Tune Arrangements	Irish	FO
	Arfryn	
	Oldcastle	
	Laudate Domine	
Be Still my Soul (Finlandia)		SATB
Carol	Joy To The World	Organ, Vl. and Horn

The Glam : Appendix 4

R.J.Sheppard Collection: Papers : File 1

1. Original Papers and Presentations
File 1 - 1949 - 1962

1949 A Survey of Instrumental Music in Glamorganshire Schools
Proposals Concerning Music Education in the Schools of Glamorgan
1950 Glamorgan Youth Orchestra
Instrumental Music in Primary Schools
1953 Music in the Schools of Wales
Teaching of Instrumental Music : Mid Glamorgan Division
1958 Training of Teachers of Music

Addresses to Concerts etc.

1960 Music in Education : Present day Problems
Presidential Address to the annual conference of the National Association of Inspectors of Schools and Educational Advisers (NAIEA)
1961 Mountain Ash Grammar School
Tabernacle, Pontycymmer
1962 Response to the article - "Key". Times Educational Supplement
1963 Mountain Ash Grammar School
1968 Grand Celebrity Concert : Treorchy Male Choir/Bryn Celynog Brass Band
1970 Grand Concert : Technical College Bridgend
UndatedMountain Ash Choral Society

File 2 : 1962 -

1966 Music
1968 Organisation of Instrumental Music in Glamorgan
1969 Music Schools - several papers - responses

Undated Papers

Music In Junior Schools
Music In Glamorgan
Music in the General Education of the Sixth Form Pupil
Music in the Grammar School
Music Sub - Panel Response - Primary Music
Music and the Raising of the School Leaving Age
Youth Music in Glamorgan

Miscellaneous Manuscript Lectures

Teaching Pianoforte To Classes
The Percussion Band
Pianoforte Accompaniment
Conducting
Music in Infant Schools
Music in the Junior School
Music in the Youth Service
Moods in Music
Music in Leisure - Youth
Musical Style

2. GLAMORGAN COUNTY COUNCIL MINUTES ETC (File 3)
Pre 1949

Glamorgan County Council unless otherwise stated
Miscellaneous items related to music policy - 1926
18.1.1948 National YO Course (Item 24)

Post 1949	To the Secondary Sub Committee unless printed in italics
11.1.1949	National YO of Great Britain (Item 8)
	National YO of Wales
	Dyffryn Residential Centre : First YO Course (Item 10)
18.1.1949	Gowerton Boys' Grammar School - Inst. Music Instruction (Item 8)
	Gowerton Girl' Grammar School - Cello Playing Instruction (Item 9)
30.1.1950	Director's letter - re Instrumental Course SP 11 at Dyffryn Res.Centre
13.6.1950	Maesteg - Teaching of Instrumental Music (Item 5)
	Dyffryn Residential Centre - Orchestral Course (Item 18)
16.1.1951	Barry Boys' GS Teaching of Instrumental Music (Item 16)
	Dyffryn Residential Centre (Item 22)
	Ogmore School Camp (Item 25)
	Festival of Britain, 1951 (Item 26)
20.3.1951	Teaching of Instrumental Music - Neath and District Division(Item 1)
	Ystalyfera GS - Instruction in Instrumental Music (Item 19)
	National YO of Wales (Item 27)
	Dyffryn Residential Centre (Item 29)
24.10.1951	Festival of Britain Orchestral and Choral Concerts (Item 3)
19.7.1954	Glamorgan CC Response to the Report on the Training of Music Teachers
11.1.1956	National YO of Great Britain (Item 19)
	National YO of Wales (Item 20)
06.1.1959	Gowerton Girls' GS - Instrumental Music (Item 4)
	Glamorgan Youth Orchestra (Item 6)
	Travelling Expenses Mr.C.T.Hannaby; Appointment of Mrs. C.E.Sheppard, Bridgend (Item 13)
	National YO of Wales
	Ogmore School Camp - School Camp Sub Committee
17.5.1960	National Youth Brass Band Course (Item 14)
	East, West and Mid Glamorgan Youth Orchestras (Item 24
20.12.1960	Travelling expenses : Mr. V.Chamberlain (Item 8)
	Teaching of Instrumental Music (Item 10)
	Glamorgan YO - West Glamorgan Section (Item 19)
	Glamorgan YO - East " " (Item 20)
	Arts Council of Great Britain - Orchestral Concert (Item 21)
	National YO of Wales, 1960 Course; Visit to Czechoslovakia (Item 22)
24.5.1974	Peripatetic Teachers of Instrumental Music
19.1.1979	Courses for 16-18 year olds in full-time education(paper as Chief Adviser)

Other Papers

1955	Mr. Aneurin Edwards
1956	County Youth Centres
1958	Music Classes In County Youth Centres
1960	Report on the Pontypridd Centre by D. Roger Jones (23.1.1960)
	Director's Letter : National Youth Orchestra of Wales (26.1.1960)
	Correspondence related to the West Glamorgan YO (15.11.1960)
	Glamorgan Education Authority : Scholarships (April 1960) (Page 3)
1961	Orchestral Courses (10.5.1961)
1976	School of Instrument Making and Repair : C.Parry (22.9.1976)
	Application : National Music Council Award to Local Authorities
1979	Full - Time teachers of Instrumental Music

Undated	**Advisory Service Papers**
	Proposals for the Structure of the Advisory Service in Mid Glamorgan
	Music In County Youth Centres
	Brass Band Playing in Schools
1974 - 1980	Miscellaneous Papers Re salary as Chief Adviser
	Various NAIEA and Burnham Papers and Reports.

Wedding Speeches etc

The Glam

Selected Bibliography

1. Primary Sources

1.1. Books

David Allsobrook	Music for Wales	Cardiff, 1992
Bernard Baldwin and Harry Rogers	Mountain Ash	Bath, 1994
Bernard Baldwin	Mountain Ash Remembered	Mountain Ash, 1994
Ed. Curtis and James	Love From Wales : An Anthology	Bridgend, 1991
D.L.Davies	History of the Cwmaman Institute	Mountain Ash.1995
Idris Davies	The Collected Poems	Llandysul, 1993
David Egan	Coal Society	Llandysul, 1987
Alice Thomas Ellis	Wales : An Anthology	London, 1991
Thomas Evans	Glanffrwd's History of Llanwynno	Merthyr Tydfil, 1950
Richard Fawkes	Welsh National Opera	London, 1986
Raymond K.J.Grant	How They Lived Then(Aberdare in the 1850s)	Bridgend, 1978
A.G.Grosvenor and G.E.Williams	The Parish of Mountain Ash and its Churches	Mountain Ash, undated
James and Allsobrook	First in the World	Cardiff, 1995
Ed. Stephens	A Book of Wales	London,1978
R.S.Thomas	Selected Poems	Newcastle, 1986
Harri Webb ed. Stephens	Collected Poems	Llandysul, 1995
Gareth Williams	Valleys of Song	Cardiff, 1998
	Hymns and Services for Secondary Schools in Wales	Oxford, 1965
JPR Williams	JPR : An Anthology	London, 1979
Robert Witkin	The Intelligence of Feeling	London, 1974

1.2. Papers, Journals, Manuscripts etc.

The Aberdare Background to the South Wales Choral Union	Glamorgan historian No.9, 1980	G.P.Ambrose
Compositions, Arrangements	Various in the Russell Sheppard Collection See Appendix 3	
Glamorgan County Council	Miscellaneous Minutes in the Russell Sheppard Collection : See Appendix 4	
Mountain Ash Parish Magazines	Volume XXVIV, October 1931 Volume XXXII, August, 1934 Volume XXXIII, February, 1935	
A History	Nat. Ass. of Inspectors and Educational Organisers, 1959	
The First Seventy Years	Nat.Ass. of Inspectors and Ed. Advisers,1989	J. Dean
Singing in The Little Valley	Coal Quarterly, Spring 1965	D. Bean

2. Secondary Sources

2.1.Books

Sir Adrian Boult	A Handbook of Conducting	Oxford, 1949
W.G.Briggs	Music and Drama in the Counties	London, 1949
Sir Walford Davies	The Pursuit of Music	London, undated
E.L.Edmonds	The School Inspector	London,1962
Charles Hooper	Playing With Music	Leeds, undated
Charles Hooper	Teaching Music To Classes	Leeds,1946
G.Kirkham Jones	Musical Appreciation in Schools	London,1945
Joseph Lewis	Conducting Without Fears	London, 1942
Joseph Lewis	Singing Without Fears	London,1939
J.B.McEwen	Foundations of Musical Aesthetics	London, undated
Stewart Mcpherson	Music and its Appreciation	London, 1940
L.G.Newton and Campbell Young	The Book of the School Orchestra	Oxford, 1936

P. Pfaff	Music Handbook For Infant Schools	Chatham, 1960
Priestley and Grayson	A Music Guide for Schools	London, 1947
Edited Watkins Shaw	Music Education : A Symposium	London, undated

2.2. Papers, Journals, etc.

Board of Education	Handbook of Suggestions	London, 1927
Department of Education and Science	Music in Schools Second Edition	London,1969
Federation of Education Committees (Wales and Monmouthshire)	Prof. H. Walford Davies	Aberdare, 1921
Incorporated Society of Musicians	An Outline of Music Education	London,1947
Ministry of Education	Pamphlet 27 : Music in Schools	London 1956
Schools Council	Music and Integrated Studies in the Secondary School	Undated
Schools Council Working Paper 35	Music And The Young School Leaver	London, 1971
Standing Conference for Amateur Music	Music And The Amateur	London, 1951
	The Scope of Instrumental Music in Schools	Plymouth,1960
	Youth Makes Music	London, 1957
	The Training of Music Teachers	London, 1954
Trinity College of Music	John Warriner : Questions on the Art of Teaching : Music	London,1929
Welsh Federation of Music Arts Clubs	"But as Yesterday" : Annual Address by A.G.Prys Jones	Cardiff, 1948